DIM SUM

DIM SUM

Fast and Festive Chinese Cooking

Ruth Law

Contemporary Books, Inc.
Chicago

Library of Congress Cataloging in Publication Data

Law, Ruth.
    Dim sum, fast and festive Chinese cooking.

    Includes index.
    1. Dim sum.   2. Snack foods.   3. Cookery, Chinese.
I. Title.
TX724.5.C5L377   1982   641.8'65   82-45410
ISBN 0-8092-5881-1 (pbk.)

Illustrations by Gretchen Hoenecke

Published by Contemporary Books, Inc.
180 North Michigan Avenue, Chicago, Illinois 60601
Manufactured in the United States of America
Library of Congress Catalog Card Number: 82-45410
International Standard Book Number: 0-8092-5881-1

Published simultaneously in Canada by
Beaverbooks, Ltd.
150 Lesmill Road
Don Mills, Ontario M3B 2T5
Canada

With love to my patient and understanding mother, Gertrude Thompson, who initiated my interest in Chinese cookery by presenting me with my first wok, and to my three children, Grant, Alison, and Sarah, who inspired, tasted, and tested recipes, and helped in so many other ways.

Contents

Preface   vii

Acknowledgments   ix

1 Introduction   *1*

2 The Chinese Kitchen: Equipment, Preparation, and Cooking
   Methods   *5*

3 Chinese Staples for Your Kitchen   *24*

4 Cooking Tips   *35*

5 Do-Ahead Dim Sum and Other Delicacies   *38*

6 Mostly Do-Ahead: Crisp and Crunchy Fare   *79*

7 Ready for Reheating: Savory, Sauced Dishes   *122*

8 Steamed Dim Sum and Other Juicy Morsels   *146*

9 Dim Sum Complements: Quick Stir-Frys   *173*

10 Wrap-Ups and Roll-Ups   *190*

11 From Teahouse to Your House: One-Dish Bounty   *204*

12 Soup with Every Meal   *223*

13 Sweet Snacks and Desserts   *233*

14 For Very Special Occasions   *246*

15 Dipping Salts and Sauces   *266*

16 Menus and Preparation Schedules   *270*

17 Chinese Ingredients   *283*

   Index   293

Preface

One Christmas years ago, my mother gave me a wok. She bought it on a whim and considered it an interesting novelty, rather than a practical gift. Yet that wok became the handiest and most-used cooking vessel in my kitchen.

When I sought creative satisfaction, I turned to Chinese cooking, although my formal training was in classic French cuisine. While looking for easy ways to entertain guests, I expanded my repertoire of Chinese dishes. Concerned about good nutrition, I introduced my children to Chinese family meals. Watching my waistline, I found that I could eat and eat the Chinese food I loved and never gain a pound.

When I needed to earn a living, the process that had begun with the gift of a wok evolved into a gratifying career as a teacher and the owner of a Chinese cooking school. I discovered that cooking with my students was even more exciting than creating recipes on my own, for my students challenged me with their diverse appetites and interests. Some simply craved Egg Rolls and Won Ton Soup, and it was delightful for me to be able to show them how to make crisp, fresh Spring Rolls and light, plump Won Tons—both unlike anything they had ever tasted in a Chinese restaurant. Others were connoisseurs of hot food and pungent spices; they wanted to discover the seasoning sources of their intrigue. Most of my students began by devouring everything we cooked and trying individual recipes at home. Then they wanted to treat their friends to home-cooked Chinese meals, and they started pressing me for more information on menus and advance preparations. To make things manageable for them, I started outlining the contents of this book.

In the meantime, I went to Taipei to continue my own studies at the Wei Chuan Cooking School, where classes were taught by master chefs from all over China. I focused on the cooking styles of Shanghai, Szechwan and Canton. Then I went on to the prestigious Hong Kong China and Gas Company Cooking School to study with Lucy Lo, the best known Chinese cooking teacher. These weeks of classes provided me with invaluable insights into the ingenuity of Chinese cooking techniques—from steaming and stir-frying to red cooking, white cooking, dry frying, and smoking.

But the most fascinating part of my education was my travels through China, where I had the opportunity to visit kitchens, markets, noodle stands, and teahouses as well as the tea commune in Hangchow. Everywhere the food was wonderfully fresh—the fish was right out of the water and vegetables had been picked the same day. Everything was cooked to perfection—never overcooked—and seasoned with fabulous imagination. In China, as in Taipei and Hong Kong, eating was a sheer delight!

I returned home with plenty of dishes beautifully suited to my students' dual demands for diverse tastes and serving convenience. Not only did I encounter less stir-frying and much greater use of other cooking methods than I had anticipated, but I also became infatuated with the noodles, dumplings, and other "fast foods" that are omnipresent in Chinese communities.

My brief overview of how this book evolved does not begin to hint at the flavors, textures, and colors that await you in the recipes. For those, you'll have to start cooking, tasting, and savoring with me the exploration of Chinese cuisines that began in my kitchen long ago and continues there every day.

Acknowledgments

This book would never have seen the light of print without the generous and extensive help of many friends and associates.

I am particularly grateful to my son Grant and his sister Sarah who always seemed to be in the right place at the right time to help their mother in her creative struggles.

Special thanks are due to my right hand, Kathy Cook, who typed manuscripts, tested recipes, and even managed to keep me organized.

And, of course, nothing would have been accomplished without a loyal cadre of tasters and testers, including Marsha and Bob Gordon, Joan Schuessler, Kathleen Euler, Nancy Laase, Beth Cada, and Harold Sholder, plus Lutz Olkiewicz, the International Culinary Olympics Gold Medal winning pastry chef of Chicago's Drake Hotel.

Others who deserve recognition for their advice, counsel, and other contributions are Bette Peters, Jean Fugo, Bobbi Bogan, Herta Lesser, Peggy Coleman, and Don Peterson, plus Keith Herbert, who suggested the book's title, Gretchen Hoenecke, who labored long hours to produce the illustrations that accompany the text. I am also extremely grateful to the students who have taken my classes through the years for all *they* have taught *me*.

I also want to give special recognition to a quartet of culinary authorities who played key roles in the development of this book:

Rhoda Yee, who first encouraged me to start teaching Chinese cookery;

Nina Simonds, who led me to Taipei and Hong Kong to further my studies of Chinese cuisine;

"Gourmet on the Go," Edward Robert Brooks, who provided inspiration and helped convert many of my scribblings into understandable English; and

the late Master Chef John Snowden, founder of Dumas Père who used just the right combination of stick and carrot to keep me progressing in the culinary arts and who also on several occasions served as my co-instructor.

DIM SUM

1

Introduction

Since I began to cook Chinese dishes I have seen some wonderful things happen in the United States. There has been an enormous growth of, interest in, and enthusiasm for, Chinese cuisine. Diners have begun to seek out the spicy excitement of Szechuan seasonings, the delicacy of steamed whole fish, the juicy satisfaction of *dim sum* dumplings, and the intrigue of multiregional Chinese menus. Wise to the low-calorie, low-cholesterol appeal of Chinese cooking, more people have turned to the wok and steamer for everyday meals. Shoppers are finding Chinese ingredients more readily available in supermarkets, and the budget weary have come to appreciate the meat-economy of Chinese recipes.

But it seems to me, one important dimension of Chinese food has been "lost in translation." What is missing is the informality of Chinese eating customs—the ad hoc indulgences at noodle stands and teahouses, as well as the relaxed pace of help-yourself dining. I find my students' enthusiasm for Chinese cooking dampened by misconceptions about menus and serving requirements. They fear being caught in a frenzy of stir-frying if they give a dinner party. They worry that flavors will go flat if the food is allowed to stand, either in the kitchen or at the table.

The problem, I believe, stems from the fact that most Americans first encounter Chinese food in restaurants, where the simultaneous stir-frying of many dishes is not only possible but more practical than advance preparation of specialties that customers may or may not order. So I caution my students that the rigors of restaurant menus were never meant for home cooks. And I assure them that the Chinese have incorporated convenience into their eating customs much more cleverly than Americans have.

It helps to realize that the Chinese regard for good food transcends formality. In China, the distinction between meals and snacks yields as often as possible to the simple pleasure of eating. "Mealtime" can be anytime—any hour the teahouse tempts appetites or sociability, any moment an irresistible aroma from a street stand evokes hunger pangs, any occasion created by a chance encounter with either a friend or a favorite food. Homestyle hospitality is no more rigid: whoever comes to visit is invited to join the family at the table. Holidays mean that more people will drop in; so a wider selection of fare is kept on hand. Moreover, the food is shared, not just served. At home, the dining style is communal, with all dishes set out at the beginning of the meal. At the teahouses, most of the "menu" takes the form of trays and carts of dishes circulated among the tables and distributed as customers beckon. The market vendors keep everything in readiness—whether it be dumplings awaiting quick immersion in broth or pickled vegetables that need only be apportioned.

The informality of Chinese meals should not be confused, however, with a casual attitude toward taste. There is no sense of compromise for the sake of convenience in Chinese cooking. There is only the practical knowledge of which foods improve with sitting, which foods can be made ahead and quickly cooked at the last minute, which foods can stand at room temperature, and which foods reheat well. Such dishes, including rice and noodles, are the kitchen mainstays of every region of China. They form a much larger repertoire than the sampling of stir-fried dishes commonly found in the U.S.

I composed this book around the serving strategy of everyday Chinese cooking. Among my recipes you will find dozens of the foods called *dim sum,* which means "touch of heart"; these are the "snacks" Chinese rely on to tide them over between meals. But the difference between a snack and a meal in China is often only a matter of quantity. Just enough dumplings or noodles to "touch the heart" is a snack. Larger portions are considered a whole lunch or dinner, especially in northern China, where noodles are a daily staple. Moreover, the assortment of *dim sum* served at elegant teahouses includes such rich morsels as Meat-Stuffed Noodle Rolls, Hot and Sour Ribs, Crisp Duck and Aromatic-Spiced Beef—any one of which would make a festive entree in either a Chinese or an American household. All of the *dim sum* recipes may be served as an American-style appetizer, a main course, or as part of a Chinese buffet.

I use the term "Chinese buffet" to refer to the custom of serving all dinner courses simultaneously, with soup and rice or noodles. This is the way Chinese people eat at home; only at banquets are the courses served one at a time. The Chinese buffet is a sit-down meal and should not be confused with American-style sideboard buffet service. Chinese buffet dishes are characterized by the fact that they stand well; they don't have to be served piping hot and consumed immediately. Indeed, many of my recipes can be served hot, cold, or at room temperature.

The versatility and scheduling flexibility of *dim sum* and buffet recipes recommends them for family meals and all kinds of informal entertaining, from brunches to open-house buffets. But the foods also fit marvelously well into more formal menus, for the flavors are fresh, light, and exciting. The recipes are as traditional as the Chinese New Year; yet the tastes are as up-to-date as the latest French nouvelle cuisine.

When you are planning a Chinese meal, take advantage of the incredible variety of Chinese regional cooking styles represented in this book. Choose among dishes both mild and spicy, crisp and sauced, steamed and fried, warm and room temperature. But do not feel that you have to offer more styles of food than you can easily prepare. It is perfectly acceptable, and typically Chinese, to sit down to a one- or two-dish meal, as well as to a more opulent array of flavor contrasts.

Let the chapter titles guide your choice of recipes. If you want to set out a large buffet without getting caught in the kitchen at serving time, select a number of salads, noodle dishes, and other delicacies from the "Do-Ahead" chapter; then fill out the menu with a hearty offering of "One-Dish Bounty." Or add one specialty from the "Mostly Do-Ahead" chapter, or one of the "Steamed Dim Sum." You will find a range of ingredients and flavors in each chapter. For more specific planning tips, see the chapter devoted to "Menu Suggestions and Preparation Schedules." You can either follow my menus step by step or use them as models for devising your own. To help you plan your own preparation schedules, every recipe is accompanied by advance preparation tips and, where applicable, directions for freezing and reheating.

With these recipes, I invite you to share the endless pleasure I take in Chinese cooking. I hope the added dimension of convenience will make it possible for you to enjoy all the other benefits of Chinese eating customs, including wise nutrition and unmatched economy. And I wish you the happiness and satisfaction that the Chinese associate, invariably, with good food.

2

The Chinese Kitchen

EQUIPMENT

Chinese Cooking requires no elaborate equipment. You can prepare Chinese meals with the cooking utensils now in your kitchen.

The pleasures of Chinese food are increased when using a few basic Chinese utensils. A wok and a Chinese cleaver will make Chinese cooking easier and I recommend that you have them. However, they are not indispensable, and there is no point in buying them until you have experimented with a few recipes and are sure you want to continue cooking in the Chinese manner.

Later, you may want to acquire a metal or bamboo steamer, and the specially designed stirring implements, the spatula and ladle.

The Wok

The wok is a bowl-shaped vessel used for stir-frying, poaching, boiling, deep-frying, and steaming.

The design of the wok has many advantages. It is shallow enough for pan frying, deep enough for parboiling, simmering, braising, deep-frying, and steaming. The wok is extremely versatile and can also be used for other types of cooking besides Chinese.

The wok lends itself easily to the constant stirring and mixing of stir-fry cooking. Its metal heats quickly, its round-bottomed shape and high sides distribute the heat evenly and permit ingredients to be stirred without spilling. Less oil is needed because it has a maximum cooking surface. It is easier to clean than conventionally shaped pans.

Many kinds of woks are available. A 14-inch wok is the best buy since most burners will not provide sufficient heat to maintain the necessary high temperature for a larger wok. Woks are made of stainless steel, copper, aluminum, and both light and heavy weight rolled steel. The heavy rolled steel wok is by far the best since it will retain and sustain the high heat essential to Chinese cookery. Most woks come with a matching ring and cover.

The wok rests on the ring during cooking. On a gas stove, the narrow side of the ring should be up, and on an electric stove, the wide side should be up to get the bottom of the wok closer to the heat source. A gas stove will give you instant heat for your wok. However, an electric stove also provides adequate heat for stir frying. When using an electric stove, set the wok and the ring on the largest burner receiving the maximum amount of heat. Turn the heat to high and let the wok heat several minutes until it is hot. On a gas range, it will not take as long. Add oil and allow it to heat before stir-frying.

Seasoning the Wok

A new wok should be carefully seasoned so that it gives the best service. Scrub the manufacturer's coating on the outside of the wok with scouring pads or a heavy cleanser. (The coating is to prevent rusting.) After scrubbing the wok, rinse it thoroughly and fill it with water. Cover and bring the water to a boil. Boil for 10 minutes. Pour out the water. Rinse the wok in fresh water and then place it for 2 to 3 minutes over medium heat until all the moisture has evaporated. Add a teaspoon of vegetable oil to the wok and rub it over the entire surface with a paper towel. Continue rubbing and adding a little oil until the towel comes out clean. Now your wok is seasoned and ready to use. With continued use, your wok will acquire a better and better cooking surface as it turns darker in color.

Cleaning the Wok

Clean your wok with hot water, a very mild liquid soap, and a soft sponge. If some food has stuck to the wok, let it sit in hot water before washing to loosen the food. Do not scrape the wok with an abrasive and do not put it in the dishwasher. After rinsing and drying, set the wok over medium heat until all the moisture has evaporated. Rub ¼ teaspoon of vegetable oil into the wok to prevent rusting. The wok will darken and mellow with age.

The Spatula and Ladle

The long-handled metal spatula and ladle are used together in stir-frying. The spatula is designed to slide easily around the sides of the pot and turn the food over. The ladle can be used with the spatula in a lifting, stir-frying motion that resembles tossing a salad; and, for more advanced cooks, it can be also used as a small bowl for mixing sauces.

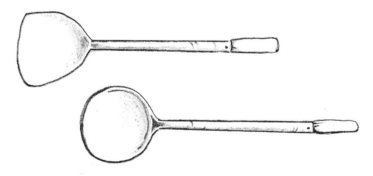

The Frying Strainer

Strainers with bamboo handles do not conduct the heat. A flat, slightly concave wire mesh is best for Chinese cooking. A larger strainer is best for straining deep-fried foods from hot oil and for boiling foods such as noodles. This is also known as a skimmer.

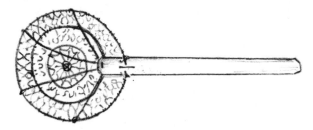

Chopsticks

Long, cooking chopsticks made of bamboo or wood are best because they can withstand high temperatures and do not conduct heat. They are used for beating, piercing, stirring, and mixing. Wooden chopsticks are as near to an extra pair of hands in the kitchen as any cook could have.

Eating chopsticks are shorter and are made from many materials. The most easily used and most durable chopsticks are wooden. Ivory has long been the favorite for refined eating. A popular Chinese wedding gift is a set of ivory chopsticks. Ivory chopsticks will last a lifetime, but they can become yellow if they are in constant contact with hot food or liquid.

Chopsticks have dictated the nature of Chinese food, which is cut into bite-size portions, making it easily graspable.

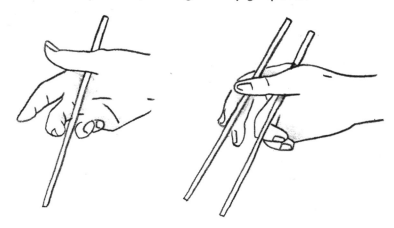

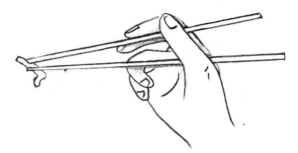

To eat with chopsticks, think of them as an extension of your hand. Place one chopstick about one-fourth of its length from the top between the thumb and the base of the index finger. The first knuckle of the fourth finger supports the chopstick. The second chopstick is held parallel above the first one resting between the second and third fingers and pressing the tip of the thumb. The first chopstick remains stationary. The top chopstick is the only one that moves.

The use of chopsticks is more easily learned by practice than by reading. Once mastered, chopsticks may well become your best friends in the kitchen and at the dinner table.

The Chinese Cleaver

A cleaver is a very important implement for the Chinese cook. Cleavers come in heavy duty, medium, and light weights. A heavy duty cleaver is better for cutting heavier meats and bones, while a medium weight one is better for slicing softer meats and vegetables. The medium weight is easier to handle and if you are only going to buy a single cleaver, choose a medium weight one. With either type of cleaver, the flat side of the blade is used for transferring chopped foods from board to bowl, for pounding and tenderizing meat, for crushing garlic, ginger, and scallions. A cleaver must always be kept razor sharp. The handle of the cleaver can also be used to grind spices in a small bowl, as with a mortar and pestle.

The Chinese Steamer

A steamer has many layers with a lid set on the top pan to contain the steam. As many layers as there are foods to be cooked are used, making this an ingenious method for steaming several dishes at once using a single heat source.

There are two basic types of Chinese steamers. One is made from bamboo and the other from aluminum.

A bamboo steamer rests upon your wok during cooking. Place 2 to 3 cups of water in the wok and place the steamer unit in the wok. Boiling water circulates steam through the steamer to cook

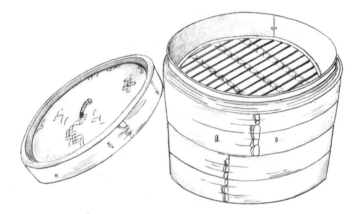

the foods that are placed in the cooking levels of the steamer.

A bamboo steamer is more pleasing aesthetically but is more difficult to clean and will not hold up as well as an aluminum steamer. To clean a bamboo steamer, use a vegetable brush and hot soapy water.

Aluminum steamers are sturdier and usually come in three different sizes. A medium-sized steamer (12 inches with at least two levels for steaming) is the smallest size you should buy. I prefer an aluminum steamer for most cooking because it is more durable and easier to clean. For steamed buns and *dim sum,* I prefer the aesthetics of the bamboo steamer.

To use an aluminum steamer, fill the bottom of the steamer pan with about 5 inches of water, heat to boiling, then place the layers with the various foods on top of one another and cover the top layer with the lid. Steam according to the recipe.

To clean an aluminum steamer, use a steel wool pad.

When using a steamer, always be sure to check the water level to make sure the water has not boiled away.

Steaming in a Wok

A wooden or metal steaming rack is available for steaming in the wok. Place the rack over boiling water in the wok. This will serve as a platform for heat-proof containers for the food. Cover the wok to contain the steam.

Improvisation of the Steamer

Remove the top and bottom of an empty can approximately 3 inches high and 4 inches wide to form a cylinder. Fill a roasting pan or Dutch oven with water to a depth of 2 to 3 inches. Stand the can up vertically in the water. Boil the water to build up the steam. Place a heatproof dish containing your food on top of the can. Cover with the top of your pan.

A regular double boiler will not work for Chinese steaming because live steam must be in contact with the food being cooked.

Pasta Machine

If you enjoy noodles, a heavy and substantial noodle machine is an excellent investment. I prefer either the Atlas or the Imperia noodle machine. They have detachable parts to vary the noodle width and can make thin sheets of noodles for egg rolls or won ton skins.

Tortilla Press

A tortilla press is excellent for pressing out wet dough for circular wrappers, such as Chinese pancakes. A press is not expensive and will save much time in rolling your dough.

PREPARATION AND COOKING TECHNIQUES

Chinese cooking techniques are quite simple to learn and to use. Most of the variety in Chinese cooking comes from the many ways in which the same ingredients can be cut up and combined in different recipes. The Chinese generally use the same cutting style for all major ingredients, in order to please the eye as well as the palate. If a recipe calls for an ingredient to be shredded, then all the other ingredients in the recipe should be shredded into the same size. The variety comes when another recipe will call for the majority of the ingredients to be diced, another will have similar ingredients chopped, and another will have foods cut into still larger pieces.

Since chopping, slicing, mincing, cubing, and shredding are so important to the aesthetics of Chinese cuisine, mastering the cleaver is of great importance. Ninety percent of Chinese cooking is preparation. Most of the cutting can be done hours ahead of the cooking time and the food stored in plastic wrap or self-locking bags.

Using the Cleaver

A cleaver should always be kept razor sharp. Wash and dry your cleaver immediately after each use.

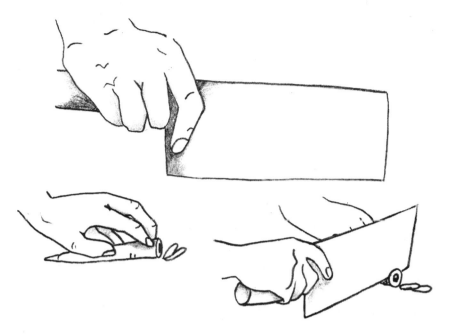

To hold the cleaver, rest the palm of your hand on top of the handle of the cleaver with the second finger curled over the cleaver blade on one side and the thumb on the other to guide the cutting edge. Grip the handle with the remaining fingers.

Hold the food with your other hand. Keep the fingers of the hand that is holding the food tucked under so that the knuckles are resting against the flat side of the cleaver with the finger tips tucked under for safety. The knuckles act as a guide for the blade. A sharp cleaver will allow the cutting to be done with an easy motion that does not require a lot of pressure.

Slicing

Meat is easier to slice if it is partially frozen first. Hold the cleaver perpendicular to the cutting board, cut straight through the food, down and away from your body. The knuckles of your other hand should act as a guide for the food as you move your hand along the food slightly after each cut. Cut the meat length-wise into strips 1½ inches wide along the grain. Then cut the meat into very thin slices against the grain on a slight slant.

Slant Cutting

Slant cutting is used for long, thin vegetables, such as carrots and asparagus and for thin pieces of meat. Instead of slicing vertically, cut at a 45-degree angle away from you.

Flat Slicing

Freeze the meat partially before you begin (10 to 15 minutes). Place the meat firmly on the chopping board and press down gently on it with the flattened fingers of the left hand. Carefully slice the meat beneath the hand using a very sharp cleaver. Hold the cleaver parallel to the cutting board. With a sawing motion, cut into the edge of the piece of meat. Continue cutting, keeping the blade parallel to the board.

Roll Cutting

Roll cutting is used for cutting a round and long item, such as carrots, turnips, and cucumbers, into larger pieces. This exposes the maximum number of sides of a raw ingredient so the piece will absorb as much flavor from the seasoning as possible while cooking.

Start by making a slant cut in the vegetable. Leaving the blade in place, roll the vegetable one quarter toward you. Then make another slant cut so the blade forms a triangle with the cut edge of the first slice. Roll the carrot another quarter turn and make a new slice, forming a new triangle. Continue rotating the vegetable, forming pieces which have triangles on some, but not all sides.

Dicing and Cubing

Cut the food into sections 2½ inches long. Then pile 2 to 4 slices on top of each other. With the length of the slices parallel to the cleaver, cut into thick slices. Then turn the long slices perpendicular to the cleaver blade and make cuts in the other direction to form squares.

Shredding

This technique is used for meat as well as vegetables. Cut the food into sections about 1½ to 2 inches long. Holding the sections on end, slice the food into slices about ⅛ inch thick. Then cut the slices lengthwise into thin shreds about ⅛ inch wide.

Mincing

The purpose of this technique is to cut ingredients into very small pieces. It is used to produce a chopped meat that will not lose its texture, which can happen when meat is ground and also for dried shrimp, garlic, ginger, etc. Start by making slices, then make shreds. Dice the food by holding the tip of the cleaver firmly

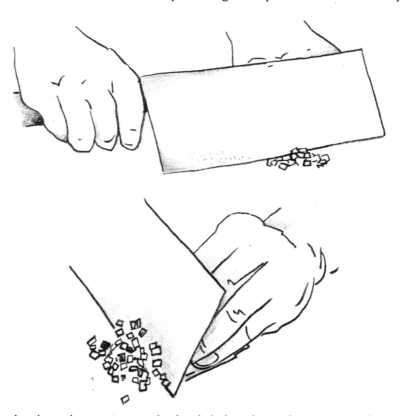

on the board pressing with the left hand on the top. Work the cleaver in a short up and down motion over the board, moving it from side to side to cover all of the ingredients. From time to time, scoop everything together into the center and continue mincing.

Fine Dicing

Another method is to slice the meat, then spread it flat on the cutting board. Hold two cleavers at once, grasping each handle with all fingers and the thumb. For hard foods, cut the food into slices, then in shreds. Mince once, then "march" chop with the 2 cleavers in a fast and even rhythm, turning the meat occasionally.

Crushing

Ginger, garlic, and scallions are crushed to release their flavor and to ensure complete cooking. Place the peeled food on the chopping block and hit firmly with the flat side of the cleaver. This should also be done before mincing the same items with the cleaver.

Scoring

The Chinese score their food to create a pattern that pleases the eye and helps to make the meat more tender. The size of the pattern and the depth of the cut vary from dish to dish. With meat it should always be done on an angle to the grain.

Scoring helps whole fish cook evenly and quickly and tenderizes seafood such as squid.

Other Uses of the Cleaver

The cleaver is used as a spatula to pick up cut food and transfer it to the wok and also to crack shells of shellfish.

The handle of the cleaver can also be used to grind spices, in a small bowl as in a mortar and pestle.

COOKING METHODS

Chinese cooking techniques are very simple to learn and take less time for preparation of a meal. Organization is the key to success.

All the ingredients must be prepared in advance. The food and seasonings such as garlic and ginger should be chopped and ready to be cooked in the wok. The sauce mixtures must be measured and ready to add within seconds. The essence of almost all Chinese cooking is speed in cooking.

An outdoor barbecue is ideal for Chinese cooking as the hot charcoal grill closely resembles the Chinese stove.

Stir-Frying

The primary use of the wok is to stir-fry. The food is cut into small pieces and cooked over high heat in a little oil. The food should move constantly so that all parts of it come in contact with the hottest part of the wok and cook quickly and evenly. The motion is similar to tossing a salad. A ladle and spatula are ideal for this as they are shaped to fit the wok.

To stir-fry, you must first heat the wok, then add 2 to 3 tablespoons of oil in a circular motion starting at the top and continuing down the sides so the oil thoroughly coats the sides of the wok. Let the oil heat. When the surface ripples slightly, it is hot enough to add the seasonings. If your oil is not hot enough, the food will stick. However, do not heat your oil to the smoking point. Until your wok is properly seasoned, the food may stick anyway. This will improve after your wok has been used 10 or 12 times.

It is important that you work quickly so the pieces of ginger and garlic do not burn and become bitter. Add the main ingredients as given in your recipe and cook until the desired doneness. Meat and vegetables are cooked separately for two reasons: they require different cooking times and the moisture in the vegetables would hinder the browning and searing of the flavorful juices in the meat. Before stir-frying, the vegetables must be absolutely dry to avoid spattering. When cooking two vegetables, add the longest cooking vegetable first and the quickest cooking vegetables last.

If you are cooking on an electric stove using a recipe that states to reduce the heat, it is best to have two burners preheated. Have one burner on high and the other on low. Then you can move the wok from burner to burner.

If doubling a stir-fry recipe, never double the oil. The purpose of the oil is just to coat the sides of the wok. Be careful not to overload the wok with food. The heat may not be hot enough in your burner to sear the food and the meat will then begin to stew instead of fry.

Stir-fry dishes cannot wait on the heat. If they are left on the stove even a minute too long, they cook in their own steam. Bright green vegetables loose their color, and crisp and delicious food becomes overcooked and soggy.

Advance Preparation for Stir-Frying

Always read your recipe first. Have all ingredients cut up, sauces prepared. Place everything on a tray for each recipe before you start to stir-fry.

The vegetables and meat may be cut up hours ahead, placed in a self-locking plastic bag and refrigerated. The use of plastic bags saves many dishes.

You may stir-fry meat, poultry, or fish several hours ahead. Stir-fry vegetables at serving time and add cooked meat and sauce mixtures at the end, blending all the ingredients and flavors.

Deep-Frying

Deep-frying produces interesting textures and seals in flavors and juices. If properly deep-fried, the food will not be greasy. The oil must be hot enough to seal the surface of the food immediately to keep the oil from penetrating. Always have the food at room temperature and dry before deep-frying.

A wok is ideal for deep-fat frying as it uses less oil than a standard pot because of its bowl shape. The wide rim also catches any splatters that might occur.

To test the temperature of heated oil, drop a cube of bread into the oil. If the bread sinks to the bottom and does not bubble, the oil is not hot enough. The oil is approximately 350 degrees (moderate) if the bread sinks to the bottom and starts to bubble immediately and floats to the surface within a few seconds. The oil is hot (375 degrees) if the bread floats to the surface immediately.

Another method of testing oil is the chopstick method. Place a clean and dry chopstick vertically in the middle of the hot oil touching the bottom of the wok. If many bubbles immediately rise along the side of the chopstick, the oil is ready for deep-frying.

The Chinese use three methods of deep-frying. To deep-fry most foods, heat the oil to the desired temperature. Carefully lower the food into the oil with chopsticks or a wire skimmer. Gently stir or turn the food while it is cooking. Remove with a wire skimmer when food is done and drain on paper towels. Fry food in several batches to maintain the oil temperature.

For many ingredients that are marinated first and then coated with cornstarch or water chestnut powder, the frying is done in two stages. The ingredients are briefly immersed in moderate oil until they are pale and golden. They are then removed and cooled while the oil is reheated. The food is then returned to the oil at a higher temperature to complete the cooking process. This makes the outside crisp and allows the inside to cook completely.

'Passing through" is a third method of deep-frying. Marinated pieces of meat are passed through oil at a low temperature (280° to 300°). The pieces are stirred with chopsticks to separate the meat. The meat is then removed and set aside to drain on paper towels. Later the meat is combined with stir-fried vegetables and a sauce mixture to blend the ingredients.

Deep-Frying a Large Piece of Food

When deep-frying a whole fish, chicken, or duck, do not turn food in the oil. The oil might splash dangerously. If the food is not fully immersed in the oil, ladle hot oil over it to baste the exposed portion.

Steaming

Steaming is the least demanding and most delicate of all Chinese cooking techniques. It is an easy method of preparing foods, is low in calories and cholesterol, and renders a multitude of services to Chinese cookery. Steaming is a marvelous cooking method since all the vitamins and minerals are preserved, rather than being boiled away in water.

Few Chinese kitchens have ovens. The steamer replaces the oven in cooking buns, dumplings, custards, vegetables, meat, and seafoods. It is used to reheat leftovers and for delicate foods.

In Chinese steaming, the food is placed in a container and suspended over boiling water in a pot or wok. The food is cooked by the steam rising from boiling water placed in the bottom of the steamer. The steam rises from the boiling water to circulate around the food and cook it by direct contact. Quite often, the steamed foods are taken to the table in their steaming container.

When you want to remove steaming heavy dishes, make a sling first. Cross two tea towels and place them under the dish. Drape them over the pot, cover and tuck them on top of the lid. To remove the food from the steamer, lift the dish with the sling.

The water should be boiling before the food is placed in the steamer. The food should be suspended at least 1½ inches above the water level and there should be at least a 1-inch space between the steaming dish and the steamer to allow the steam to circulate properly. Check the water level occasionally, making sure the water has not boiled away. The steaming dish should be heat-proof, but the heat created by the steam is not great enough to damage most china. For chicken or other large pieces of food, use a bowl to hold the savory juices and seasonings during the steaming.

Dumplings are more attractive when steamed and served in a bamboo steamer. Place a layer of cabbage leaves beneath the dumplings or line a bamboo steamer with wet cheesecloth to prevent sticking.

Red-Cooking

Red-cooking is a favorite method of cooking whole poultry and large cuts of pork and beef. The method derives its name from the rich red-brown sauce produced by soy sauce. The meat is usually seared or browned in oil first and then simmered covered over low heat until it becomes rich, mellow, and very tender. Sherry, ginger, and scallions are usually added. Foods cooked in this way can be reheated and taste even better when rewarmed a day or two later. The meats can be served with their sauces or the sauces can be used on noodles or rice. In China, these sauces are saved and reused for the next cooking. The more meat that is cooked in the sauce, the more the sauce takes on the flavors of the meat, making it richer with each cooking. These sauces are saved for one to two hundred years and are known as "master sauces." They are given to a new restaurant owner as a treasured gift and are passed on from generation to generation.

Red-cooked meats can also be served chilled with their jellied sauces used as an aspic. If you plan to chill a meat, do not use vegetables, as the sauce will not be clear.

Slow Steeping

Delicate foods such as chicken or fish can be cooked by slow steeping. Very gentle heat is used to cook the meat of the chicken. The food simmers for a short period, then the heat is turned off, the pot tightly covered, and the food left to steep to finish cooking the pieces. It is then plunged into ice water to firm the flesh, trap the juices, and stop the cooking process.

Slow steeping produces a unique texture. The meat is extremely moist with a satiny texture.

MISCELLANEOUS COOKING TECHNIQUES

Blanching

This method calls for ingredients to be plunged into boiling water and cooked rapidly. It is primarily used for vegetables, to reduce their cooking time in stir-frying. It is also used to remove the skins of tomatoes. Blanching also reduces the bitter tastes of some vegetables, such as cabbage and onions.

Dry-Frying

This is a way of preserving meats or vegetables. The food is cut up and simmered in oil or water until it dries out completely. The food then needs no refrigeration.

Roasting

Roasting is rarely done in Chinese homes as there usually is no oven. There are central roasting pits where roasted meats are prepared by suspending the meat over an open pit. Chinese-style roasting can be accomplished in the United States by marinating the meat first. Place the meat on a rack in the oven with ½ inch of water in the pan. The water provides moisture and prevents the drippings from burning. Cover as little of the meat as possible so that most of it is exposed to the direct heat. It is crucial to elevate the meat from the pan and the water so the heat can circulate all around the meat.

For smaller meats, such as barbecued pork, hang the meat vertically on hooks with a pan of water underneath. (See Index for Barbecued Pork recipe.)

Barbecuing

This is a variation of roasting. The marinated meat is suspended over an open fire and a container of water is placed under the meat to keep the air around it moist. Barbecuing may be accomplished by hanging the meat from the top rack of the oven with hooks. (See Index for Barbecued Pork and Ribs.)

Smoking

Smoking is a way of flavoring foods after they have been cooked by other methods. The aromatic qualities of the smoke are enhanced by the burning of brown sugar, and seasonings such as ground anise, cinnamon, and black tea leaves. This may be done in a foil-lined wok or on an outdoor barbecue grill.

Marinating

Marinating generally affects the texture more than the taste of the meat. It gives the raw ingredient a velvety texture and also tenderizes the food. One of the few exceptions to this rule is barbecued pork, where the meat is flavored by the marinade.

3

Chinese Staples for Your Kitchen

If you keep the following staples in your cupboard, you will be prepared to serve Chinese dishes with just a quick trip to a nearby grocery store for perishables.

The Chinese Grocer, 209 Post Street, San Francisco, CA., 94108, has a complete line of Chinese mail-order foods.

See Glossary of Ingredients for descriptions of these Chinese staples.

Basic Dry Ingredients

Chinese dried black mushrooms
Five spice powder
Dried shrimp
Tiger lily buds (lily flowers)
Tree ears, cloud ears
Salted black beans (fermented
   black beans)
Glutinous rice (sweet rice)
Chinese dried egg noodles
Bean threads or rice noodles
Chinese tea

Basic Staples

Bamboo shoots, canned
Water chestnuts, canned
Cornstarch

Dry sherry or Chinese rice
   wine (shaoshing)
Rice vinegar
Fresh ginger
Fresh garlic

Basic Seasonings

Light soy sauce (thin soy sauce)
Dark soy sauce (thick soy sauce,
   black soy sauce)
Oyster-flavored sauce
Chinese sesame oil

Optional Seasonings

Bean sauce
Sesame seed paste
Plum sauce

Items for the Freezer

Shanghai spring roll wrappers
Won ton wrappers

Spicy Dried Ingredients and Seasonings

Dried chili peppers

Szechuan peppercorns
Chili paste with garlic or hot chili sauce
Hot bean sauce
Hot chili oil
Szechuan preserved vegetables

VEGETABLES

The Chinese consider vegetables very important. They are inexpensive, nutritious, and a major part of their diet.

Vegetables may be stir-fried, braised, steamed, or deep-fried. Stir-frying is the most popular method. The technique of cooking is most important and the vegetable used, secondary. One vegetable can easily be substituted for another. Ginger and garlic are quite often used for seasoning the oil. Vegetables are also cooked, cooled, and served as a salad course. When cooked, vegetables should look as fresh as they did before cooking; they should be crisp, with a bright color and an excellent flavor.

Hard and semihard vegetables, such as broccoli, carrots, cauliflower, and green beans may be cooked in advance and reheated. Stir-fry briefly in oil, add ¼ cup liquid and cook, covered, over medium heat until nearly done. Remove cover. Let liquid cook away. Cool the vegetable. When ready to use, stir-fry in a little hot oil just enough to reheat. Almost all vegetables should be purchased fresh. Frozen peas are the only exception. Defrosted and cooked with other ingredients just long enough to warm them, they add a nice touch of color to a dish.

PORK

The predominant meat for the Chinese is pork. It is so important to the Chinese that the Chinese word for meat and for pork is the same. Pork may be stir-fried, deep-fried, braised, red-cooked, white-cooked, steamed, ground for fillings, or dried and salted. It is combined easily with other foods to produce perfect culinary harmony. The feet, innards, and even the brain are all cooked in various methods. Slow cooking of pork produces a dish that is jellylike in tenderness. The fat and skin in these dishes is highly savored as a delicacy. There is absolutely no waste.

Any lean cut of pork will do nicely for Chinese cooking. The part of the animal the meat comes from does not make a difference as the meat is uniformly tender and good tasting. The major difference between the various cuts is the ratio of fat to lean meat. Buy the leanest piece you can, but not necessarily the most expensive cut. Trim most of the solid fat before cooking. Pork shoulder and pork loin are best for American use. The easiest and most practical way to purchase pork is to buy a large piece of meat and cut it up into smaller portions, weighing approximately 8 ounces each. Wrap the meat and freeze it. This is economical and a great time-saver. If you do not have meat in the freezer, purchase pork chops and shred or slice them for a recipe requiring a small amount of pork.

POULTRY

Chicken is a major part of the Chinese diet. Chicken is extremely versatile and may be stir-fried, steamed, deep-fried, poached, braised, simmered, roasted, or smoked. It is often cooked by a combination of methods such as simmering and roasting or steaming and deep-frying. These methods were designed to conserve fuel by shortening the cooking time. Purchase chickens that are fresh and weigh at least 3 pounds. The larger roasting chickens, about 4 to 5 pounds, are richer in flavor and easier to bone. Always check to be sure you are buying a roasting chicken and not a stewing or baking hen.

When buying duck, a fresh bird is best. However, a frozen duck is acceptable. Thaw a frozen duck (4½ to 5½ pounds) by letting it stand at room temperature for 6 to 8 hours, or allow a day for it to thaw in the refrigerator. The Chinese prefer duck with the head and feet attached. These can be found in Chinese markets and they are preferable, though not essential, for making Peking Duck (see Index).

BEEF

Beef is rarely used in Chinese cooking because of the scarcity of cattle. Flank steak and top round are best for stir-frying. For braising, brisket or chuck can be used. Beef can be substituted for pork in most meat and vegetable dishes.

Beef should never be stir-fried longer than 2 minutes before the vegetables are added, as the meat will toughen.

FISH

The Chinese like their fish as fresh as possible. The best way to judge the freshness of a fish is by its eyes—they should be bright and clear. Lift the gills to make sure that they are red and clean. The scales should be tight and flat against the body. When buying a slice of a larger fish, you can tell the freshness by look, smell, and feel. The flesh should be moist and close-textured and should not have a strong odor. The flesh should be firm and resilient when pushed with a finger. If freshwater fish is not available, sea bass, red snapper, flounder, or any firm white-fleshed fish will do. Fish may be steamed, poached, fried, pan-fried, or stir-fried.

To test fish for doneness: smaller fish should flake easily with a fork. For a larger fish, make a cut to the bone in the thickest part close to the head with a chopstick or small sharp knife. The fish is done if the meat is white and opaque.

Abalone, crab, lobster, oysters, scallops, shrimp, snails, and squid are also used by the Chinese. They are cooked fresh or used dried as a flavoring ingredient. Most of the crab and shrimp are fresh-water harvests from the many rivers, canals, and ponds; they are sweeter and more delicate than the saltwater varieties.

All types of seafood are briefly cooked by stir-frying, steaming, or deep-frying. Overcooking toughens seafood. If you buy frozen seafood, thaw it completely and drain before using.

RICE

Rice is the main food in most regions of China and is eaten with every meal. In the morning soft rice or congee (porridge) is eaten for breakfast. A familiar Chinese greeting is "Have you had your rice yet?", which means "Have you had your meal?"

Many types of rice are used in China; however, the two main types are long-grain white rice and short-grain glutinous rice, also called sweet rice. Glutinous rice is stickier than long-grain white rice. It is used for stuffing because it holds together so well.

The Chinese wash their rice several times before cooking or until the water runs clear. This is to remove any loose starch so the grains will separate after cooking. American rice purchased from a supermarket need not be rinsed. However, the grains will not stick together as much if it is rinsed. Rice purchased in Chinatown should be rinsed several times until the water is clear.

Rice should be cooked *al dente*—not too soft but with a bite to it. It should be starchy enough for the grains to hold together but not be sticky.

Cooking Rice

Quantities: ½ cup raw rice per person is generally sufficient since rice increases in volume when cooked. Use 1 cup long-grain rice to 1½ cups water. This will make 3 cups cooked rice.

Wash the rice by putting it in a colander and rubbing the grains together between the palms of your hands. Continue doing this until the water runs fairly clear.

Place the well-drained rice in a saucepan. Add the appropriate amount of water. Heat the rice over high heat until it comes to a boil. Boil 1 minute, reduce heat to very low and cover the saucepan. (For electric burners, preheat a second burner to low. Transfer the rice to the second burner.) Cook without stirring for 15 minutes. Immediately remove the saucepan from the heat and let it stand for 10 minutes. DO NOT LIFT THE COVER. During this standing period the heat in the saucepan will finish the cooking and absorb any remaining moisture. With chopsticks or a fork, fluff the rice to separate the grains.

Cooking time varies from stove to stove and from pan to pan. The precise cooking time comes from experience. Freshly cooked rice will stay warm in a saucepan for 45 minutes. Automatic rice cookers are available to cook the rice and keep it warm several hours.

NOODLES

Noodles are the primary staple in northern China where the climate is more suitable to growing wheat. Here, rice is seldom served. The Chinese eat noodles with as much passion as Italians eat pasta. In the North, for breakfast, a bowl of piping hot noodles might be served to start the day with a warm stomach, since houses do not have central heat. During the day, noodles take many snack forms including dumplings, buns, and pancakes. They are the main meal for dinner. As one-dish meals they are the filling kind of inexpensive entrees you might serve to your family. If the meal needs to be stretched, more noodles are added. Quite often a meal might be composed exclusively of many dumplings in broth, such as Won Ton Soup, or Peking Pan-Fried Dumplings. Many other pastries and breads might occupy a place on the menu also.

Experienced chefs prepare noodles by hand. Other versions are machine made in the neighborhoods with fascinating wooden devices. Each community has a noodlemaker. He makes noodles, won ton skins, and dumpling wrappers. In northern China, noodles are made with flour and water. The Cantonese prefer the addition of egg to their noodles.

There are many different kinds and shapes of noodles. They are made from wheat flour, rice flour, or bean flour. The noodles can be either boiled or fried and served dry with a sauce or simmered in a bowl of soup. They can also be eaten cold. They cook quickly and are an inexpensive filler.

Because they are the symbol of longevity, noodles are served as the main dish at birthday parties all over China. Chinese noodles are very long, since to cut them would be considered symbolic of cutting off one's life. Sometimes they are served in place of rice as the final course of a large dinner, in keeping with the Chinese tradition of ending a meal with a starch.

Noodles made from rice flour are known as rice noodles or rice sticks and are popular in the eastern and southern regions of China. In the United States, these noodles are available in 8- and 16-ounce bags in dry form and will keep indefinitely in an airtight container.

Bean threads, cellophane noodles, or pea starch noodles are made from mung beans that are soaked, ground to a smooth puree, mixed with water, and strained to obtain a liquid. The liquid is made into translucent noodles or dried in sheets; either way, the noodles are transparent and have a smooth gelatinous texture.

The dried rice or bean thread noodles must first be soaked in warm water to soften. They are used in soups, stir-fried with a sauce, or served in cold platters and salads. Unsoaked, they may be deep fried in hot oil to make a light, crisp "noodle nest," which may be used as a base for a stir-fried dish. Fresh egg noodles, made with wheat flour, are available in most Chinatown grocery stores. They are supplied daily by noodle factories. You can buy them in quantities, as these noodles freeze well. Dried noodles are also available in Chinese markets. American or Italian packaged noodles such as flat linguini or spaghettini may be substituted. But there is no comparison in flavor between the dried and fresh egg noodles. Fortunately, you can also make the fresh noodles at home.

Boiling Fresh Egg Noodles

Fresh thin noodles cook very rapidly. It is better to undercook rather than overcook noodles. If they are to be recooked, slightly undercook the noodles the first time.

To cook 8 to 10 ounces of fresh egg noodles, bring 4 quarts of water to a rapid boil over high heat. Add the noodles; turn the heat to medium. Stir immediately to separate. Cook until barely done, or *al dente*. Test for doneness by biting into a single strand. The outside should be tender while the inside is firm and hard. DO NOT OVERCOOK. The cooking time depends upon the noodles. As a general rule, fresh noodles take 2 to 3 minutes and most dried noodles take 6 to 8 minutes. If they are to be cooked again, reduce the original cooking time.

Drain the noodles in a colander. Rinse immediately with cold water to prevent the noodles from continuing to cook in their own heat. This also washes off the starch and prevents sticking together. Drain again.

Separate the noodles on a flat plate. Mix well with a little oil, preferably Chinese sesame oil (1 tablespoon), and set aside until needed. To reheat, plunge into boiling water. Drain.

Preparing Noodles in Advance

Many recipes call for chilled, parboiled noodles. Cook the noodles, drain them, and toss them with about 1 tablespoon of oil, preferably Chinese sesame oil. This will prevent them from sticking together. Store cooked noodles in a tightly covered container or plastic bag in the refrigerator. They will keep for a day or two.

CHINESE BREADS

Particularly in northern China, breads are served instead of rice. They are also often offered as snacks in *dim sum* teahouses either as a light meal or as sweets.

Most of the breads are steamed, but some are deep-fried. Very few are baked. In many Chinese restaurants, you will find one chef whose specialty is preparing steamed breads along with savory and sweet pastries. He is able to form the dough very deftly into many different shapes in minutes. It might seem that steamed buns would be heavy, but the use of baking powder and a lengthy rising period produce a light, fluffy product.

SOUPS

Soup is an integral part of a Chinese meal. Since the Chinese rarely drink water, soup is the beverage most often served during an informal meal. Tea is served only before and after the meal. Soup is offered to quench one's thirst and as a source of nourishment. It is usually placed in a tureen in the center of the table and left there throughout the meal. Except at banquets, all dishes are served simultaneously, with the soup as an accompaniment. Each person helps himself to a little soup during the meal. It is spooned into a soup bowl and then drunk as a beverage. It also serves as a palate cleanser.

SWEETS

Sweets are reserved for snacks and banquets in China. They are served in the many "teahouses" and during lavish dinner parties, as a change of pace, as well as palate-refreshers between courses and after the meal.

Since very few homes have ovens, flaky pastries must be purchased from commercial sources and are enjoyed only on very special occasions. Steaming and deep-fat frying are the methods used for preparing the more common sweet treats. At banquets, sweet soups may also be served.

Fruits, both dried and fresh, and nuts play a prominent role in Chinese sweets. In the winter, there are oranges, tangerines, and kumquats; in the spring, peaches and red grapes; in summer, sweet melons, pineapple, mangoes, papayas, and bananas; and in fall, pears, apples, and persimmons. A bowl of fresh fruit is considered one of the nicest endings to a Chinese meal.

TEA

Tea has been the most popular beverage in China for more than a thousand years. The drinking of tea originated with the fact that boiled water was healthier and tea leaves were added to make the water more palatable.

The Chinese connoisseur of tea is very much like a student of wine. He can tell the life history of a tea from just a sip and enjoys sniffing, savoring, and talking about tea. A truly fine cup of tea is never served with a meal. It can be quite expensive and is reserved for very special occasions. The rarest teas are like vintage wines or fine brandies.

Fine tea is clear and pale gold in color. It has a natural sweetness and should never be flavored with sugar, milk, or lemon. The bouquet is exquisite and leaves a pleasant aftertaste.

Tea is rarely served during a family meal in most of China. It is served only at the end of the meal to soothe the stomach and help digestion. In southern China, around Canton, however, tea is served with the meals. During elaborate formal dinners tea is served throughout the dinner to refresh the diner and make him appreciate each new dish.

Chinese teas vary greatly in character, flavor, and aroma. Most come from plants which are varieties of the camellia family. The major differences between teas are derived from the locale, climate, time of harvest, and processing.

There are two basic kinds of tea, green and black, plus a combination of the two, oolong, which is a semifermented tea.

Green teas are unfermented and are made from young tender leaves, which are baked in the sun as soon as they are picked.

They produce a pale golden tea with a natural bouquet and a refreshingly delicate taste. One of the great green teas of China is Lung Jen, translated as "Dragon Well." It is grown in the outskirts of Hangchow in east-central China. The tea was named for a famous natural spring, which is now a spa in the beautiful resort city. One of the highlights of my trip to China was a visit to the Lung Jen tea commune. The picturesque setting, the sight of the tea pickers with their bamboo baskets to hold the tea leaves, and the taste of the tea, fresh from the bush, was indeed a treat. The best grade of Lung Jen is harvested in April. It should be served with highly-flavored foods.

Black tea is fermented. Its leaves are permitted to wither on the bush. They are then gathered, rolled, fermented, and dried. The fermentation process alters the chlorophyll content and changes the color from green to brownish black, strengthening its flavor. It produces a full bodied, rich tea. Black tea is also called "red" tea because of the color of the brewed beverage. It is a pungent tea popular in winter, especially in northern China. Serve it with deep-fried foods. Keemun is one of the best black teas.

Semifermented teas, such as oolong tea, are partly dried and partly fermented. They are allowed to ferment briefly in the sun before being dried, sorted, and packed. Oolong combines the richness of the black tea with the delicateness of the green tea. It goes well with heavy foods and the evening meal. Black Dragon is most common for family use.

Fresh or dried flowers and fruit blossoms are often blended with teas. Jasmine and lychee tea are two of the best known. Chrysanthemum tea, often sweetened with rock sugar, is usually served with pastries.

Brewing of Tea

Green teas are usually more potent and require fewer tea leaves. However, the number of cups of tea brewed determines the quantity of tea leaves to use. The greater the amount of boiling water, the greater the amount of heat on the leaves, giving a stronger infusion. If a larger amount of water is used, fewer tea leaves are needed per cup. As a general rule, use one teaspoon of tea leaves to one cup of boiling water.

To brew tea:

1. Start with a good quality tea. Store the tea in an airtight container.

2. Scald the teapot with boiling water; drain. Keep the pot warm. Use a heavy porcelain or earthenware teapot. Metal pots distort the flavors.

3. Bring freshly drawn cold water to boiling and immediately pour the water over the leaves. The tea leaves will rise to the top

quickly and then sink to the bottom. If the water has not boiled, the tea leaves will remain floating on the top.

4. Cover the pot and let the tea steep for three to five minutes. Green tea will be pale gold, semifermented tea will be amber, and black tea a rich red color.

Good quality tea can be brewed at least twice. Add a little more tea to the pot and pour more boiling water over the leaves. Cover and let the mixture steep for another three to five minutes. Some tea connoisseurs feel the second brewing of the tea is superior to the first.

WINES

Chinese wines and spirits are made from rice and other grains. Some are mild, others quite strong.

Shaoshing wine is made from rice and is probably the best known type. It is also called yellow wine. It is somewhat similar in taste to sherry. The best grade is used for drinking and the lower grades for cooking. A dry sherry can be substituted.

Mao-tai from the western region is made from wheat and millet. It is a colorless, very strong liquor, and is usually served only at formal dinners.

There are many other rice wines as well as wines flavored with lichee and plums. The latter are sweet and make good after-dinner drinks. A dry, white wine goes well with Chinese food. Chinese beer, available in the United States, may also be served.

4

Cooking Tips

1. Always read the recipe completely before starting.
2. Measure ingredients accurately. A kitchen scale is helpful. Have two sets of measuring spoons, one for dry ingredients, one for wet. Always use level spoon measurements. Even a slight variation in the amount of an ingredient can alter the flavor and may make the dish too bland or too salty.
3. Follow the advance preparations specified under each recipe.
4. Cut up all ingredients uniformly so they will cook evenly. The size and shape of the pieces of meat usually determine the size and shape of other ingredients.
5. You may cut up the meat, poultry, seafood, and vegetables in advance. Meat, seafood, and poultry are easier to cut up if they are still partially frozen (about 30 minutes in the freezer). For stir-frying, cut the meat against the grain. After pieces are cut up, place them in a bowl, cover, and refrigerate. Instead of a bowl, you can use self-locking plastic bags, disposable cups, paper plates, aluminum foil, and plastic wrap, saving much cleanup time.
6. When marinating meat, seafood, or poultry, remember that marinating flavors the meat, gives it texture, and acts as a tenderizer so that it will not harden and shrink when it comes in contact with hot oil. Cover the meat if you're marinating it ahead of time. Do not marinate more than 3 hours unless the recipe specifies a longer period.
7. Limit meat, seafood, or chicken, as well as vegetables, to one pound per stir-fry. If you increase a recipe, cook the meat and

35

vegetables in separate batches of about 1 pound each, or you will end up with a stew. The heat will not become hot enough in a wok to accommodate more food. Combine the cooked vegetables and meat in the wok with the heated sauce and reheat all together at serving time.

8. Always purchase firm-skinned ginger. Ginger is best stored in the refrigerator, in the vegetable crisper, or in a cool, dry place. If you're not planning on using all the ginger within 3 to 4 weeks, wash, dry, and place the extra portion in a jar. Cover with dry sherry and seal tightly, then refrigerate. Flavors are released when ginger and garlic are smashed with the flat side of a cleaver before cooking.

9. Ginger, garlic, and scallions can be cut up hours in advance and wrapped in plastic wrap or a plastic bag. All of these are easier to cut if they are crushed with the cleaver first. If cooking more than one recipe, cut up the ginger, garlic, and scallions for all the recipes at one time. Divide the ingredients for each recipe before storing. To save time, you may chop up a large amount of garlic in advance, immerse it in sesame oil, and refrigerate it until you need it for a recipe.

10. Cooking oils include corn oil, peanut oil, and other vegetable oils. Do not use sesame oil for stir-frying unless specified. Sesame oil is a seasoning. The Chinese never use olive oil.

11. Vegetables (carrots, broccoli, string beans) may be blanched before stir-frying. To blanch, bring at least 2 quarts of water to a boil. Add prepared vegetables, bring the water back to a boil, and cook the vegetables until they are crisp textured or "al dente." Remove the vegetables and rinse with cold water immediately to stop cooking. Drain and dry before stir-frying. This may be done hours in advance. To test for doneness, taste a piece. It should be resistant, but not raw. Do not overcook or you will lose texture, color, and important vitamins. At serving time, stir-fry the blanched vegetables with the cooked meat and sauce to heat through.

12. Always wash and dry vegetables before putting them in hot oil. Do not overcook.

13. For each recipe, prepare the sauce mixture before you start cooking. If a cornstarch mixture is used, it should also be prepared in advance. If you are not using the mixtures immediately, cover them with plastic wrap. It is important to blend (recombine) each

sauce mixture thoroughly before adding it to the recipe. After adding the sauce mixture, stir rapidly to prevent lumps until the sauce thickens evenly.

14. Have an emergency container of cornstarch and water beside your stove, two tablespoons cornstarch to four tablespoons water. If a sauce is too thin, you will have your thickener at hand ready to use.

15. Arrange all the ingredients on a tray in order of use. A cookie sheet is good. The order is usually: the aromatic ingredients such as ginger and garlic, then the vegetables, the marinated meat, the dry seasonings, premixed sauce mixtures, cornstarch mixture, if used, and finally the garnishes. Cooking oil and utensils should be within easy reach. After measuring and mixing, put away all the bottles not being used.

16. In stir-frying, always heat the wok to very hot. Add the cooking oil. Heat the oil. Add the meat. If the meat sticks to the pan, either your wok is not well enough seasoned, the oil is not hot enough, or you may need more oil.

17. Follow the directions for each individual recipe. The cooking times may vary because each stove heats differently and you will have to adjust to this variation.

18. Oil for deep-frying can be reused if you strain it through several layers of cheesecloth or a coffee filter and then refrigerate. Leftover oil from deep-frying can later be used for stir-frying. Discard the oil when it becomes heavy and dark or when it starts to foam when heated.

19. Soy sauces vary from brand to brand. A Chinese soy sauce is best.

20. Batters and doughs are temperamental. Weather and types of flour greatly affect them. Always add liquid ingredients gradually. More water is needed in dry weather than in humid weather. Use your own judgment.

21. When a recipe calls for half an egg white, lightly beat the egg white. It will be easier to divide.

5

Do-Ahead Dim Sum and Other Delicacies

Variety is the greatest temptation—especially when it takes the form of many little dishes designed to "touch the heart." *Dim Sum* that can be prepared completely ahead of time and served at room temperature or chilled set an easy pace for a most tantalizing spread.

I especially like to greet guests with the spectacular colors of Happy Shrimp Rolls, which slice to reveal layers of egg sheet, shrimp, carrots, and purple laver. Hot and Sour Shrimp add a Chinese "Good luck!" to the greeting with the symbolic color of their red pepper garnish. Jade Salad, Asparagus Sesame Salad, and Green Beans with Peanuts can brighten the table at any point in the meal—and create a balance of cool, crisp texture, as well.

All of the noodle dishes in this chapter make marvelous warm weather buffet fare with few additions to the menu needed. Steamed Rice Noodle Rolls with Hot Spicy Sauce can be refrigerated for a quick picnic pack-up anytime. But the breeziest outdoor feast is Tangy Noodles with Vegetables, since you can prepare the noodles and vegetables separately and let everyone toss their own combination at mealtime. Szechuan Sesame Chicken Shred Noodles and Cold Noodles with Chicken and Shrimp are other cold delights to serve. If you like to cook outdoors, the scent of smoldering tea leaves and burnt sugar will alert diners that Smoked Tea Chicken and Scallion Smoked Fish make outstanding barbecue fare. And best of all, they can be prepared indoors also!

I favor the spiciness of Hacked Chicken Szechuan Style but cannot resist the delicacy of Lemon Chicken arrayed on a bed of shredded lettuce. Both can be served as appetizers or entrées. I have found Aromatic Spiced Beef to be equally superb on an appetizer platter or in a lunchtime sandwich. Chinese Barbecued Pork deserves a special place among these do-aheads because it fits beautifully on an appetizer platter, but you'll also want to keep it on hand for Barbecued Pork Lo Mein and Barbecued Pork Filled Buns (see Index).

Anise-Boiled Peanuts

In China, you'll find these peanuts on many restaurant tables when you arrive. The soy sauce and star anise produce fragrant, licorice-flavored peanuts, which are an unusual accompaniment to a meal. The peanuts are easily prepared and can be cooked in advance and refrigerated.

2 **cups raw peanuts**
6 **slices ginger, the size of a**
   quarter, crushed
4 **whole star anise**

4 **teaspoons Szechuan**
   peppercorns
3 **tablespoons dark soy sauce**
1 **teaspoon salt**
   Water to cover

Combine all the ingredients in a saucepan; cover with water. Heat to boiling; reduce heat. Simmer for 1 hour or until the peanuts have absorbed most of the cooking liquid. Stir occasionally while cooking. Taste for seasoning after peanuts have cooked for 1 hour. Add more salt, if necessary. Refrigerate peanuts until ready to serve.

Makes 6 to 8 servings.

Sweet Fried Nuts

One of the appetizers that usually precede a Chinese banquet is fried nuts. They are delicious with cocktails and can be made in advance. You may use shelled pecan halves, shelled walnuts (no skin), or raw cashews.

2 **cups shelled raw cashews**	3 **tablespoons honey**
1 **cup water**	5 **cups oil**
3 **tablespoons sugar**	

1. Put the nuts in a pan. Cover with boiling water. Heat to boiling. Reduce to simmer. Simmer for 1 minute. Pour off all water. Add sugar. Stir until the nuts are evenly coated and the sugar is practically dissolved. Spread the nuts out evenly on waxed paper. Let dry overnight.
2. Heat oil in wok to 375°. Add nuts. Fry until the sugar coats the nuts with a rich brown glaze. Transfer the nuts to an oiled plate. Separate in a single layer to cool.

Makes 6 to 8 servings.

Tea Eggs

Tea eggs are seen everywhere in China. They are wonderful as a snack, an appetizer, or for a buffet. The cracks in the shells allow the sauce to flavor the egg and also produce a pretty design.

1 **dozen small eggs**	2 **tablespoons dark soy sauce**
2 **tablespoons loose black tea**	2 **teaspoons light soy sauce**
1 **whole star anise**	1 **tablespoons salt**
1 **cinnamon stick**	1½ **teaspoons sugar**

1. Rinse the eggs carefully to remove any blemishes.
2. Place the eggs in a saucepan and run cold water over them. Slowly heat eggs to boiling over low heat to prevent shells from breaking. Reduce heat and simmer about 15 minutes. Cool eggs and drain.
3. Tap each egg lightly with a spoon until it is covered with many fine cracks.
4. Place the cracked eggs in a saucepan; add enough water to cover. Add the remaining ingredients; heat to boiling. Reduce heat and simmer gently for 1½ to 2 hours. Drain eggs and cool. If serving immediately, remove the shell from each egg and cut into 6 wedges lengthwise before serving. If you are going to serve the eggs later, refrigerate and remove the shells before serving.

Makes 8 to 12 servings.

Steamed Rice Noodle Rolls with Hot Spicy Sauce

The combination of barbecued pork wrapped with cold rice noodles and smothered with a spicy sauce creates delightful taste sensations. This is a marvelous dish for a picnic or a buffet.

Rice Noodle Batter
2⅔ cups flour
⅔ cup rice flour
1 teaspoon salt
½ cup minus 1 tablespoon oil
4 cups cold water

Meat Filling
2 cups barbecued pork or ham,
   shredded into 1½-inch shreds
⅔ cup scallions, shredded into
   1½-inch shreds
Light soy sauce
Chinese sesame oil

Sauce Mixture
1 clove garlic, minced
1 teaspoon ginger, minced
1 teaspoon sugar
4 tablespoons light soy sauce
3 tablespoons oil
2 tablespoons Chinese sesame
   oil
2 tablespoons rice vinegar
1 teaspoon hot chili oil
   (optional)
Salt to taste

Garnish
4 tablespoons dry roasted
   peanuts, chopped
¼ cup scallions, sliced

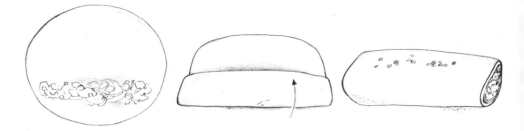

1. To make batter: Mix flour, rice flour, and 1 teaspoon salt in a bowl. Make a well in the center and add the oil and cold water gradually. Whisk batter or use a blender and mix until there are no lumps and the batter is smooth. Ladle approximately ⅓ cup of the batter into a lightly oiled 9-inch pie pan. (The batter should be ⅛ inch thick.) Steam for 4 to 5 minutes until solid.

Cool. Remove noodles to oiled plates. Wipe the pie pan clean. Re-oil pan and cook the remaining noodles. (It is easier to work with two pie pans, rotating them.)

2. Combine sauce mixture. Set aside. Place 2 to 3 tablespoons of the pork and scallions down the center of each noodle. Sprinkle very lightly with soy sauce and a few drops of sesame oil. Fold the noodles into thirds and place them seam side down on plates. Spoon the sauce mixture over the noodles and sprinkle with chopped peanuts and sliced scallions. Cut into thirds. Serve at room temperature.

Advance Preparation: Prepare sauce and assemble the filled noodle rolls. Cover with plastic wrap. Refrigerate for 1 day. Bring to room temperature before serving. Spoon sauce over noodles and sprinkle with peanuts and scallions.

Variations: Use cooked chicken or shrimp instead of pork.
   Steam filled noodles over high heat until warmed. Pour sauce over hot noodle rolls. Serve.

Makes 10 to 12 noodle rolls. (Serve 2 rolls per person as part of a *dim sum* meal or cut up rolls and serve as part of a buffet.)

Chinese Barbecued Pork

Barbecued pork is a Cantonese specialty and a basic component in many dishes. Sliced, it can be used as an appetizer. It is also a common ingredient in soups, stir-fried dishes, and stuffings. Since few Chinese homes have an oven, it is usually purchased from stores specializing in barbecuing. The Chinese barbecue meat by hanging it in the oven with a pan of water beneath. The pan of water catches the fat as well as producing humidity, which prevents the meat from drying out.

Barbecued pork strips can be made in advance and frozen. Spareribs can be barbecued in the same manner.

2 pounds boneless pork butt or loin, excess fat trimmed, sliced lengthwise with the grain into strips 2 × 1 × 6 inches

Pork Marinade
3 tablespoons light soy sauce
2 tablespoons brown bean paste
2 tablespoons hoisin sauce
2 tablespoons dry sherry

(marinade continued in next column)

2 tablespoons ketchup
2 tablespoons sugar
1 tablespoon garlic, minced
1 teaspoon five-spice powder

Glaze
3 tablespoons honey
1 tablespoon light soy sauce
1 tablespoon Chinese sesame oil
1 tablespoon boiling water

1. Place the pork strips in a bowl. Combine marinade ingredients and mix well with pork. Marinate at room temperature for 5 hours or overnight in the refrigerator. (Do not marinate longer than 8 hours or the meat will become tough.)
2. Remove all the racks from the oven but the top rack. Put a large pan on the floor of the oven and fill it with 1 inch of water. Preheat the oven to 350°.
3. Insert a meat hook, skewer, or drapery hook into one end of each strip and hook the strips onto the top rack over the drip pan. Roast the pork for 45 minutes, basting occasionally with the marinade. Increase the heat to 425° and roast for 10 minutes longer.

4. Combine the glaze ingredients. Generously brush the upper side of the pork strips with the glaze. Roast for 5 minutes more. Pork is done when a meat thermometer inserted in pork registers 170°. Remove the meat and take out the hooks. Let the strips cool to firm and slice them crosswise against the grain into ½-inch slices. Arrange the pork slices on a platter. Serve warm or cold with reheated marinade, plum sauce, or Chinese mustard.

Tips: Pork strips may be placed on a rack over a shallow roasting pan containing a few inches of water if hooks are unavailable. Turn the meat several times if not suspended.

Marinate pork strips. Cook on a hibachi or charcoal grill about 15 minutes on each side.

Advance Preparation: Store pork in the refrigerator 2 to 3 days or in the freezer 2 to 3 months. Do not slice pork if not using it immediately. Slice at serving time.

Makes 4 to 6 main-course servings.

Smoked Tea Chicken

This recipe uses a variation of an ancient Chinese method of smoking meats. Sugar and tea burned together provide an unusual and appealing flavoring for the chicken. Fish may also be cooked in this manner. This dish is delicious hot or cold.

2½ tablespoons coarse salt
1 tablespoon Szechuan peppercorns
1 2½-pound chicken
2 slices ginger, flattened with a cleaver
2 scallions, crushed with side of a cleaver

½ cup loosely packed light brown sugar
3 tablespoons fresh dark colored tea leaves, such as oolong
1 tablespoon Chinese sesame oil mixed with 1 tablespoon light soy sauce

1. Toast the salt and peppercorns in an ungreased pan over medium heat for 4 minutes, stirring steadily. The peppercorns should be fragrant and the salt slightly browned. Crush the mixture between two layers of waxed paper using a rolling pin.
2. Remove any excess fat from the cavity of the chicken. Rinse the chicken under running water and pat dry with paper towels. Rub the chicken inside and out with the peppercorn mixture. Wrap the chicken in a plastic bag and refrigerate for 6 hours or overnight.
3. Place half the ginger and scallions in the cavity and the remainder on top of the chicken. Steam the chicken over boiling water for 45 minutes or until done, and juices run clear. Remove the chicken from the steamer and pat dry with paper towels.
4. Line the wok with heavy aluminum foil. Sprinkle foil with sugar and tea. Place steamer rack or chopsticks in the wok to keep the chicken above the tea mixture. Rest the chicken on the rack about 2 inches above the tea mixture.
5. Heat the wok over medium heat for about 5 minutes or until tea mixture begins to smoke. Lower the heat slightly. Smoke the chicken, covered, for 7 minutes. Turn the chicken breast side down and smoke for 8 minutes. Remove wok from heat. Let stand, covered, for 10 minutes. Remove chicken to chopping block. Brush skin with sesame oil-soy sauce mixture. Carve the chicken American-style or chop it into bite-size pieces leaving in the bone which is the Chinese manner.

Tip: This recipe is even better prepared 1 day in advance. A covered barbecue grill is perfect. Place the tea leaves and brown sugar in a pie plate and set it directly on the charcoal ashes. Place chicken on grill above the charcoal. Cover. Smoke 20 minutes.

Makes 3 to 6 servings.

White-Cooked Chicken

Slow steeping of chicken is particularly helpful when you are preparing many dishes. The chicken is first simmered, then allowed to steep in ginger and scallions, and finally plunged into ice water. This produces a chicken that is firm and flavorful with fantastic succulence.

This chicken may be served cold with a ginger-scallion dipping sauce or stir-fried with a spicy sauce and served hot or at room temperature.

1 **whole roasting chicken or 1½ pounds chicken breasts**	2 **2-inch scallions, crushed with the side of a cleaver**
2 **pieces fresh ginger, the size of a quarter, peeled, crushed with the side of a cleaver**	1 **teaspoon salt** **About 3 quarts water** 3 **trays ice cubes**

1. Place chicken breast side down in a deep heavy pan into which the chicken fits snugly. Add ginger, scallions, salt, and water to cover. Heat to boiling; reduce heat. Simmer, skimming off residue that rises to the surface. When all the residue is gone (about 10 minutes), cover and let the chicken simmer gently for 25 minutes. (The Chinese like the chicken slightly pink. Simmer the chicken 10 minutes longer if desired.)
2. Remove the pot from the heat; let chicken steep, covered, for 45 minutes.
3. Fill a large bowl with ice water and the ice cubes. Remove the chicken from the pot and plunge it into the bowl. Let the chicken remain in the ice water for 15 minutes, turning it to chill it thoroughly. (This forces the juices to retract into the chicken, making it extremely juicy.) Remove chicken and pat it dry with

paper towels. Place chicken in a bowl and refrigerate for at least 2 hours.
4. Carefully remove the breast meat from the chicken and cut into pieces 3 × 1 inch each. Remaining chicken may be reserved for other dishes.

Tip: The best results come from a whole chicken. If you are using the breasts only, boil them in water with the ginger and scallions for 10 minutes. Turn the breasts frequently so the thickest part of the breast is no longer puffy when pressed with a spoon. Cover the pot. Remove from the heat and let steep 15 minutes. Drain and plunge in ice water until well chilled. Drain, dry, and chill.

Makes 3 main-course servings.

White-Cooked Chicken with Spicy Sauce

This is an unusual dish, and easy to prepare in advance. It makes a delicious appetizer or can be used as one of the entrées in a multicourse dinner.

1 **recipe white-cooked chicken, cut into pieces 3 × 1 inch each (see preceding recipe)**
2 **tablespoons oil**
½ **teaspoon Szechuan peppercorns, crushed**
¼ to ½ **teaspoon red pepper flakes**
½ **tablespoon finely shredded ginger**
2 **scallions, shredded into 2-inch shreds**

Sauce Mixture
¼ **cup chicken stock**
1½ **tablespoons light soy sauce**
1½ **teaspoons sugar**
1 **tablespoon dry sherry**
¼ **teaspoon salt**

1½ **teaspoons rice vinegar**
½ **teaspoon sesame oil**

1. Prepare chicken. Combine sauce ingredients.
2. Heat wok over medium heat until hot. Add 2 tablespoons oil to the wok. Let heat. Add the peppercorns; heat for 5 seconds.

Add the red pepper, ginger, and scallions. Stir gently for 5 to 10 seconds until fragrant. Add the chicken to the wok. Stir-fry carefully for 3 minutes, keeping the chicken intact.

3. Add sauce mixture to the wok and cook until the liquid comes to a boil. Taste. Add more sugar if necessary.

4. With a Chinese strainer or slotted spoon, remove the chicken and arrange it on a serving platter. Sprinkle it with vinegar and sesame oil. Then pour the sauce from the wok over the chicken. Serve immediately or at room temperature.

Tip: White-Cooked Chicken may be made 1 to 2 days in advance and refrigerated. The chicken and sauce mixture may be combined 3 to 4 hours before serving.

Makes 3 main-course servings or 8 to 12 appetizer servings.

White-Cooked Chicken with Ginger Scallion Dipping Sauce

Serve the chicken cold or at room temperature with this flavorful dipping sauce.

4 scallions, white part only, shredded
1 tablespoon ginger, finely minced
2 tablespoons light soy sauce
1 tablespoon dry sherry
3 tablespoons oil

Combine the scallions, ginger, soy sauce, sherry, and salt in a small heatproof bowl. Heat the oil in a small saucepan until it begins to smoke. Immediately pour the oil over the scallions to release their fragrance.

Advance Preparation: Prepare completely 1 to 2 days ahead.

Lemon Chicken

This recipe makes a lovely lemon-flavored sauce, which can be mildly seasoned with green peppers or turned into a spicy-flavored treat by the addition of hot peppers. It can be served cold or at room temperature and can easily be made ahead.

4 to 5 large lemons
1 whole chicken

Sauce Mixture
1 cup chicken broth
¼ cup sugar
½ cup lemon juice
Salt to taste

2 tablespoons oil

6 dried Chinese black mushrooms, soaked in hot water until spongy, stems discarded
2 tablespoons peeled, finely shredded ginger
⅓ cup long hot peppers, or fresh green peppers, shredded
1½ cups lettuce, shredded

1. Peel skin of lemons; shred finely to make ½ cup shreds. Grate lemon to make 1 tablespoon grated lemon rind. Squeeze lemon to make ½ cup juice, slice remaining lemon into slices for garnish. Prepare sauce. Mix 1 cup reserved chicken broth, ½ cup lemon juice, sugar, and salt.
2. Steam chicken in a heat-proof bowl over boiling water for 45 minutes or until tender. Let the chicken cool in the cooking liquid. Remove the chicken and strain the broth. Reserve broth.
3. Remove the breast meat from the chicken and cut into bite-size pieces. Chop the remaining wings, legs, and thighs into bite-size pieces leaving in the bone.
4. Heat oil in wok. Add the ginger and press into the oil until lightly browned. Add mushrooms, lemon shreds, grated lemon, and peppers. Cook until the flavors release, about 30 seconds. Add the sauce mixture. Cook until the sugar dissolves. Add the chicken. Cook until heated through.
5. To serve, place the shredded lettuce on a platter and arrange the chicken pieces symmetrically on the lettuce. Pour the sauce over the chicken and let stand until room temperature.

Variation: Two whole chicken breasts may be substituted for the whole chicken. However, the flavor will not be at its optimum. Steam the breasts for 20 minutes.

Advance Preparation: Prepare completely one day in advance.

Cover. Refrigerate. Bring to room temperature before serving.

Makes 4 servings.

Drunken Chicken

This simple but elegant dish takes its name from the quantity of wine used in its preparation. High quality ingredients are essential to this dish—particularly a good dry rice wine or sherry. Drunken chicken should be made ahead because the flavor improves upon standing. The recipe may be easily doubled or tripled.

1 4-pound chicken	**1½ cups chicken broth**
4 to 5 tablespoons coarse salt	**Chopped coriander or scallions**
3 cups Chinese rice wine or dry sherry	**to garnish**

1. Place chicken in a deep dish that will fit in the top of a steamer or on steaming rack of wok. Place the dish, uncovered, into the steamer top or on wok steaming rack over boiling water. Cover. Steam chicken until tender and juices run clear, about 45 minutes. Let stand with the steamer cover on until cool.
2. Transfer the chicken to a chopping block. With cleaver, remove the wings, legs, and thighs of chicken. Cut away and discard the backbone, then chop the breasts into two pieces along the breastbone.
3. Sprinkle salt on the chicken pieces on all sides. Place the pieces in a shallow baking dish large enough to hold them in 1 layer.
4. Combine the wine and chicken broth. Pour over the chicken. Cover the dish with plastic wrap. Refrigerate for 1 to 3 days, turning the pieces occasionally.
5. Cut the chicken into bite-size pieces and arrange on a serving dish. Sprinkle with reserved wine mixture. Garnish with coriander. Serve cool.

Variation: Three whole chicken breasts may be substituted for the whole chicken. Steam breasts 15 to 20 minutes or until tender and firm.

Advance Preparation: Must be made 1 to 3 days ahead.

Makes 4 main-course servings or 8 to 10 servings when part of a Chinese meal.

Hacked Chicken, Szechuan Style

A famous Szechuan dish, this chicken has a wonderful blending of flavors. It can be served at room temperature or cold as an appetizer or main dish. It is a marvelous buffet dish, as it can easily be doubled or tripled.

2 **large chicken breasts**
¼ **cup raw peanuts**
1 **cup oil**
1 **cucumber**
2 **scallions, shredded into ½-inch lengths**

Sauce Mixture
2 **tablespoons sesame seed paste or creamy peanut butter**

2 **tablespoons Chinese sesame oil**
2 **tablespoons dark soy sauce**
1½ **tablespoons rice vinegar**
About 1 to 3 teaspoons hot chili oil
1½ **teaspoons sugar**
1½ **teaspoons ginger, finely minced**
1½ **teaspoons garlic, finely minced**

1. Place chicken in a saucepan and add water to cover. Heat to boiling; simmer chicken until tender but firm, about 15 minutes. Do not overcook. Remove from heat; let chicken stand in cooking liquid until cool. Drain the chicken. Cool. Tear into strips, 3 × ¼ inch each.
2. Make sauce. With a whisk, beat sesame seed paste and sesame oil in medium-size bowl until smooth. Add soy sauce, vinegar, hot chili oil, and sugar. Mix well into smooth paste. Add ginger and garlic. Mix. Set aside.
3. Deep-fry peanuts in 1 cup oil until golden brown. Drain and cool. Place peanuts in a plastic bag and crush them with a rolling pin. Set aside.
4. Cut cucumber in half lengthwise; remove seeds wih a spoon. Slice thinly to form half crescent shapes. Arrange cucumber around the edge of a plate. Place any remaining cucumber in the center of the plate. Place the chicken in the center. Pour some of the sauce on top. Garnish with scallions and chopped peanuts. Present this attractive platter to your guests. Toss all ingredients together at the table. Add remaining sauce.

Tip: This dish may be served on dried cellophane noodles. Soak 2 ounces noodles in very warm water for 15 minutes or until they just soften. Drain well. Place noodles on a platter. Arrange the chicken on top of the noodles. Pour sauce on top. Garnish with scallions and chopped peanuts.

Advance Preparation: The chicken and the sauce may be prepared 1 day ahead of time. Assemble the platter 3 to 4 hours before your guests arrive. Pour sauce on dish and garnish when serving.

Makes 3 main-course servings or 8 to 12 appetizer servings.

Chicken in Mustard Sauce

The following is a very attractive Chinese "salad" which may be made ahead and served at room temperature.

Chicken Mixture
2 **chicken breasts, boned, skinned, cut into matchstick strips**
1 **egg white, lightly beaten**
4 **teaspoons cornstarch**

4 **ounces raw peanuts**
1 **cup oil**
2 **cups celery cabbage, shredded**
6 **scallions, shredded into 1½-inch strips**
2 **cups cucumbers, halved, seeded, cut into ⅛-inch slices**
½ **red bell pepper, chopped**

Sauce Mixture
2 **tablespoons dark soy sauce**
2 **tablespoons Chinese red vinegar**
2 **tablespoons Chinese sesame oil**
4 **teaspoons water**
4 **teaspoons dry mustard powder**
4 **teaspoons sugar**

½ **red bell pepper, shredded**

1. Combine chicken, egg white, and cornstarch. Let marinate for 20 minutes.
2. Deep-fry the peanuts in 1 cup hot oil until lightly browned. Drain on paper towels. Place the nuts in a plastic bag and crush with a rolling pin.
3. Add the chicken shreds to 1 quart boiling water. Turn off the heat. Stir to separate the pieces. Let chicken remain in the water 1 minute. Pour into a strainer. Rinse with cold water. Drain well.
4. Combine sauce ingredients and mix into smooth sauce. Do 10 minutes before serving; mustard loses its power if left standing too long. Arrange the celery cabbage strips, and half the scallions in the center of a platter. Place the cucumber slices and bell pepper around the edge. Top with the chicken shreds. Pour the mustard mixture over the chicken evenly and garnish with the remaining scallions, crushed nuts, and red bell pepper. Serve at room temperature.

Variation: Curry may be substituted for the mustard. Carrots may be substituted for red pepper.

Makes 4 main course servings.

Beef Jerky

This flavorful beef snack is dried slowly in the oven and is best made several days in advance.

1½ **pounds flank steak, partially frozen, cut in half lengthwise, sliced diagonally crosswise into paper-thin slices, 4 × 1½ inches each**
¼ **cup light soy sauce**
3 **tablespoons honey**

2½ **tablespoons dry sherry**
1 **tablespoon Chinese sesame oil**
2 **teaspoons garlic, minced**
2 **teaspoons ginger, minced**
2 **teaspoons crushed red pepper flakes**

1. Combine all ingredients. Let marinate overnight.
2. Heat oven to 250°. Place wire racks on 2 large baking sheets. Arrange the meat on the racks in single layers. Bake 30 minutes. Reduce heat to 200°; turn meat and bake 30 minutes. Reduce heat to 175° and bake 40 to 60 minutes. Do not burn meat. Let the meat continue to dry on racks at cool room temperature overnight before packing into jars. Brush lightly with sesame oil for more flavor.

Advance Preparation: Prepare dish completely 2 to 3 days in advance.

Cinnamon-Flavored Beef

The following beef dish with a hint of cinnamon can be served hot or at room temperature, making it ideal for entertaining. The flavor improves if the meat is prepared a day or two in advance.

Beef Mixture
1½ pounds flank steak, cut into strips 2 × 1½ × ¼ inch each
3 tablespoons dry sherry
2 slices ginger, the size of a quarter, flattened with the flat side of a cleaver
¾ teaspoon salt

Sauce Mixture
1 cup chicken broth
3 tablespoons dry sherry
3 tablespoons sugar
2 tablespoons light soy sauce

3 cups oil
3 tablespoons Chinese sesame oil
4 dried chili peppers
12 Szechuan peppercorns
1 star anise
2 tablespoons dried tangerine peel, soaked in hot water 20 minutes, shredded into matchstick strips
3 to 4 inch cinnamon stick
1 tablespoon Chinese sesame oil
1 teaspoon rice vinegar

1. Combine meat, 3 tablespoons sherry, the ginger, and salt. Let marinate 3 hours. Combine sauce ingredients. Set aside.
2. In wok, deep-fry the beef in 3 cups hot oil until the pieces separate and change color. Remove. Drain the oil in the wok.
3. Heat 3 tablespoons sesame oil in the wok. Add the dried peppers, peppercorns, and star anise. Stir-fry 30 seconds or until they are fragrant. Add the beef, tangerine peel, cinnamon stick, and sauce mixture. Heat to boiling; simmer 20 to 30 minutes or until the liquid is reduced by two-thirds. Stir-fry mixture over high heat for 3 minutes or until the sauce is reduced to a syrup. Add 1 tablespoon sesame oil and 1 teaspoon rice vinegar. Toss. Serve hot or room temperature.

Variation: Substitute 1 tablespoon finely grated orange rind for the dried tangerine peel.

Advance Preparation: Prepare dish completely 1 day in advance. Bring to room temperature at serving time or heat in a 325-degree oven for 15 to 20 minutes if serving hot.

Makes 3 to 4 servings as an entrée or 6 to 8 dim sum servings.

Aromatic Spiced Beef

A Chinese banquet often begins with cold, aromatic spiced beef. The beef is cooked with star anise, chilled until firm, and sliced paper thin with a sauce spooned over the meat.

The meat keeps well and the flavor improves by the second or third day. It can be served on a cold mixed platter or as part of a cold stirred vegetable dish.

2 **pounds boneless shin beef, in 1 piece**
4 **tablespoons oil**
3 **slices ginger, the size of a quarter, peeled**
2 **scallions, cut into 2-inch lengths**
⅓ **cup dark soy sauce**
½ **cup dry sherry**

½ **teaspoon salt**
3 **tablespoons crushed rock sugar or 2 tablespoons granulated sugar**
2 **whole star anise**
4 to 5 **cups boiling water or to cover the beef**
Coriander

1. Trim the beef of any fat and tough membrane covering.
2. Heat a heavy pot that will hold the meat securely. Add oil and heat. Add ginger and scallions; stir for 30 seconds. Add the beef and brown on all sides. Reduce the heat; add the soy sauce and turn the meat to color it. Add the sherry, salt, sugar, star anise, and boiling water to cover. Stir. Reduce the heat. Skim off the residue. Simmer, covered, for 1½ to 2 hours, turning the meat every 30 minutes. Adjust the flavor the last 30 minutes by adding a little more soy sauce or sugar to taste—the flavor should be extremely mellow. The water should cover the meat entirely and when the meat is done, it should be saturated by the sauce. There should be 1 cup of sauce remaining. If the meat gets too dry during cooking, add 1 tablespoon water mixed with 1 tablespoon soy sauce. The meat should not be cooked to the point of falling apart. The texture should be firm, neither soft nor hard.
3. Transfer the beef to a bowl. Strain the sauce into another bowl. Cool the beef and the sauce. Cover and refrigerate. Cut the meat into ¼-inch or slightly thicker slices. Arrange on a platter. Garnish with fresh coriander. Serve cold with the sauce.

Tip: If there is more than 1 cup of sauce remaining after cooking the beef, reduce it by boiling the liquid to 1 cup.

Makes 8 to 12 servings or 16 to 20 dim sum servings.

Cold Lamb in Aspic

This elegant dish is very popular during the Chinese New Year. It makes a wonderful hors d'oeuvre, or first course, or even a picnic treat. Serve cold.

1 **pound lean boned leg of lamb, trimmed, cut into 8 uniform pieces**
Water to cover the lamb
2 **cloves garlic, crushed**
2 **scallions, flattened with the flat side of the cleaver**
4 **slices ginger, the size of a quarter, flattened with the flat side of a cleaver**
1 **whole star anise**

2 **3-inch cinnamon sticks**
1 **teaspoon sugar**
1 **teaspoon salt**
3 **tablespoons light soy sauce**
3 **tablespoons dry sherry or rice wine**
2 **tablespoons gelatin**
¾ **cup cold water**
Coriander
3 **tablespoons ginger, peeled, finely shredded**

1. Cook the lamb covered with water in a heavy medium-sized saucepan. Heat the water to boiling and cook 3 minutes. Drain. Rinse lamb well and return to the pan. Skim off any residue if necessary to make a clearer sauce. Add garlic, scallions, ginger slices, anise, cinnamon, sugar, salt, soy sauce, and sherry. Heat to boiling; reduce heat. Simmer, covered, until the meat is very tender, for 1½ to 2 hours. The meat should be soft enough to be shredded with chopsticks. Remove the lamb, reserving the liquid and let cool for 10 minutes. Cut it into small 1-inch cubes.
2. Strain the reserved liquid through a fine sieve. Discard the solids. Measure 1 cup and return to the saucepan.
3. Sprinkle the gelatin over ¾ cup cold water to soften for 15 minutes. Add to the strained liquid and heat gently, stirring until the gelatin dissolves.
4. Rinse a loaf pan mold, 8 × 4 inches, with cold water. Pour a quarter inch of the liquid in the mold. Refrigerate. Place the lamb in the mold, pour remaining liquid over it and chill the mold, covered, for at least 6 hours or until it is set.
5. To serve, remove any fat formed on top of aspic. Run a thin knife around the inside of the mold to loosen the jellied lamb around the edges and dip the bottom of the mold in hot water for a few seconds. Wipe the outside of the mold completely dry. Invert a serving plate on top and invert the mold onto the plate.

Rap the plate on a table and the jellied lamb should easily slide out of the mold. Cut the lamb into ½-inch slices and arrange these in a row down the center of the platter, overlapping them slightly. Serve chilled garnished with coriander. Sprinkle the shredded ginger on top.

Tip: Prepare lamb 1 day in advance.

Makes 3 to 4 main-course servings or 6 to 8 servings as dim sum.

Shrimp with Scallions

The flavor of this marvelous cold dish improves upon standing. It is very popular for Eastern buffets. The shells are left on, giving the shrimp a savory texture and aroma. The finished dish may be served hot or cold.

1 pound very small shrimp with shells	**10 scallions, finely chopped**
3 tablespoons oil	*Sauce Mixture*
2 tablespoons ginger, peeled, minced	**¼ cup light soy sauce**
	¼ cup dry sherry
4 medium cloves garlic, crushed, peeled	**4 teaspoons sugar**
	½ teaspoon Chinese sesame oil

1. Wash shrimp; remove legs. Cut the shrimp about ½ inch through the shell along the back (leave shells intact). Remove the black vein. Dry thoroughly.
2. Combine sauce ingredients. Set aside.
3. Heat wok. Add oil and heat. Add the ginger and garlic and stir about 10 seconds. Add the shrimp and stir rapidly until the shrimp turn pink and the tails are bright red, about 30 to 45 seconds. Add the scallions and stir 20 seconds. Add the sauce mixture. Stir-fry 1 minute until the sauce flavors the shrimp. Serve immediately or let the shrimp cool and refrigerate. To eat, bite into the shell and extract the meat.

Makes 2 to 3 servings as a main course or 6 to 8 servings as dim sum.

Happy Shrimp Rolls

These delightful rolls are very pretty and are shaped in the form of the Chinese symbol of happiness. In China, they are saved for weddings, banquets, and birthdays. The rolls can be made in advance and served hot or at room temperature.

1½ teaspoons water
3 eggs, slightly beaten
pinch salt
1 teaspoon cornstarch

¼ teaspoon salt
¼ teaspoon white pepper
½ teaspoon Chinese sesame oil
½ egg white, lightly beaten
1 tablespoon cornstarch

Shrimp Mixture
¾ pound shrimp, shelled, deveined, minced to a paste
1 ounce pork fat, minced to a paste
½ teaspoon ginger, minced
1 tablespoon scallions, minced
12 water chestnuts, minced
2 teaspoons dry sherry

2 purple laver or nori sheets
1 carrot, blanched in water 2 minutes, cut into matchstick pieces ¼ inch thick, the length of the egg sheet
1 tablespoon flour
1 tablespoon water

1. Combine water and cornstarch and add to slightly beaten eggs and salt. Set aside.
2. Combine shrimp and pork fat. Add ginger, scallions, water chestnuts, sherry, salt, pepper, sesame oil, ½ egg white, and cornstarch. Combine until the mixture is sticky and a spreadable paste. If using food processor, do not overprocess.
3. Heat wok or 10-inch skillet. Lightly grease wok with oil. Pour in one-third the egg mixture, tilting and rotating the wok to form a thin layer. Cook over medium heat until egg is set. Turn the egg sheet over and cook for 15 seconds more. Transfer to plate and make 2 more egg sheets.
4. Trim the egg sheet to make an even square. Sprinkle egg sheet lightly with cornstarch. Spread a thin layer of the shrimp paste on it. Place purple laver on top. Trim purple laver to fit egg sheet. Sprinkle lightly with cornstarch and spread shrimp paste on purple laver. Place 2 carrot sticks on each end. Roll closest edge of egg sheet to center and roll the opposite edge to center to make a scroll shape. Prepare remaining shrimp rolls. To

secure, brush roll edges with flour and water. Place on lightly greased, heat-proof plate, seam side down. Steam 10 minutes on medium heat. Remove, and cut into ¾-inch slices at serving time.

Variation: Substitute sliced ham for the purple laver.

Tip: To make crispy shrimp rolls, steam as above. Dust with cornstarch. Sauté in hot oil until crisp. Cut into slices.

Advance Preparation: Completely prepare 1 day in advance. Refrigerate. Slice and serve at serving time. To serve warm, steam ahead. Reheat by steaming at serving time.

Makes 6 to 8 appetizer servings.

Hot and Sour Shrimp

This is an unusually attractive cold dish combining a colorful array of shrimp, cucumber, red peppers and black mushrooms. It may be prepared well in advance and is certain to be a big hit with your guests.

1 **pound unpeeled shrimp (about 20)**
1 **firm cucumber**

½ **cup red wine vinegar**
½ **cup sugar**
Salt

Sauce Mixture
¼ **cup Chinese sesame oil**
2 **tablespoons oil**
2 to 3 **dried red peppers**
1 **teaspoon Szechuan peppercorn powder**

8 **Chinese dried black mushrooms, soaked in hot water until spongy, stems removed, shredded**
1 **red pepper, shredded**

1. Drop shrimp into boiling water to cover. When water returns to boiling, cook 45 seconds or until shrimp turn pink. Drain shrimp. Rinse under cold water to chill and stop cooking. Remove shells, devein, and split the shrimp in half. Refrigerate.
2. Cut cucumber in half. Scoop out seeds with a spoon. Do not remove the skin. Slice the cucumber thinly and set aside.
3. Prepare sauce. Heat the sesame oil and oil in wok. Add the dried peppers and peppercorn powder. Cook, stirring until the dried peppers turn blackish. Remove wok from heat and strain the hot seasoned oil, removing spices. Wipe out wok.
4. Return the seasoned oil to the wok. Combine the vinegar and sugar; add to the wok. Add salt to taste. Heat to boiling and let bubble, stirring until the sugar dissolves. Let the mixture cool and pour into a container.
5. Arrange the cucumber on a platter. Place the shrimp in the center of the platter on top of the cucumber. Place the shredded black mushrooms and red pepper around the edge of the platter in a decorative fashion.
6. Cover with plastic wrap and refrigerate until ready to serve. When serving, pour the sauce over the dish and toss at the table.

Advance Preparation: Prepare sauce 3 to 4 days in advance. Prepare the shrimp 1 day in advance. Cut up the vegetables the morning of serving.

Makes 4 servings as a main course.

Vegetable Rolls

These Vegetable Rolls are cool, refreshing snacks with a piquant flavor. Make ahead and serve cold.

12 leaves Chinese cabbage
2 carrots, shredded
½ teaspoon salt
½ pound Chinese turnip, peeled, shredded
1 teaspoon salt

2 tablespoons ginger, shredded, peeled
2 teaspoons rice vinegar
2 teaspoons sugar
1 teaspoon Chinese sesame oil
Dash pepper
2 hot red peppers, shredded

1. Rinse cabbage leaves. Cook in boiling water until soft, about 1½ minutes. Remove cabbage and plunge into cold water to stop cooking. Cut off hard stems and cut each leaf into 5-inch pieces. Remove all excess moisture.
2. Place shredded carrots in a colander. Add ½ teaspoon salt and let soften about 10 minutes. Rinse with water; drain and squeeze well, removing any excess water.
3. Place shredded Chinese turnip in colander. Add 1 teaspoon salt to Chinese turnip in colander. Repeat process as in carrots.
4. Combine carrots, Chinese turnip, ginger, vinegar, sugar, sesame oil, and dash pepper. Let stand 10 minutes.
5. Place cabbage leaf on flat surface. Place carrot-turnip mixture in middle of each cabbage leaf. Place 1 slice hot red pepper on top of mixture. Roll like a spring roll. Cut each roll in half. Serve.

Tip: Chopped, soaked wood ears can be used to garnish the vegetable rolls. Substitute 1 teaspoon hot oil for sesame oil.

Makes 24 half-rolls.

Scallion Smoked Fish

This is a marvelous preparation of fish. The Chinese smoking method of burning sugar and tea together provides an intriguing flavoring. The fish is first steamed, then smoked, making it particularly succulent. It tastes even better the next day served cold. Either a whole fish or fillets are wonderful.

1 **whole fish (flounder, fluke, walleye pike, whitefish, or any centrally boned fish)**

1 **tablespoon salt**
1 **tablespoon dry sherry**
1 **tablespoon light soy sauce**

Fish Marinade
2 **pieces ginger, the size of a quarter, peeled, smashed with the flat side of a cleaver**
2 **scallions, smashed with the flat side of a cleaver**
1 **tablespoon Szechuan peppercorn powder**

½ **cup loosely packed brown sugar**
¼ **cup black tea leaves**
8 **large whole scallions, crushed lightly with a cleaver**
Chinese sesame oil
Shredded lettuce for garnish

1. Clean the fish, leaving the head and tail on. Rinse and dry thoroughly. Rub the ginger, scallions, peppercorn powder, salt, sherry, and soy sauce into the fish on both sides and the inside as well. Let the fish marinate refrigerated for 2 hours.
2. Place 3 chopsticks lengthwise on a heat-proof platter. Place the fish on top of the chopsticks so that it will not lie directly on the platter during steaming.
3. Steam the fish over medium-high heat for 8 to 10 minutes. Remove to a dry plate. Dry with paper towels.
4. Line the wok with heavy-duty aluminum foil. Sprinkle the foil with sugar and tea. Place an oiled rack in the wok and lay the whole scallions on the rack. Place the fish on top of the scallions. Cover the wok; wrap excess foil around wok cover for tight fit. Heat wok over moderate heat 5 minutes or until mixture begins to smoke. Cook over medium heat and smoke about 8 minutes until the fish turns light brown. Turn the fish over; cover and smoke about 6 minutes more. Let fish stand, covered, in the wok for 15 minutes.
5. Place the smoked fish on a chopping board and brush both

sides lightly with sesame oil. Serve fish whole or cut it crosswise into 4 large pieces and serve reassembled into a whole fish. Garnish the plate with shredded lettuce.

Variation: Make a bed of charcoal in the barbecue and ignite. When the surface turns to ash, set a metal pie plate containing the smoking ingredients on the coals. Cover it with a grate and set the fish on the grate. Cover the grill and smoke the fish for 15 minutes or until evenly browned. Check the coals to make sure they do not die down.

Tips: Serve fish cold with soy mayonnaise, by combining the following ingredients:

Soy Mayonnaise

1 cup mayonnaise
2 teaspoons light soy sauce
$\frac{1}{2}$ to 1 teaspoon rice vinegar
Lemon juice and white pepper
    to taste

When cooking fillets the best types are $\frac{1}{2}$-inch thick carp, haddock, whitefish, or lake trout. Use fillets with the skin. Steam the fillets for 6 minutes. Smoke the fish for 10 minutes. Do not oversteam the fish as it will fall apart.

Makes 4 servings.

Spiced Eggplant

This spiced salad, which can be served hot or cold, is composed of soft eggplant strips in a delicious sauce. Eggplant is extremely versatile and soaks up sauces readily. Chinese eggplants are usually smaller than American ones; they are about the size and shape of zucchini. If little Italian eggplants are available, use them. In any case, avoid large overripe eggplants, which tend to be spongy and have too many seeds.

1¾ pounds baby eggplant

Sauce Mixture
3 tablespoons light soy sauce
2 tablespoons red wine vinegar
2 tablespoons Chinese sesame oil
1 tablespoon dry sherry

1½ tablespoons sugar
1 tablespoon hot chili oil
1 tablespoon garlic, minced
1 tablespoon ginger, minced
1 tablespoon scallion, minced
1 tablespoon white sesame seeds
Salt to taste

1. Steam the eggplant in a heat-proof bowl for 20 minutes or until the eggplant is tender and in a slightly collapsed condition. Cool. If the eggplant is mature, remove skin.
2. Combine soy sauce, vinegar, sesame oil, sherry, sugar, hot chili oil, garlic, ginger, and scallion. Set sauce mixture aside.
3. Toast sesame seeds in a pan over medium-low heat, shaking the pan and stirring the seeds until they are pale brown. Remove from the pan. Let cool.
4. Pull the eggplant into shreds. If seeds are tough because the eggplant is too mature, discard them. Pour sauce mixture over the eggplant. Sprinkle with sesame seeds. Serve hot or cold.

Tip: Larger, more mature eggplants may require more sugar.

Makes 4 to 6 servings.

Hot and Sour Cucumbers

These crisp and tangy cucumbers, combined with red peppers, are a cool, refreshing addition to any meal.

2 firm, slender, unwaxed cucumbers (about 1 pound)	2 to 4 dried chili peppers
1 red bell pepper, cut into strips (½ cup)	2 tablespoons rice vinegar
3 tablespoons oil	*Sauce Mixture*
1 large clove garlic, peeled, lightly crushed	1 tablespoon light soy sauce
	2 tablespoons sugar
	½ teaspoon salt

1. Trim off the ends of cucumbers. Cut cucumbers lengthwise in half. Scrape out the seeds with a small spoon and cut each half lengthwise into 4 strips. Cut each strip lengthwise into 4 sections.
2. Prepare sauce. Mix light soy sauce, sugar, and salt in a large bowl. Set sauce mixture aside.
3. Heat wok. Add 3 tablespoons oil. Add garlic and chili peppers (2 for a mild dish, 4 for hot). Cook until garlic is light brown and peppers have darkened.
4. Add cucumbers and red pepper. Stir-fry for 30 seconds until cucumber skin is bright green. Add sauce mixture. Stir for 5 seconds to combine mixture and dissolve sugar. Do not brown sugar. Pour into a dish. Let cool; cover and refrigerate until cold, stirring a few times for even marinating.
5. Drain and transfer mixture to a serving dish. Add the vinegar; toss to mix well and serve.

Makes 4 main course servings or 8 appetizer servings.

Asparagus Sesame Salad

A cool, refreshing, easily made salad, this dish can be made several hours in advance and refrigerated until serving time.

1 bunch asparagus, stems peeled, tough ends removed, cut diagonally into 1½-inch pieces (1 pound)
1 scallion, shredded into 1½-inch lengths
¼ cup toasted white sesame seeds

Lettuce (optional)

Sauce Mixture
2 tablespoons lemon juice
2 tablespoons oil
Salt to taste
Dash white pepper

1. Steam asparagus for 2 minutes over water. Remove. Rinse with cold water. Cool. (The asparagus should just be slightly cooked.)
2. Mix lemon juice, oil, white pepper, and salt to taste. Pour mixture over the asparagus. Garnish with scallion shreds. Refrigerate until cold.
3. Serve asparagus on a bed of lettuce. Garnish with sesame seeds.

Tip: To toast sesame seeds, heat a small pan over medium-high heat. Add the sesame seeds and toast, stirring occasionally, until lightly browned.

Makes 4 servings.

Bean Sprout Salad

Delicious and refreshing, this salad is a crisp, light, inexpensive addition to any meal. Be sure to use fresh white bean sprouts.

½ **pound bean sprouts**
½ **cup ham, shredded into 1½-inch shreds**
½ **medium cucumber, pared, halved, seeded, shredded into 1½-inch shreds**

Dressing Mixture
1 **tablespoon light soy sauce**
1 **tablespoon Chinese sesame oil**
1 **tablespoon rice vinegar**
1 **tablespoon sugar**
½ **teaspoon salt**

1. Heat 1½ quarts water to boiling. Remove from heat. Immerse bean sprouts in the water for 45 seconds. Drain. Rinse with cold water until chilled. Drain well. Place bean sprouts on a platter. Scatter ham and cucumber on top.
2. Combine dressing ingredients in a bowl. Pour the mixture over salad. Serve immediately.

Variations: Substitute ¼ cup finely shredded carrots for the ham.
Omit the ham and cucumber and serve bean sprouts alone as a salad.
Makes 4 servings.

Spicy Vegetable Salad

Crisp vegetables combine nicely with a tangy sauce to produce a real palate pleaser.

¼ **pound snow peas, strings removed**
2 **medium cucumbers, pared, halved, seeded, cut into ¼-inch slices**
2 **small celery stalks, peeled, cut into 2-inch matchsticks**
1 **medium red bell pepper, shredded**
2 **tablespoons oil**

1 **tablespoon chili paste with garlic**

Dressing Mixture
¼ **cup light soy sauce**
¼ **cup rice vinegar**
2½ **tablespoons Chinese sesame oil**
4 **tablespoons brown sugar**

1. Blanch snow peas in boiling water 30 seconds. Rinse with cold water; drain. Shred into 2-inch shreds. Combine snow peas, cucumbers, celery, and red pepper.
2. Mix dressing ingredients. Set aside.
3. Heat wok. Add 2 tablespoons oil. Add chili paste and stir-fry until heated. Add dressing mixture. Mix well. Remove and set aside.
4. Combine the vegetables and dressing 1 hour before serving. Cover and refrigerate until serving time.

Tips: Any desired vegetable can be substituted for the vegetables called for in the recipe.

This salad is also delicious when the vegetables are marinated 6 to 8 hours. This allows the dressing to penetrate the vegetables, imparting a different texture and taste.

Makes 4 servings.

Tomato and Cucumber Salad

A hot cooked sauce poured over the uncooked vegetables creates an interesting combination of tastes and textures.

2 tomatoes
1 cucumber, halved, seeded, cut into ½-inch slices

Sauce Mixture
2 tablespoons sugar

2 tablespoons rice vinegar
1 tablespoon ketchup
1 teaspoon cornstarch dissolved in 1½ tablespoons water
½ teaspoon Chinese sesame oil

1. Dip tomatoes in hot water for 2 minutes. Peel; cut into wedges.
2. Combine sauce ingredients. Cook over low heat until thickened.
3. Arrange cucumber slices in the center of a platter. Place tomato wedges around the edge. Pour hot sauce over the vegetables.

Makes 4 servings.

Lotus Root Salad

Fresh lotus root is available in late summer and fall. It is extremely pretty with its delicate, lacy appearance. This salad is served often around Hangchow, Soochow, and Shanghai where the lotus root is plentiful.

1½ pounds fresh lotus root, peeled, cut crosswise into ⅛-inch slices, placed in ice water to prevent darkening
2 red peppers, cut into julienne strips

Dressing Mixture
2 tablespoons rice vinegar
1½ tablespoons sugar
1 tablespoon Chinese sesame oil
½ teaspoon salt
½ teaspoon hot chili oil

1. Combine dressing ingredients. Stir until sugar is dissolved. Set aside.
2. Blanch lotus root in boiling salted water for 1½ minutes. Drain. Rinse under cold water. Drain well.
3. Combine lotus root with the red peppers and the sauce mixture. Stir until vegetables are well coated. Refrigerate, covered, for 20 minutes.

Makes 4 servings.

Jade Salad

This high-protein salad may be served either as an appetizer or as a main course. The addition of the Szechuan preserved vegetable gives the salad a spicy taste. It is best when made ahead of time so the flavors can blend.

1 pound fresh spinach, rinsed, tough part of stems removed

2 squares seasoned pressed bean curd, cut into shreds ¾ × ⅛ × ⅛ inch each

3 tablespoons cooked Smithfield or Westphalian ham, minced

2 tablespoons Szechuan preserved vegetables, minced (optional)

Sauce Mixture

2 tablespoons light soy sauce

1 tablespoon Chinese sesame oil

1 teaspoon hot chili oil

½ teaspoon cider vinegar

1 teaspoon sugar

Egg Sheet

2 teaspoons oil

1 egg combined with pinch salt, beaten lightly

1. Blanch spinach in 6 cups boiling water for 45 seconds. Drain. Rinse with cold water. Drain. Blot with a towel to remove excess moisture. Chop into pieces 1 inch long each. Place spinach in a serving bowl. Combine sauce ingredients. Mix well.
2. Add the bean curd, ham, and preserved vegetable to spinach. Mix well. Pour the sauce mixture over the spinach mixture. Cover and refrigerate 4 hours or a day in advance.
3. To make egg sheet: Prepare shortly before serving to maintain a fluffy consistency. Heat a 9-inch skillet until hot; add the oil. Heat. Pour out any excess oil. Add the egg; tilt over medium low heat to spread the egg thinly over the bottom of the skillet. When the egg sheet is light brown, turn and cook the other side for 10 seconds. Remove to a chopping block. Let cool. Cut egg sheet into ¾ × ⅛ inch shreds. To serve, sprinkle the egg shreds over the top of the spinach mixture.

Variation: Omit the ham, seasoned pressed bean curd, and preserved vegetables. Use baked ham or bacon.

Makes 4 servings.

Chilled Red Radishes

Colorful with a peppery and piquant flavor, this appetizer should be chilled slightly before serving. Use only firm-fleshed round red radishes.

8 ounces firm red radishes, sliced
1 teaspoon salt
1 teaspoon rice vinegar

Dressing Mixture
1 teaspoon sugar
3 teaspoons light soy sauce
1½ tablespoons oil
1 tablespoon Chinese sesame oil

1. Sprinkle the radishes with the salt in a large bowl; mix well. Cover the bowl with plastic wrap; let stand 6 hours or overnight in the refrigerator, stirring occasionally.
2. Combine the dressing ingredients. Drain the salt water; rinse the radishes briefly under cold running water. Press them with a kitchen towel to extract their moisture. Add to the dressing mixture. Chill slightly before serving.

Note: For a sharper taste, add more vinegar.

Makes 4 to 6 servings.

Green Beans with Peanuts

This easily prepared vegetable dish may be served hot, cold, or at room temperature. Oyster-flavored sauce enhances the flavor of the vegetables.

2 tablespoons oil
1 teaspoon garlic, minced
½ pound fresh green beans, cut into julienne strips
3 tablespoons dry roasted peanuts, crushed

Sauce Mixture
3 tablespoons oyster-flavored sauce
3 tablespoons rice vinegar

1. Mix oyster-flavored sauce and vinegar. Set sauce mixture aside.
2. Heat wok. Add oil. Heat. Add garlic and stir-fry 10 seconds. Add green beans. Stir-fry 1½ minutes, until crisp but tender. Add sauce mixture. Toss together and cook until heated through. Garnish with peanuts. Serve.

Tip: Substitute frozen julienned green beans. Thaw beans. Dry before stir-frying.   Makes 3 to 4 servings.

Stir-Fried Cabbage

Cabbage takes on a whole new flavor dimension when prepared in this ancient Chinese manner.

1½ pounds cabbage
2 tablespoons oil
2 pieces ginger, the size of a quarter, peeled, sliced

1 teaspoon salt
1 teaspoon sugar
2 teaspoons Chinese sesame oil

1. Core the cabbage; cut it into strips ½-inch wide. Rinse with water; drain.
2. Heat wok. Add oil. Heat. Add the ginger and press the slices around the pan. Add the cabbage and stir-fry for 3 minutes. Add the salt and sugar. Reduce heat to low; cover and cook the cabbage for 10 minutes. Uncover, stir and cook for another 10 minutes. Cook, covered, for an additional 10 minutes. (Total cooking time is 30 minutes.) Add the sesame oil. Stir and serve.

Makes 4 to 6 servings.

Cold Noodles with Chicken and Shrimp

An extremely attractive presentation of crisp vegetables and noodles on a serving platter, this recipe makes an excellent one-dish meal or it can be served as part of a multicourse dinner. Quantities can be easily increased to serve large groups.

10 ounces thin Chinese fresh egg noodles
1 tablespoon Chinese sesame oil
1 chicken breast, skinned and boned
2 slices ginger the size of a quarter, smashed with the side of a cleaver
2 tablespoons dry sherry
½ pound shelled, deveined shrimp
1 cucumber, halved, seeded, shredded

1 red bell pepper, shredded
2 cups bean sprouts
3 scallions, shredded into 1-inch lengths
4 teaspoons roasted peanuts, chopped

Sauce Mixture
6 tablespoons light soy sauce
4 teaspoons Chinese red vinegar or red wine vinegar
2 tablespoons sugar
1 tablespoon salt
1 tablespoon Chinese sesame oil

1. Cook noodles in 3 quarts water until al dente. Remove. Rinse with cold water. Drain. Toss with 1 tablespoon sesame oil. Refrigerate.
2. Heat 2 quarts of water in a saucepan to boiling. Add chicken breast; return water to boiling. Reduce heat to low and simmer for 20 minutes. Remove from heat. Drain, cool, and refrigerate. Cut into ½-inch strips.
3. Heat 4 cups water to boiling. Add ginger and sherry. Add shrimp and cook 45 seconds or until pink. Turn off heat. Drain shrimp. Cool. Refrigerate.
4. Combine sauce ingredients.
5. Place noodles on a large platter. Arrange cucumber and red pepper around the edge of the platter. Place bean sprouts in the center of the platter over the noodles. Place chicken on top of the bean sprouts. Garnish with shrimp and scallions.
6. Pour sauce over the dish. Sprinkle peanuts on top. Present this attractive dish to your guests. Toss the mixture lightly at the table to combine the ingredients before eating.

Variations: Use all chicken or all shrimp for the dish. Cubed ham may be substituted for the chicken and shrimp. Shredded carrots may be substituted for the red pepper. For a special dish, add 1 to 2 teaspoons hot chili oil.

Advance Preparation: Cook chicken, shrimp, and noodles 1 day in advance. Toss noodles in sesame oil. Place in plastic bag and refrigerate. Noodle dish may be assembled several hours in advance. Cover with plastic wrap. Refrigerate.

Makes 8 servings.

Cold Szechuan Sesame Chicken Shred Noodles

Perfect for a buffet, cold noodles and crispy vegetables combined with a peppery hot sesame-based sauce, make a very pretty and tasty dish. This recipe can be doubled easily and prepared well in advance. It also makes a very refreshing one-dish meal.

8 ounces fresh thin Chinese egg noodles
1 tablespoon Chinese sesame oil
2 chicken breasts, skinned and boned
2 cups bean sprouts

Sauce Mixture
½ cup dark soy sauce
¼ cup Chinese red vinegar or red wine vinegar
2½ tablespoons sesame seed paste or creamy peanut butter
2 tablespoons sugar

2 tablespoons Chinese sesame oil
2 tablespoons oil

1 to 3 dried chili peppers
1 tablespoon ginger, peeled, minced
2 teaspoons garlic, minced
½ teaspoon Szechuan peppercorn powder
2 cups Chinese cabbage, shredded
1 cup scallions, shredded into 1-inch pieces

2 cups cucumbers, halved, seeded, shredded
1 red bell pepper, shredded into 1½-inch lengths
⅓ cup roasted peanuts, chopped

1. Cook noodles in 3 quarts water until al dente. Rinse with cold water. Chill. Drain well. Toss with 1 tablespoon sesame oil. Place in a plastic bag. Chill.
2. Heat 2 quarts of water to boiling in a saucepan. Add chicken breasts and return the water back to boiling. Reduce heat to low; simmer for 20 minutes. Remove from the heat. Cut into ½-inch strips.
3. Heat 1½ quarts water to boiling. Remove from heat. Add bean sprouts. Let stand for 45 seconds. Drain. Rinse with cold water. Drain and chill.
4. Combine soy sauce, vinegar, sesame seed paste, and sugar. Mix well with a whisk. Heat wok. Add sesame oil and oil. Heat the oils. Add the dried peppers, and press against the side of the wok until peppers have darkened. Add ginger, garlic, and peppercorn powder; brown them slightly. Stir in the sauce mixture; cook, stirring for about 10 seconds until blended.

Remove from the heat. Let cool to room temperature. (This may be done well in advance.)

5. Place chilled noodles on a serving platter. Sprinkle the cabbage, bean sprouts, and half the scallions on the noodles. Arrange the chicken breast strips neatly on the cabbage mixture. Place the shredded cucumber around the edge of the platter. Pour the sauce over the chicken just before serving. Sprinkle the remaining scallions, red pepper, and peanuts over the top in a decorative fashion. Serve at room temperature. Let guests see your lovely creation, then toss the salad just before eating.

Variations: Substitute 1 cup shredded carrots for the red pepper. Substitute 1 pound cooked shrimp for the chicken.

Advance Preparation: Prepare all ingredients in advance. Assemble dish several hours before serving time. Cover with plastic wrap. Refrigerate. Pour sauce over dish at serving time.

Makes 8 servings.

Tangy Noodles

There are two ways to serve these noodles. Both preparations are made ahead and served at room temperature or chilled. The noodles may be presented with sauce alone or with vegetables.

1 pound fresh Chinese egg noodles
2 tablespoons scallions, sliced

Sauce Mixture
3½ tablespoons dark soy sauce
2 tablespoons Chinese sesame oil

1½ tablespoons Chinese black vinegar or red wine vinegar
½ to 1 tablespoon hot chili oil
3 tablespoons sesame seed paste or creamy peanut butter
1½ tablespoons sugar
2 teaspoons salt

1. Cook noodles until al dente. Do not overcook. Separate noodles as they cook. Drain immediately. Rinse with cold running water. Drain well. Place in a large bowl.
2. Combine sauce ingredients. Add to noodles; mix well. Add the scallions. Mix well. Serve at room temperature or refrigerate several hours and serve cold. The flavor is even better when made a day ahead.   Makes 8 servings.

Tangy Noodles with Vegetables

The noodles can be made into a meal. Place vegetables along with sauce in separate dishes so that each person can mix according to individual taste. This recipe is also a wonderful picnic dish. In any case, do not cut the noodles. They symbolize longevity.

½ **pound fresh Chinese egg noodles**
Sauce recipe as prepared in Tangy Noodle recipe above
1 **tablespoon Chinese sesame oil**
An assortment of vegetables and meat of your choice, such as:

2 **cups fresh bean sprouts**
1 **large cucumber, pared, halved, seeded, shredded**
2 **cups romaine lettuce, shredded**
1 **cup celery, shredded**
1 **red bell pepper, shredded**
1 **cup ham, cubed (optional)**

1. Cook noodles until firm. Drain. Rinse under cold water. Toss with sesame oil. Refrigerate until completely cold. Arrange on a serving platter.
2. Arrange the vegetables and meat in serving dishes along with the Tangy Noodle sauce mixture and place in the center of the table. Serve the noodles to each person. Allow each guest to choose his vegetables, meat, and sauce.

Variations: Serve several sauces, such as Spicy Sauce from White-Cooked Chicken.

Sprinkle ¼ cup dry roasted peanuts, chopped, on top of the noodles.

Tip: Chinese black vinegar produces a mellow sauce, red wine vinegar gives a mild sauce, and white distilled vinegar, a sour flavor.

Makes 8 servings.

6

Mostly Do-Ahead: Crisp and Crunchy Fare

The title of this chapter is meant to dispel the beginner's Chinese cooking syndrome I call "fear of frying." The inimitable tastes of Spring Rolls, Barbecued Ribs, Peking Pan-Fried Dumplings (Pot Stickers), and Crisp Scallion Cakes should be enough to spur you on. But just in case you hesitate at the prospect of deep-frying batches of quick-disappearing foods at the last minute, I offer this reminder: all of these recipes can be prepared up to the point of final cooking well ahead of time. Some can be fried once in advance and refried just to heat before serving; others can be held in a warm oven. Still others are meant to be fried twice for maximum crispness—and hours can elapse between fryings.

This convenience explains the penchant I have for keeping a supply of Pressed Duck or Phoenix Dragon Chicken—a batter-crunched "sandwich" of chicken and ham—in the freezer. It also makes it possible to indulge predinner appetites with a heaping platter of meltingly delicate One Hundred Corner Deep-Fried Shrimp Balls, Deep-Fried Jade Meatballs, or Hot and Sour Ribs.

The best *dim sum* sensation comes when you bite into a light, crisp "pot sticker" or won ton to savor the moist, seasoned meat within. So I have included instructions for making the wrappers, although you may substitute prepared, fresh ones from a Chinese market. Lightness and fresh taste make all the difference in the world between homemade versions of these treats and those encountered in run-of-the-mill Chinese restaurants. The same holds true of Yangchow Fried Rice, a popular Chinese snack that would not be unwelcome at dinner.

79

Some of these recipes are not fried at all, but need only be placed under the broiler or in the oven prior to serving. Barbecued Ribs promise pure pleasure when baked, after marinating, indoors or out. Salt Roasted Chicken takes time to cook to juicy tenderness, but requires almost no attention until you're ready to serve. Crisp Scallion Cakes can be kept frozen for weeks, but should not be forgotten when you need a warm, crusty accompaniment for any meat dish.

Egg Noodles, Egg Rolls, and Won Tons

The Chinese usually purchase freshly made noodles. They are sold in 1-pound packages in Chinese grocery stores and can be refrigerated for 1 to 2 days or frozen 2 to 3 months. Do not defrost frozen noodles before cooking. Wrappers are also available in Chinese markets and are fresh and well made. Wrappers from American supermarkets are sometimes too thick. The wrappers freeze well and keep for 2 months. They can be easily made at home.

2 **cups unsifted all-purpose flour**
½ **teaspoon salt**
2 **jumbo eggs, lightly beaten**

2 **teaspoons oil**
Flour for dusting noodles
Cornstarch for dusting wrappers

HAND METHOD:
1. Place the flour in a mound on a pastry board. Make a well in the center and put in the egg, oil, and salt. With fork, mix the egg, oil, and salt together. Begin to incorporate the flour from the inner rim of the well, always incorporating fresh flour from the lower part of the well.
2. When half the flour has been absorbed, start kneading, using the palms of your hands. Continue until almost all of the flour has been incorporated.
3. Knead for about 5 minutes, dusting with flour when necessary, until the dough is smooth and no longer sticky. Cover with a damp cloth. Let dough rest for 30 minutes.
4. Divide the dough in half. Dust a flat surface with flour. Roll the dough out as thin as you desire with a rolling pin. (A desirable thickness is 1/16 inch.)

PASTA MACHINE METHOD:
1. Complete steps 1 and 2 above.
2. In the pasta machine, start the kneading process on the widest setting. Pass the dough through the rollers. Fold the dough into thirds and press down. Sprinkle with flour and repeat the rolling and folding 8 to 10 times until the dough is very smooth.
3. Move the wheel to the next notch. Pass the dough through the rollers once. Do not fold. Move the wheel to each successive notch, each time passing the dough through the rollers once. Sprinkle a little flour on the dough each time when passing through the rollers. Stop when the dough reaches the thickness desired. (A desirable thickness is $\frac{1}{16}$ inch.)

FOOD PROCESSOR METHOD:
1. Combine egg, oil, and salt in food processor. Process 10 seconds to mix. Scrape down container. Add flour. Process with 5 or 6 one-second pulses until small beads form that hold together when pinched and texture of mixture is crumbly. If beads do not form, add 2 tablespoons additional flour and process with several more one-second pulses to mix until beads form.
2. Empty container on a sheet of plastic wrap; press dough together. Fold plastic wrap around dough and let stand at room temperature for 30 minutes. Roll out on pasta machine as above.

SHAPING OF THE DOUGH:
For egg rolls, cut dough into 7-inch squares.
For won tons, cut dough into 3-inch squares.
Dust each wrapper with cornstarch lightly to stack them without sticking together.
For noodles, cut dough into the desired width. Sprinkle with flour lightly to prevent noodles from sticking together.

Tips: The wrappers and noodles can be stored in a well-sealed plastic bag in the refrigerator for 2 to 3 days or in the freezer for several months. The wrappers must be completely defrosted before using. Noodles may be cooked when frozen.

This dough may be used as an alternate wrapper for Steamed Dumplings and Peking Pan-Fried Dumplings.

The amount of flour needed to make dough varies with the brand of flour and the weather. More liquid is needed in dry weather than in humid weather.

Pork and Shrimp Fried Won Tons

Fried won tons make a wonderful appetizer. Various fillings may be used, such as pork, pork with shrimp, seafood, curried beef. They can be fried ahead, frozen and warmed in the oven, or refried just before serving, which is preferable.

25 to 30 won ton wrappers

Filling Mixture
½ pound pork, ground
4 ounces shrimp, shelled, chopped
8 water chestnuts, minced
4 Chinese dried black mushrooms, soaked in water until spongy, chopped
1 scallion, minced
1 egg, lightly beaten
(filling mixture continued in next column)

1 tablespoon dark soy sauce
1 teaspoon salt
⅛ teaspoon Chinese sesame oil
1 teaspoon dry sherry
1 teaspoon ginger, minced

1 tablespoon cornstarch dissolved in 2 tablespoons water
1 egg, lightly beaten
3 cups oil

1. Make the dough or purchase the dough for the wrappers.
2. Combine the filling ingredients in a bowl. Heat wok over high heat. Add 2 tablespoons of the oil and heat for 30 seconds. Add the filling mixture. Stir for about 1 minute, to mingle well. Recombine the cornstarch and pour into the wok. Stir until the mixture is smooth and slightly thickened. Pour onto a plate to cool before wrapping.
3. Place ¾ teaspoon of the pork mixture in the center of each wrapper. Moisten the wrapper edges with egg. Bring 1 corner up over the filling to the opposite corner, folding the wrapper at an angle so that 2 overlapping triangles are formed, with their

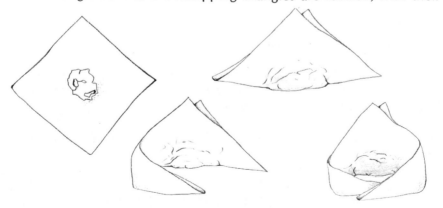

points side by side about ½ inch apart. Press edges together. Pull the two bottom corners of the folded triangle forward and below the folded edge so that they meet one another and slightly overlap, creating a frame around the mound of the filling. Moisten with egg and pinch the ends together. Place finished won tons on a plate and cover with a towel until ready to cook.

4. Heat 3 cups oil in wok to 350°. Cook the won tons, a few at a time, until crisp and golden. Remove and drain.
5. Serve with a dipping sauce, such as Soy Vinegar Sesame Dipping Sauce or Spicy Soy Vinegar Dipping Sauce.

Advance Preparation: Cooked or uncooked won tons can be kept in the refrigerator 1 to 2 days covered with plastic wrap or in the freezer 1 to 3 months.

Reheat cooked won tons in a preheated 350° oven on a rack over a baking pan for 20 minutes or until heated through and crispy. Turn once while heating. Frozen won tons may take longer. For optimum results, heat by frying just before serving.

Makes 25 to 30 won tons.

Fried Seafood Won Tons

25 to 30 won ton wrappers

Filling Mixture
½ pound raw shrimp, shelled, deveined, minced
½ pound fish fillet (sole or flounder) chopped, minced
6 water chestnuts, minced
1 scallion, chopped
1 tablespoon light soy sauce

1 tablespoon dry sherry
½ teaspoon sugar
¼ teaspoon salt
Dash white pepper

1 tablespoon cornstarch dissolved in 2 tablespoons water
1 egg, lightly beaten
3 cups oil

1. Heat wok. Add 2 tablespoons of the oil. Heat oil. Add shrimp and fish. Stir-fry until shrimp turns pink, about 30 seconds. Add water chestnuts, scallions, soy sauce, sherry, sugar, salt, and white pepper. Stir to mingle the flavors. Add cornstarch and water. Cook until translucent. Remove from wok. Let filling cool before filling.
2. Follow the procedures for wrapping and cooking of Pork and Shrimp Won Tons above.

Peking Pan-Fried Dumplings (Pot Stickers)

These scrumptious dumplings are often served as a meal in northern China. They acquire a dual texture through the combined processes of shallow frying and steaming, making them delightfully soft on the top and crisp on the bottom. In other parts of China, they are served as an appetizer or snack. They are generally offered with a variety of light sauces. The most common is vinegar and soy sauce; and, if you desire spice, add some shredded ginger and hot chili oil to the sauce.

1 recipe for Basic Hot Water Dough (recipe follows) or commercially purchased won ton wrappers cut into 3-inch circles

Filling Mixture
½ pound pork, ground
1 cup celery cabbage, finely chopped
1 scallion, minced
4 to 6 Chinese dried black mushrooms, soaked in hot
(filling mixture continued in next column)

water until spongy, minced
4 teaspoons ginger, minced
1 tablespoon light soy sauce
1 tablespoon dry sherry
½ teaspoon sugar
½ teaspoon salt
1 tablespoon Chinese sesame oil
2 teaspoons cornstarch
Dash pepper

4 tablespoons oil
¾ cup boiling water

1. Make dough.
2. Combine the filling mixture in a bowl. Mix well.
3. To fill the dough, put a heaping teaspoon of pork filling in the center of each circle. Fold the circle in half, forming a filled crescent. Starting at one end, with your forefinger and thumb, make 2 to 3 pleats on the back side, then pinch them together

with the front side of the dough to seal the filling in. Do the same at the other end until the opening is completely closed.

If the edges are hard to seal, wet the inside edge with water. Press and pinch the edges to seal tightly so the juice of the filling will not leak out during cooking. Tap the finished dumpling on a flat surface to make a flat bottom. Repeat procedure with remaining dough and filling.

4. Heat a large, heavy skillet over high heat until hot. Add 4 tablespoons oil; swirl and heat for 30 seconds. Reduce heat to medium. Arrange dumplings with sides just touching and pleated side up in a winding circle. Tilt the pan around a little to grease the outer sides of the dumplings with oil. Cook about 2 minutes or until the bottoms are golden.

5. Add ¾ cup of boiling water to the skillet and cover with lid immediately. Simmer over medium heat 10 minutes. Uncover; heat slightly to evaporate any remaining water. Let dumplings fry two minutes until the bottoms are crisp and golden brown. Tilt the pan a few times to prevent the dumplings from sticking. Remove dumplings with a spatula to a hot platter.

6. Serve with Soy Vinegar Sesame Dipping Sauce or Spicy Soy Vinegar Dipping Sauce (see Chapter 15).

Variation: Fill dough with chopped beef, onions, and a touch of curry powder.

Tips: To prevent pot stickers from actually sticking to the bottom of the pan, use a well-seasoned heavy skillet or a commercial aluminum skillet.

Boiled dumplings: Heat 2 quarts of water to boiling in a 4- to 5-quart pan. Drop in the dumplings and turn them in water once with chopsticks to prevent sticking. Cover the pot and cook over high heat until the water comes to a boil. Immediately pour in 1 cup cold water, recover the pot, heat the water to boiling again. Repeat this process twice more, adding 1 cup cold water each time. Remove with a bamboo strainer.

Advance Preparation: Dumplings may be cooked 1 hour ahead. Leave in pan. Reheat at serving time. Add more oil if they are sticking.

Dumplings may be frozen uncooked on a well-floured tray. Be careful dumplings do not touch each other. Once frozen, transfer to a well-sealed plastic bag. Freeze 1 to 2 months. They may be cooked without defrosting.

Basic Hot Water Dough

2 cups all-purpose flour
1 cup boiling water

1. Place the flour in a mixing bowl and make a well. Quickly pour in the boiling water while stirring with a wooden spoon or a pair of chopsticks. Let the dough cool slightly and form the warm dough into a ball with your hands. Let the dough rest covered with a tea towel about 30 minutes.
2. After the dough has rested, knead it on a lightly floured board for about 5 minutes until soft and smooth.
3. Roll the dough into a long sausage, 1 inch in diameter and 30 inches long. Cut into 30 equal portions. Roll each portion into a round ball, then flatten it. Roll each flattened ball into a thin circle, 3 inches in diameter, with a rolling pin. Keep the circles covered with a towel as you work to prevent them from drying out.

Spring Rolls

Spring rolls are an excellent cocktail appetizer with very delicate, light, crisp skins. They are a relative of the American egg roll which has a heavy and doughy wrapper, but the relation ends with the fact that both are deep-fat fried filled pastries.

On Chinese New Year's Day, spring rolls are served because they resemble gold bars and are symbols of prosperity.

Spring roll skins, ready to fill, are available in Oriental markets raw or frozen. Buy several packages as they freeze well.

Spring rolls may be served whole or cut into thirds as an appetizer.

Pork Mixture
10 ounces pork, shredded into matchstick strips about ¼ inch thick each
4 teaspoons cornstarch
1 teaspoon dark soy sauce

Shrimp Mixture
3 ounces raw shrimp, cleaned, deveined, cut into thirds
½ teaspoon cornstarch
1 teaspoon dry sherry

2 tablespoons oil
6 Chinese dried black mushrooms, soaked in hot water until spongy, stems removed, shredded
1 cup bamboo shoots, shredded

1 cup bean sprouts
½ cup carrot, shredded
3 tablespoons cornstarch combined with ½ cup chicken stock
1½ cups celery cabbage, shredded
2 scallions, shredded

20 square spring roll skins
1 egg, beaten

Sauce Mixture
2 tablespoons light soy sauce
1 tablespoon sherry
1 tablespoon dark soy sauce
1 tablespoon Chinese sesame oil

1. Combine pork, 4 teaspoons cornstarch, and 1 teaspoon dark soy sauce. Set aside. Combine shrimp, ½ teaspoon cornstarch, and 1 teaspoon sherry. Set aside. Combine sauce ingredients. Set aside.
2. Heat wok. Add 2 tablespoons oil. Heat. Add pork mixture and stir-fry until shreds change color. Add the black mushroom shreds, stir-fry for 5 seconds until fragrant, add the bamboo shoots, bean sprouts, carrots, and shrimp mixture. Stir-fry for 1 minute. Add sauce mixture. Cook 30 seconds. Recombine corn-

starch and chicken broth. Add to wok. Cook until sauce begins to thicken. Add celery cabbage and scallions. Toss lightly and transfer mixture to a platter. Refrigerate until cool.

The Wrapping Procedure:

1. Take one spring roll skin, one corner pointing toward you and spoon approximately 2 tablespoons of filling onto the lower corner of the spring roll in a sausage shape. Cover remaining spring rolls with a damp towel.

2. Fold the corner of the skin pointing at you over the filling until just covered. Turn again to enclose the filling securely.

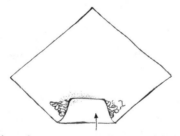

3. Moisten the left and right corners of the triangle with beaten egg, fold over the corners and press down firmly to seal, making an envelope.

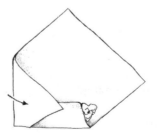

4. Moisten the flap of the envelope with the egg and turn, rolling it into a cylinder, sealing it firmly. Set aside and repeat until all the filling has been used.

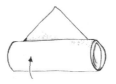

5. Heat 4 cups oil to 375° in a wok. Cook the spring rolls, a few at a time, until crisp and golden. They may be served whole or cut into thirds as an appetizer.

Makes 18 spring rolls.

Tips: Traditionally the fillings are shredded. To save time, chop the ingredients. The filling may be cooked 1 day in advance.
   Spring roll wrappers are made in China. Chinese pancakes rolled thinner than the recipe specifies may be substituted. The thinner the wrapper, the lighter the roll. Egg roll wrappers may be substituted, but will not be as crisp as spring roll wrappers.

Advance Preparation: If the spring rolls are not cooked immediately, place roll on a plate sealed side down. Keep the rolls separated and cover with plastic wrap. Refrigerate for a few hours until ready to cook.
   Spring rolls may be fried ahead of time and drained. They may be refried at serving time to heat them or preheat a 400° oven. Place the spring rolls on a rack resting on a shallow roasting pan or cookie sheet and heat for 8 to 10 minutes. They are best when fried and served immediately.

Crisp Scallion Cakes

In China, scallion cakes are street food and you will see vendors making them all day long.

Thin, crisp, and aromatic, these pancakes are extremely versatile. They can be served with soup, during cocktail hour, or with a buffet.

2 cups flour
1 teaspoon salt
1 cup lukewarm water
2 tablespoons lard
⅔ cup scallions, chopped

8 strips bacon, slightly cooked, chopped (optional)
¼ cup oil
Coarse salt

1. Mix the flour and salt. Add water, a little at a time, to make a lumpy dough. (Some flours require more water than others.) The dough should just hold together when pressed into a ball. Knead on a floured surface for 5 minutes or until smooth. Place dough in a bowl. Cover and let rest for 30 minutes.
2. Roll the dough into a thick sausage and cut it into thirds. Roll each piece of dough into a round ball and cover with a damp towel to prevent drying.
3. Roll each ball of dough on a lightly floured surface into a large, thin pancake (about 11 to 12 inches in diameter). Spread a thin layer of lard on each pancake evenly to within ½ inch of rim. Sprinkle each pancake with 3 tablespoons of scallions and 2 tablespoons bacon. Roll each pancake into a sausage as you would roll up a jelly roll. Pinch the ends to seal the filling. Pick up the dough sausage and twist it like a rope, then hold it upright with 1 end on the table and coil to form a round cake. Dust the cake with a little flour and roll it into a thin cake about 10 inches across. Prepare two more cakes. Store cakes between wax paper.

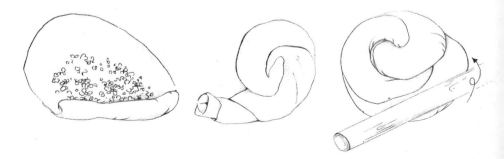

4. Heat a large skillet; pour in enough oil to cover the bottom generously. When the oil is hot, cook the scallion cake in the oil on one side until it is lightly browned and then turn over. Reduce the heat and brown the other side. Drain on paper towels. Add more oil; fry the remaining cakes. Sprinkle with coarse salt.
5. Cut the cakes into 6 pie-shaped wedges. Serve immediately.

Tip: The traditional version of the scallion cakes does not have bacon. Do not overcook the bacon or the flavor will be lost. The coarse salt is not traditional either, but it imparts a nice flavor.

Advance Preparation: The cakes may be made ahead and frozen. If frozen, defrost first. Reheat for 5 minutes at 400° or fry in a skillet until crisp.

Makes 3 10-inch round cakes.

Turnip Dumplings

In China, turnip dumplings are seen in many roadside stands. They have a crunchy texture and make a very interesting appetizer or dim sum.

2½ cups Chinese turnip (about 1 pound), pared
4 ounces raw sweet potato, pared
2 Chinese pork sausages, finely minced
⅔ cup scallions, shredded into 1½-inch lengths
1 cup chicken broth
1 cup flour
1 cup cornstarch
½ teaspoon salt
4 cups oil
Soy Vinegar Dipping Sauce (see Index)

1. With a potato peeler, shave turnip and sweet potato into thin strips. Combine turnip, sweet potato, sausage, scallions, broth, flour, cornstarch, and salt.
2. Heat oil in wok to 350°. Pour in a scant ¼ cup turnip batter to make one dumpling. Deep fry, turning, until light golden in color. Two or three dumplings may be fried at one time. The dumplings should be crisp on the outside, but soft inside.
3. Serve dumplings hot with Soy Vinegar Dipping Sauce.

Makes 6 servings.

Taro Dumplings

The salty filling combined with the sweet taro wrapper makes an interesting combination in this recipe. The dumplings are crispy on the outside and have a soft texture inside.

Pork Mixture
4 ounces pork loin, diced
½ tablespoon light soy sauce
2 teaspoons sugar
1 teaspoon cornstarch
½ teaspoon salt

Shrimp Mixture
2 ounces raw shrimp, shelled,
   cleaned, deveined, diced
1 teaspoon sugar
1 teaspoon Chinese sesame oil
1 teaspoon dry sherry
½ teaspoon salt
White pepper to taste

Sauce
1 tablespoon dark soy sauce
1 teaspoon sugar
¼ teaspoon black pepper
1 teaspoon Chinese sesame oil

½ tablespoon cornstarch
   dissolved in 3 tablespoons
   cold water

2 tablespoons oil
1 chicken liver, blanched for 45
   seconds, cooled, diced
⅓ cup bamboo shoots, minced

Taro Wrapper
1 pound raw taro root peeled,
   thinly sliced
3 tablespoons lard
¾ cup cornstarch, sifted
1 tablespoon sugar
½ teaspoon salt
Dash five-spice powder
Boiling water, if needed

4 cups oil

1. Mix pork, light soy sauce, sugar, cornstarch, and salt. Toss and let marinate for 20 minutes. Mix shrimp, sugar, sesame oil, sherry, salt and pepper. Let marinate for 20 minutes.
2. Combine sauce ingredients.
3. Heat wok. Add 2 tablespoons oil and heat. Add the pork mixture. Stir-fry until grayish in color. Remove. Add the shrimp mixture. Stir-fry until the color changes. Add the liver and bamboo shoots; stir. Add the pork and the sauce mixture. Toss lightly until the sauce thickens. Remove. Refrigerate until firm.
4. Steam the taro for 30 minutes until tender. Drain well, removing all excess moisture. Remove and mash with a rolling pin. Discard hard pieces. Add the lard, cornstarch, sugar, salt, five-spice powder, and boiling water, and mix to work into a smooth

dough. Add more cornstarch if it is too moist. Add more boiling water if too dry. Roll into a long roll. Cut the roll into 24 pieces. Roll each into a ball and flatten with the palm of your hand to a 3-inch circle. Place 1 tablespoon filling in the center of each circle, gather the edges together, folding the circle over in half to form a half-moon shape. Pinch the edges to seal. Repeat for the remaining circles.

5. Heat 4 cups oil to 325°. Add the dumplings and deep-fry in several batches for about 2 minutes until golden brown and crisp. Remove; drain. Serve immediately.

Variations: Substitute presoaked, chopped Chinese dried black mushrooms for the liver.

Sweet potatoes may be substituted for the taro, but it will not have the same texture.

Advance Preparation: Uncooked dumplings can be made 1 day in advance and refrigerated.

Cooked dumplings will keep in the refrigerator 2 to 3 days, and in the freezer 2 months. Reheat in a preheated oven (250°) for 20 minutes.

Makes 6 to 8 servings as a side dish.

Sesame Seed Buns

These typically northern Chinese buns are served with Mongolian Firepot or other meat dishes. They are flat with a crusty outside and a soft inside. They have a nutty flavor that comes from the sesame seed topping as well as the filling. The buns are eaten for breakfast by the Northerners and when cut in half, each piece forms a pocket for food stuffing.

1½ teaspoons active dry yeast
½ cup warm water (110° to 115°)
1 tablespoon sugar
3 cups all-purpose flour
1 teaspoon salt
½ cup plus 1 to 2 tablespoons warm water

3 tablespoons sesame paste or creamy peanut butter combined with ½ teaspoon salt
1 tablespoon corn syrup mixed with 1½ tablespoons water
½ cup sesame seeds

1. Sprinkle yeast on ½ cup warm water. Sprinkle sugar over the yeast. Let stand for 3 to 5 minutes until the yeast bubbles up and doubles in volume.
2. Stir the yeast mixture into the flour in a large bowl. Add the salt and warm water. Knead for 10 minutes on a lightly floured surface, pushing and turning with the heel of your hand until the dough is smooth. Shape it into a ball. Place in a mixing bowl and cover closely with a towel. Let rise in a warm place for 45 minutes.
3. Knead the dough again on a lightly floured surface for 1 to 2 minutes. Divide dough in half. Roll out one portion at a time into a rectangle, 15 × 8 inches. Spread half of the sesame paste mixture over each portion of the dough. If the sesame seed paste is too thick to spread, thin it with Chinese sesame oil. Roll it into a 15-inch-long jelly roll and cut into 6 sections.
4. Seal each section at both ends by pinching together. Stand on end. Flatten with palm of the hand. Roll each section with a rolling pin into a 4-inch round. Brush the top with the corn syrup mixture. Dip the top into the sesame seeds until generously coated. Press the seeds lightly into the dough. Cook immediately. The dough should not rise again before cooking.
5. Cook buns covered in a skillet over low heat for 10 minutes. Increase the heat to medium and cook another 5 minutes until

the bottom is golden in color. Turn the buns over; cover and cook until the sesame seeds are golden, about 4 minutes. Serve hot.

Variation: Bake buns seeded side up on a lightly oiled baking sheet covered with aluminum foil at 450° for 10 to 15 minutes or until the bottom of the buns are golden brown.

Tip: The buns can be refrigerated for 3 to 4 days or frozen 1 to 2 months. Rewarm in a covered skillet over low heat.

Makes 12 buns.

Water Chestnut Rolls

The combination of crunchy water chestnuts, bacon, and ham lend a nice change of pace in taste and cooking methods.

24 water chestnuts	2 scallions, cut into 1-inch
¼ cup chicken broth	pieces
3 tablespoons light soy sauce	1 slice cooked ham, cut into
1 tablespoon dry sherry	strips, 1 × ½ inch each
1 tablespoon sugar	12 slices lean bacon, cut in half
1 tablespoon honey	

1. Combine water chestnuts, chicken broth, soy sauce, sherry, sugar, and honey. Let marinate 2 to 3 hours.
2. Wrap 1 piece each of water chestnut, scallion, and ham in half a bacon strip. Insert a toothpick to hold together.
3. Heat oven to 375°. Bake water chestnut rolls on a rack over a baking pan, 15 to 18 minutes. Serve with sweet and sour or plum sauce.

Tips: Assemble early in the day.
  Rolls may be kept warm in a 200° oven for 15 to 20 minutes.

Makes 6 servings.

Stuffed Eggplant Slices

Stuffed eggplant slices are perfect for a Chinese buffet. They may be fried in advance and refried just before serving. The eggplant is equally tasty when served at room temperature.

1½ pounds baby eggplant or Italian eggplant
2 teaspoons salt
3 cups oil

Batter
3 large eggs, slightly beaten
6 tablespoons cornstarch
2 tablespoons flour
3 tablespoons cold water

Pork Mixture
½ pound pork, ground
2 tablespoons ginger, minced
1 scallion, minced
4 water chestnuts, minced
2 tablespoons Chinese sesame oil
1 tablespoon light soy sauce
2 teaspoons cornstarch
¼ teaspoon black pepper

1. Cut the eggplant into slices ¼ inch thick. Cut the center of each slice three-fourths of the way through, forming a V-shaped pocket. In a colander, toss the eggplant with salt; let drain for 15 minutes. Rinse with cold water; pat dry with paper towels.
2. Combine batter ingredients. Whisk until well blended and the batter has no lumps. Let rest for 20 minutes.
3. Mix pork, ginger, scallion, water chestnuts, Chinese sesame oil, soy sauce, cornstarch, and the black pepper in a large bowl. Place ½ to ¾ teaspoon pork mixture into each eggplant pocket. Do not overstuff or the filling will not cook thoroughly.
4. Heat wok over medium heat. Add 3 cups oil. Heat oil to 375°. Dip eggplant slices into the batter. Deep-fry for 2 to 3 minutes until golden and the filling is cooked. Serve with Szechuan peppercorn salt (see Index).

Variation: Substitute small zucchini for the baby eggplant.

Advance Preparation: Fry 2 to 3 hours ahead. Cool and refry until heated at serving time.

Makes 4 to 6 dinner servings.

Deep-Fried Jade Meatballs

These spinach-filled meatballs are excellent fried or steamed and can be used for a main dish or as an appetizer.

6 ounces frozen chopped spinach, thawed, drained	1 tablespoon dark soy sauce
1 tablespoon light soy sauce	½ teaspoon sugar
1 teaspoon sugar	½ teaspoon salt
1 pound lean pork, ground	1 egg, lightly beaten
1 scallion, minced (white part only)	2 tablespoons cornstarch
1 tablespoon Chinese sesame oil
1 tablespoon dry sherry	4 cups oil

1. Combine the spinach, light soy sauce, and 1 teaspoon sugar. Set aside.
2. Combine the pork, scallion, sherry, dark soy sauce, ½ teaspoon sugar, and salt. Mix well. Add the beaten egg and mix. Sprinkle the cornstarch on the mixture and mix until completely smooth. Divide into 20 portions.
3. Squeeze the spinach mixture in a tea towel to remove all moisture. Add 1 tablespoon sesame oil and mix well. Divide into 20 portions. Roll each portion into a ball.
4. Grease your palms with oil. Place 1 portion of the meat in your palm and flatten it into a small round with your fingers. Place a portion of the spinach in the center. Fold the meat over and roll it lightly into a ball. Repeat procedure until all the balls are made.
5. Heat 4 cups oil to 325°. Deep-fry the meatballs, a few at a time, spinning constantly for 4 minutes. Remove the meatballs. Increase the heat to high and fry them all together for 2 minutes until they are brown. Drain. Serve immediately with Soy-Vinegar Dipping Sauce (see Index).

Tip: The meatballs may be fried at 325° 1 to 2 hours before serving. Fry the second time at 375° at serving time.

Variations: Meatballs may be filled with cooked carrot or zucchini.
   Steamed Meatballs: Steam over high heat for 15 minutes.
   Jade Pearl Balls: Soak ½ cup glutinous rice in warm water for 4 hours and drain. Roll each ball in rice and steam for 40 minutes. Serve with soy-vinegar dip or plum sauce.   Makes 20 meatballs.

Barbecued Ribs

Barbecued ribs are one of the most popular Chinese appetizers. Purchase lean ribs from the butcher. Generally, there is too much fat and gristle in the ribs from the grocery store.

2 pounds pork spareribs, fat and gristle trimmed

Rib Marinade
4 tablespoons hoisin sauce
3 tablespoons dark soy sauce
2 tablespoons ketchup
2 tablespoons dry sherry
2 tablespoons sugar

1 teaspoon five-spice powder
½ teaspoon garlic, minced
½ teaspoon ginger, minced

Glaze
2 tablespoons honey
1 tablespoon Chinese sesame oil
1 tablespoon light soy sauce

1. Combine marinade ingredients. Set aside.
2. Make a cut between, but not through, each sparerib. Place the ribs in a shallow pan and pour marinade over, rubbing into the slits between the ribs. Refrigerate for 4 to 6 hours, basting and turning from time to time. Drain, reserving marinade.
3. Heat oven to 375°. Place marinated ribs on a metal rack over a roasting pan filled with 1 inch of water or suspend ribs high in the oven with skewers or as in barbecued pork (see Index). Roast 45 minutes. Turn ribs, basting with reserved marinade at 15 to 20 minute intervals for even browning. Increase the heat to 450°, cook 10 minutes longer to crisp the ribs.
4. Remove the ribs from the oven. Glaze ribs with the honey glaze. Return to the oven for 2 minutes or until crisp and a glaze forms. To serve, cut through the entire rib.

Tips: To barbecue on an outside grill, sear the ribs over high heat initially and raise the grill height for a thorough, slow cooking.
To keep ribs warm, heat in a 200° oven for 30 minutes.

Advance Preparation: Roast the ribs as above. Let cool. Wrap in foil and refrigerate. Before serving, heat the wrapped ribs 10 to 15 minutes in a 350° oven.
To freeze, roast ribs as above. Let cool. Seal tightly in foil and freeze. When ready to use, heat the wrapped ribs 30 minutes in a 400° oven. Do not thaw first.

Makes 8 dim sum servings or 4 dinner servings.

Hot and Sour Ribs

Easily prepared, spicy and piquant, these ribs stand up well on a buffet table. The contrast between the flavorings of the ribs and the crunchy texture is extraordinary. This is a superb dish!

Rib Mixture
1½ pounds meaty spareribs, chopped by your butcher into 1-inch pieces
2 slices ginger, the size of quarter, smashed with the side of a cleaver
2 scallions, cut into 2-inch lengths, smashed with the side of a cleaver
2 tablespoons rice wine or dry sherry
1 tablespoon light soy sauce
⅛ teaspoon salt
½ cup cornstarch

3 cups oil

Sauce Mixture
3 to 4 dried whole chili peppers
1 large clove garlic, minced
1 teaspoon ginger, peeled, minced
1 tablespoon scallions, finely chopped
4 tablespoons sugar dissolved in 4 tablespoons red wine vinegar

1 tablespoon Chinese sesame oil

1. Combine ribs, ginger, scallions, rice wine, soy sauce, and salt. Let marinate for 20 minutes. Drain well. Toss the ribs in a plastic bag with the cornstarch. Cover well. Remove. Place on a plate. (This should be done just before deep-fat frying.)
2. Heat 3 cups oil in wok to 350°. Shake off any excess cornstarch and drop the ribs into the hot oil a few at a time. Deep-fry for 6 minutes, reduce the heat slightly after 2 minutes. Rotate the ribs with a skimmer for even frying. Remove the ribs from the oil and cool for 2 minutes. Reheat the oil over high heat to 375°. Return ribs to the oil and deep-fry again, stirring and turning for 1½ to 2 minutes until crisp and brown. Remove from oil and drain.
3. Pour out all but 2 tablespoons of the oil from wok. Add the dried chili peppers; press and turn them over low heat until blackened. Add the ginger, garlic, and scallions. Stir-fry for a few seconds. Recombine the sugar and vinegar mixture. Add, stirring, until the sauce has dissolved. Add ribs. Cook until heated through. Add sesame oil. Stir. Place on a serving dish. Serve.

Advance Preparation: Prepare the sauce 1 to 2 days in advance. Refrigerate. The first frying of the ribs may be done up to 4 hours in advance. Drain ribs on paper towels in a single layer. Cover. Fry the second time at serving time. Reheat in the sauce and serve.

Makes 4 main-course servings or 8 dim sum servings.

Spicy Chicken Dumplings

Traditionally, these dumplings, topped with a spicy sauce, are served in the noodle stands on the streets of China.

Chicken Mixture
1 chicken breast, skinned, boned, cut into 1-inch cubes
½ egg white
3 tablespoons water
1 tablespoon dry sherry
1 tablespoon cornstarch
½ teaspoon sugar
Salt

Sauce Mixture
4 tablespoons garlic, minced
4 tablespoons Szechuan preserved vegetable, minced
8 scallions, chopped
8 tablespoons hot chili oil
2 tablespoons sugar
8 tablespoons light soy sauce
4 tablespoons red wine vinegar

1 package won ton skins, cut into 2½-inch rounds, or 1 recipe Basic Hot Water Dough (see Index)

1. Mix chicken, egg white, water, sherry, cornstarch, sugar, and salt to taste. Spoon a teaspoon of the chicken filling into the center of each round, fold the round over to enclose the filling and seal the edges using a little water. Press the edges together to make a filled crescent.
2. Combine sauce ingredients. Set aside. Heat 6 quarts water to boiling. Add the dumplings and ½ cup cold water. Cook dumplings until they come to the surface. Cook a few seconds longer. Drain. Place on a platter. Pour the sauce over the dumplings.

Variation: Deep-fat fry the dumplings.

Advance Preparation: Prepared dumplings may be refrigerated 1 to 2 days or frozen 2 months. If frozen, cook while still frozen. Cook an additional 5 minutes.

Makes 60 dumplings.

Skewered Chicken with Bacon

This easily prepared appetizer is broiled in the oven.

Chicken Mixture
½ **pound chicken breast, sliced paper thin**
3 **tablespoons light soy sauce**
1 **tablespoon dry sherry**
1 **tablespoon brown sugar**
1 **teaspoon ginger, minced**

Glaze
2 **tablespoons light soy sauce**
2 **tablespoons honey**

10 **water chestnuts, sliced**
½ **pound bacon, cut into 1-inch pieces**
4 **to 6 wooden skewers, soaked in cold water for 1 hour**

1. Combine chicken, light soy sauce, sherry, brown sugar, and ginger. Let marinate for 2 hours. Mix light soy sauce and honey for glaze. Set aside.
2. Thread chicken, water chestnuts, and bacon on skewers. Brush with glaze.
3. Preheat oven. Broil until chicken is tender, turning once.

Variation: Substitute chicken livers for the chicken breast. Deep-fry in 3 cups hot oil or cook on a hibachi.

Makes 4 to 6 servings.

Paper-Wrapped Chicken

Chicken wrapped in parchment paper is an old Chinese dish. The wrapped juicy morsels of chicken combined with the crunchy snow peas and ham are sure to be a conversation piece.

Chicken Mixture
1 large chicken breast, skinned, boned, cut into 2½ × 1 inch pieces
2 tablespoons dry sherry
2 teaspoons light soy sauce
½ teaspoon salt
¼ teaspoon sugar
Dash white pepper

4 scallions, shredded into 1-inch pieces

8 snow peas, shredded on the diagonal into pieces 1¼ × ½ inch.
Ginger, peeled, slivered thinly into ½-inch pieces (optional)
Smoked ham , slivered into 1-inch pieces (optional)
20 6-inch squares parchment or waxed paper
2 teaspoons Chinese sesame oil
3 cups oil

1. Combine chicken, sherry, soy sauce, salt, sugar, and white pepper. Let marinate for 20 minutes; drain marinade.
2. Wrap one piece of marinated chicken, scallion, a snow pea, ginger, and ham in the paper, envelope style.

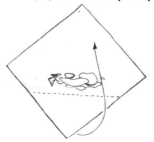

3. Place each square with the lower corner pointing toward you. Grease paper with a drop of sesame oil. Place ingredients below the center line of the square.

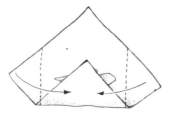

4. Fold up the lower corner to cover the filling. Fold the lower section again to the center. Fold the right corner over and the left in. Fold the top corner down and tuck in securely like an envelope flap.

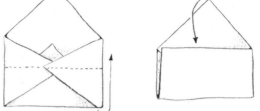

5. Heat 3 cups oil in wok over high heat to 375°. Deep-fry chicken packages, a few at a time, for 2 to 3 minutes. Turn once. Drain. Serve hot in wrappers. To eat, the diner breaks open the paper envelopes with chopsticks or a fork.

Tip: Keep warm in a 200° oven for 15 minutes. Do not overcook chicken or it will toughen.

Makes 20 packages.

Phoenix Dragon Chicken

The bird is symbolic of female beauty and the dragon a symbol of male virility in Chinese mythology. The delicate white meat of the chicken breast, considered feminine, joined with the red ham, regarded masculine, indicates that the male and female have joined together in harmony and bliss.

The ham is put between 2 layers of chicken which are enclosed in a crunchy batter, deep-fried and served with a sprinkling of roasted Szechuan peppercorn salt. This is indeed a party dish!

4 **large chicken breasts,**
   skinned, boned
8 **⅛-inch-thick slices cooked**
   Smithfield ham or 16 slices
   baked ham

4 **cups oil**
Szechuan peppercorn salt

Batter
1 **cup all-purpose flour**
2 **teaspoons baking powder**
¼ **teaspoon salt**
1 **egg**
¾ **cup water**

1. Freeze the chicken breasts until firm, about 2 hours, for easier cutting. Remove the fillets and cut off the thin tapered ends of the breasts. Place 1 of the 8 pieces of chicken on the cutting board. Pressing hand on top, start at the thicker side and slice horizontally through the middle of the meat to within ½ inch of the far end, yielding two flaps of meat with the end attached. This will form a pocket. Repeat with the other breast halves.
2. Open the flap of each chicken breast, line neatly with a slice of ham; close. (If you use baked ham, insert 2 slices as it is milder.)
3. Prepare batter. Combine the flour, baking powder, and salt. Lightly beat the egg and water together. Add the egg mixture to the flour, gradually stirring, until it is as smooth as a thin pancake batter. Set aside.
4. Heat wok. Add 4 cups oil and heat to 350°. Stir the batter. Dip 1 chicken breast into the batter, holding together the open end. Let the excess batter drip off a little, then quickly slip the breast into the hot oil. Repeat with 3 other breasts. Fry them for 1 minute, then turn. Reduce the heat to medium and fry for 3 minutes, turning constantly until they are crisp and brown. To test for doneness, press the breast. If it feels mushy, it needs further cooking. Remove and drain the chicken. Coat and fry the other 4 breasts. Reheat the oil to 350°. Refry all the chicken together for 1 minute. Remove. Slice crosswise diagonally into ½-inch pieces. Serve with Szechuan peppercorn salt.

Advance Preparation: The ham-filled chicken breasts may be refrigerated 1 day or frozen 1 to 2 months.

The chicken may be prepared ahead and fried once earlier in the day. Refry the second time at serving time. The crisp coating stands well at room temperature.

Makes 6 to 8 main-course servings or 12 to 14 appetizer servings.

Chicken Lollipops

The wings are one of the most succulent parts of the chicken. They are economical and can be marinated a day in advance.

12 large chicken wings

Chicken Marinade
2 tablespoons light soy sauce
2 tablespoons dark soy sauce
1½ tablespoons sugar
1 tablespoon dry sherry
1 tablespoon Chinese sesame oil

Batter
2 tablespoons cornstarch
1 tablespoon flour
¼ teaspoon salt
1 egg, well beaten
1 tablespoon water

4 cups oil
Szechuan peppercorn salt or plum sauce

1. Cut off and discard the wing tips. Disjoint the upper part of the wing at the first joint and save the lower section for stuffed chicken wings. Cut around the tip of the smaller end of the bone to release the skin and meat. Scrape and push the meat toward the thick end. Holding the meat down with the cleaver, pull the bone so the meat wraps around the thick end. You now have a "lollipop." Repeat procedure for all wings.
2. Mix soy sauce, sugar, sherry, and sesame oil. Marinate the wings in the mixture at least 2 hours or overnight.
3. Combine batter ingredients. Mix well. Let batter rest for 10 minutes. Heat 4 cups oil to 350° over medium-high heat. Dip the wings into the batter. Deep-fry for 3 to 4 minutes until the meat is firm and brown. Serve with Szechuan peppercorn salt or plum sauce.

Advance Preparation: The "lollipops" may be deep-fried and then frozen. Spread frozen chicken on a cookie sheet and reheat for 15 minutes in a preheated 425° oven or deep-fry to heat through in hot oil.

Makes 12 "lollipops."

Salt Roasted Chicken

Chicken roasted in salt allows the meat to cook to tenderness in its own juices. In this recipe, the chicken meat is succulent and the skin has an unusual texture. It is firm but not really crisp, soft but not moist. The chicken is not at all salty. The chicken's cavity is filled with a tasty marinade, then the chicken is wrapped in cheesecloth. It may be prepared a day ahead as the chicken is wonderful hot, cold, or at room temperature. This dish is excellent for a picnic. It is also my daughter Sarah's favorite dish.

1 **roasting chicken (about 4 pounds)**

Chicken Marinade
3 **slices ginger, smashed with a cleaver**
3 **cloves garlic, lightly crushed**
1 **tablespoon oil**
3 **scallions, cut into 2-inch sections**
1 **whole star anise**

1 **teaspoon whole Szechuan peppercorns, roasted**
¼ **cup chicken broth**
2 **tablespoons light soy sauce**
1 **tablespoon bean sauce**
1 **tablespoon rice wine or dry sherry**
1 **tablespoon sugar**

1 **large piece cheesecloth, oiled**
5 **to 6 pounds coarse salt**

1. Remove the fat from the chicken cavity. Rinse and dry inside and out. Sew up the neck cavity.
2. Stir-fry the ginger and garlic in 1 tablespoon hot oil for 2 to 3 seconds. Reduce the heat and add the remaining marinade ingredients. Simmer the mixture for 2 to 3 minutes. Pour into a bowl to cool.
3. Pour the marinade into the chicken cavity and truss the opening very tightly with a skewer or sew with a needle and thread. Let dry for 1½ hours.
4. Wrap the chicken in a large piece of cheesecloth soaked in oil.
5. Heat the coarse salt in a large, heavy pot or wok on top of the stove over a low heat or in the oven at 350° for at least 1 hour. Pour off some of the salt, leaving just enough to cover the bottom of the pot. Place the chicken on top of the salt in the pot and cover it with the remaining salt. Cover the pot and bake the chicken at 350° in the oven or in a wok or top of the stove for 1½ hours.

6. Remove the chicken from the salt. Carefully unwrap the cheese-cloth. Untruss the cavity and pour the marinade into a bowl. Cut the chicken into bite-sized pieces or carve it Western style. Serve it with the marinade.

Variation: Two fresh Cornish hens may be prepared in this manner. Roast 1 hour.

Tip: To serve the chicken cold, keep the marinade inside the chicken to keep it moist. Wrap the chicken in plastic wrap and refrigerate. It should not be reheated. Bring to room temperature when serving.

Makes 4 dinner servings or 8 dim sum servings.

Pressed Duck

One of the most popular dishes in Chinese restaurants in the U.S., this Cantonese specialty originated in the northern part of China. Pressed duck is an excellent way to serve duck. There are two cooking stages, allowing most of the preparation to be done in advance. I make several ducks at a time and freeze them. When unexpected guests arrive, you can take the ducks from the freezer and impress your company.

This makes an excellent buffet dish as it can be made ahead and refried just before serving. Two sauces can be served with the duck, the traditional brown sauce or the sweet and sour sauce, which I prefer.

1 duck (about 4½ to 5 pounds)

Marinade
3 to 4 slices ginger
1 tablespoon sugar
1 tablespoon light soy sauce
1 tablespoon dry sherry
1 tablespoon honey
1 teaspoon salt
**1 piece dried tangerine peel,
    soaked in water 30 minutes**

2 egg whites, lightly beaten
**½ cup water chestnut flour
    combined with ½ cup
    cornstarch**
4 cups oil

Sweet and Sour Sauce
5 tablespoons sugar
4 tablespoons rice vinegar
3 tablespoons light soy sauce
3 tablespoons ketchup
2 tablespoons dry sherry
½ cup chicken broth
½ teaspoon salt
2 tablespoons oil
**1 large clove garlic, crushed
    with the side of the cleaver**
**1 tablespoon cornstarch
    dissolved in 2 tablespoons
    water**
**1 tablespoon Chinese sesame
    oil**

2 cups lettuce, shredded
**4 tablespoons almonds, fried in
    4 tablespoons oil until
    golden, chopped.**

1. Discard the fat from the duck cavity. Cut off the wing tips and tail. Mix the ginger, sugar, soy sauce, sherry, honey, and salt.

Rub the mixture over the duck skin. Pour the remainder inside the cavity, moving it around to coat the interior. Drain off the excess and discard. Place the tangerine peel inside the cavity.

2. Heat 2 quarts of water to full boiling in the bottom of a large steamer. Place the duck in the top section of the steamer without a plate so that the duck fat will drop into the water during steaming. Steam over high heat for 1 hour. Remove from the steamer.

3. When the duck is cool enough to touch, cut in half lengthwise through the back. Spread out flat and remove all the bones, being very careful to keep the skin intact. Place the boned duck on a flat cutting board or large platter. Cover with a plate. Using both hands, press down on the duck, flattening it to a ¾-inch thickness to loosen the meat so that the texture is lighter and crisper when deep fried. Cut each half crosswise just beyond the thighs so that you have 4 pieces of duck meat.

4. Dip the pieces of meat in the beaten egg whites, then coat evenly with the water chestnut flour and cornstarch mixture. Place pieces on a heat-proof plate; steam over medium heat for 20 minutes. Transfer to a dry plate. Let cool and refrigerate. (This may be done 1 to 2 days in advance.)

5. Prepare sweet and sour sauce. Mix sugar, rice vinegar, soy sauce, chicken broth, ketchup, and sherry, for sauce mixture. Heat a large, heavy skillet or wok over high heat; return heat to medium. Add 2 tablespoons oil; heat. Add the garlic and let it season in the oil for a few seconds. Add the sauce mixture, stirring until the liquid comes to a boil. Reduce heat; add the cornstarch mixture, stirring until the sauce begins to thicken. Stir until the sauce is smooth. Add the sesame oil and remove from the heat. Discard the garlic. Serve over the duck.

6. Place the shredded lettuce on a serving platter. Set aside.

7. Heat 6 cups oil in wok to 375°. Fry 2 pieces of the duck at a time for about 5 minutes or until all the pieces are crisp and brown. Drain on paper towels. Let cool slightly, then cut the duck into 1½-inch squares, each with some skin. Keep warm.

8. Arrange the duck pieces on top of the lettuce. Stir the sauce; heat sauce to simmering. Pour the sauce over the duck and sprinkle with chopped almonds. Serve.

Brown Sauce for Pressed Duck

2 **cups chicken broth**
2 **tablespoons dry sherry**
1 **tablespoon light soy sauce**
2 **tablespoons cornstarch
    dissolved in 4 tablespoons
    water**

2 **teaspoons Chinese sesame oil**
Dash white pepper

Heat the broth to simmering in a small saucepan. Add the sherry and soy sauce. Recombine the cornstarch mixture and pour into the broth. Stir until thickened. Remove from the heat. Add sesame oil and white pepper to taste.

Tips: When planning your meal, choose your sauce for the duck. If you already have dishes with a sweet and sour flavor, serve the duck with the brown sauce.
  If water chestnut flour is unavailable, you may use cornstarch throughout.

Advance Preparation: Coat the duck with water chestnut flour mixture. Refrigerate until set, about 4 hours. Wrap the duck tightly and freeze. Duck may be refrigerated 1 to 2 days or frozen 1 to 2 months.
  Deep-fry the duck until almost brown the morning of your dinner and prepare sauce. At serving time, fry the duck until crisp and warm for 1 to 2 minutes. Reheat sauce. Pour over duck.

Makes 4 to 6 servings.

Sesame Beef Strips

Simple to make and cooked in the broiler, the beef strips make a pleasant appetizer.

Beef Marinade
¾ **cup oil**
½ **cup Chinese sesame oil**
⅔ **cup light soy sauce**
⅔ **cup dry sherry**
⅔ **cup brown sugar, firmly packed**
2 **cloves garlic, finely minced**

¾ **teaspoon ginger, minced**

1½ **pounds flank steak, cut across the grain into paper-thin slices 2 × 1 inch**

Bamboo skewers soaked in water

1. Mix oils, soy sauce, sherry, sugar, garlic, and ginger. Marinate beef strips in mixture, turning to coat. Cover and refrigerate at least 2 hours or overnight.
2. Heat broiler. Thread the beef onto skewers. Brush with the marinade, coating heavily. Place on a rack and broil for 1½ minutes. Remove from the heat. Turn over. Brush with the marinade. Broil on the second side to desired doneness. Serve hot or at room temperature.

Makes 12 appetizer servings.

Skewered Lamb

This lamb is skewered and broiled in a Chinese shish kebab.

Lamb Marinade
2 tablespoons light soy sauce
1 tablespoon dry sherry
1 clove garlic, minced
2 teaspoons ginger, peeled, minced
1 teaspoon Chinese sesame oil
½ teaspoon five-spice powder

½ teaspoon Szechuan peppercorn powder

1 pound boneless lamb shoulder, trimmed, cut into 1-inch cubes

4 8-inch bamboo skewers, soaked in cold water for 1 hour

1. Mix soy sauce, sherry, garlic, ginger, Chinese sesame oil, five-spice powder, and peppercorn powder. Marinate lamb in mixture for 3 hours.
2. Thread lamb onto the skewers. Do not crowd. Reserve marinade.
3. Heat broiler. Arrange skewers on the rack of a broiler pan; broil lamb under the broiler 4 inches from the heat, turning and basting with the reserved marinade. Broil 8 to 10 minutes for medium rare.

Tip: Skewered Lamb may be cooked on an outside grill or hibachi.

Makes 6 to 8 servings.

Shrimp Toast

Shrimp Toast is a popular snack and buffet dish. The Shrimp Toast is puffy, crisp, and crunchy and often appears during a Chinese banquet.

8 pieces very thin sliced homemade-type white bread, crusts removed, cut into triangles

Shrimp Mixture
½ pound fresh shrimp, shelled, deveined, cleaned, dried, minced to a fine paste
1 tablespoon pork fat or bacon fat, minced to a fine paste
1½ teaspoons ginger, finely minced
6 water chestnuts, minced

2 scallions, minced
1 egg, lightly beaten
1 teaspoon dry sherry
2 teaspoons cornstarch
1 teaspoon sugar
½ teaspoon salt
Dash white pepper

3 tablespoons white sesame seeds
4 cups oil

1. Dry bread triangles on a rack overnight or for 2 hours in a 200° oven.
2. Combine shrimp, pork fat, ginger, water chestnuts, scallions, egg, sherry, cornstarch, sugar, salt, and pepper. Throw mixture lightly against the inside of a bowl to mix thoroughly. Spread the shrimp paste on the bread, making a slight mound in the center of each piece. Sprinkle with sesame seeds.
3. Heat oil to 325°. Place the toast in the oil in batches of 6 to 8, shrimp side down. Deep-fry for 2 minutes. Turn over gently and fry for 45 seconds or until brown and crisp. Drain on paper towels. Keep warm in the oven while cooking remaining shrimp toast.

Advance Preparation: Cooked Shrimp Toast can be frozen for 1 to 2 months. Deep-fry while still frozen or reheat frozen in a 350° oven on a rack over a baking pan for 20 minutes. Turn once during heating.

The shrimp mixture may be spread on the bread, placed on a cookie sheet in a single layer, covered with plastic wrap, and refrigerated 2 hours before deep-fat frying. For optimum results, fry at serving time.

Makes 32 pieces of Shrimp Toast.

One Hundred Corner Deep-Fried Shrimp Balls

These attractive, delicate balls are often served as a banquet dish. They are crispy on the outside with delicate shrimp puff inside, making an excellent combination and are so named because of the many corners of the bread cubes.

20 thin slices of homemade-
  type bread, crusts removed,
  cut into ¼-inch cubes
1 pound raw shrimp, shelled,
  deveined, cleaned, dried,
  minced into a paste
1½ ounces pork fat, minced to a
  paste
⅓ cup water chestnuts, finely
  minced
1 egg white, lightly beaten

1½ teaspoons ginger, peeled,
  finely minced
1½ teaspoons scallions, finely
  minced
1 teaspoon Chinese sesame oil
1 teaspoon cornstarch
1 teaspoon salt
Dash white pepper
4 cups oil
Szechuan peppercorn salt or
Soy Vinegar Sesame Dipping
  Sauce

1. Dry bread cubes for 2 hours, turning occasionally.
2. Combine shrimp, pork fat, water chestnuts, egg white, ginger, scallions, Chinese sesame oil, cornstarch, salt, and white pepper. Compact shrimp mixture. Form the shrimp mixture into balls 1 inch in diameter, dipping your hands in oil for easier formation of the balls. (Balls are easier to shape if you let the mixture set in the refrigerator for 2 hours.) Roll the balls in the bread cubes, pressing the cubes into the balls slightly to make them adhere. (Do not make the balls too large or they will not cook through.)
3. Heat 4 cups oil in wok to 325°. Add the shrimp balls, a few at a time, and fry. Turn the balls as they are frying and fry until they are deep golden brown. Drain the balls; place them in a preheated very low oven until the others are done.

Tip: Serve Shrimp Balls with Szechuan peppercorn salt.

Advance Preparation: Cooked Shrimp Balls may be frozen. Reheat frozen balls in a 350° oven on a rack over a baking pan for 15 to 20 minutes until heated through. Turn once during cooking. For optimum results, fry at serving time.

Makes 32 balls.

Shrimp Balls Steamed or Fried

Steamed and fried shrimp balls can be served as appetizers or as a main course. They can be cooked with vegetables and other ingredients to create many dishes. They are very delicate and are often served during a banquet. Also delicious in a soup.

1 **pound small or medium shrimp, shelled, deveined, minced into a paste**
6 **water chestnuts, very finely minced**
2 **scallions, white part only, finely minced**
2 **tablespoons pork fat or bacon fat, finely minced**
1 **tablespoon dry sherry**

¼ **teaspoon ginger, minced**
Dash white pepper
½ **teaspoon salt**
2 **teaspoons Chinese sesame oil**
½ **teaspoon sugar**
3 **tablespoons water**
3 **tablespoons cornstarch**
1 **large egg white, beaten until very foamy**

1. Combine the shrimp, water chestnuts, scallions, and pork fat. Mix in a circular motion until well blended. Add remaining ingredients. Mix well. (If using a food processor, do not over-process.)

Fried Shrimp Balls:
2. Heat 3 cups oil in wok to 350°. Have a small bowl of oil handy. Moisten hands with oil; form the paste into walnut-size balls. Slip the shrimp balls one by one into hot oil. When they are brown, about 3 minutes, remove. Do not fry too many at once or the oil will cool down and they will not fry properly.

Steamed Shrimp Balls:
2. Have a bowl of ice water beside the shrimp mixture. With wet hands dipped in cold water, form the paste into balls about 1 inch in diameter. Place shrimp balls on a lightly oiled heatproof plate, and steam over water for 10 minutes or until done.

Tip: Serve with Szechuan peppercorn salt or the mustard sauce of the Steamed Shrimp in Mustard Sauce. (See Index.)

Advance Preparation: Both the Steamed and Fried Shrimp Balls can be kept in the refrigerator for one day or can be frozen. Do not store uncooked. Steamed balls can be resteamed until heated through. Fried Shrimp Balls can be rewarmed in a 350° oven for 15 minutes or until heated through. Do not overcook, as shrimp will get tough and dry. They are best when fried and served immediately, however.   Makes 30 balls.

Shrimp Stuffed Bananas

The contrast of textures and tastes produces a marvelous dish. Use firm bananas.

2 medium, firm bananas, cut into 3 sections across, then cut into 4 pieces lengthwise
2 tablespoons cornstarch

Filling
4 ounces shrimp, shelled, deveined, cleaned, dried, minced
1 slice bacon, slightly cooked, minced
1 teaspoon dry sherry
(filling mixture continued in next column)

½ teaspoon Chinese sesame oil
½ teaspoon light soy sauce
⅛ teaspoon white pepper

Batter
½ cup flour
6 tablespoons water
¼ teaspoon salt
½ teaspoon baking powder
1 tablespoon oil

4 cups oil

1. Combine filling ingredients.
2. Coat the cut surface of the banana pieces with cornstarch. Spread the filling on 12 sections and top the sections with another banana slice.
3. Combine batter ingredients. Mix until a smooth batter is formed.
4. Heat 4 cups oil to deep-fry temperature, 350°. Dip each sandwich in the batter and deep-fry a few at a time over medium heat for 3 minutes until golden brown. Serve hot.

Tips: If too many banana sandwiches are fried at one time, the oil temperature will lower and they will not fry properly.
Flours vary. If batter is too thick, thin with ½ tablespoon water.

Makes 12 sandwiches.

Deep-Fried Squid

The dry, crisp squid are a nice complement to wine as an appetizer or when served as part of a buffet.

1 **pound fresh squid**	1 **teaspoon dry sherry**
3 **slices ginger, smashed with**	1 **teaspoon salt**
the side of a cleaver	¾ **cup cornstarch**
2 **scallions, smashed with the**	3 **cups oil**
side of a cleaver	**Szechuan peppercorn salt**

1. Clean and skin squid. Remove the thin membrane. Score lengthwise and crosswise in a diamond-shaped pattern on the inside of squid sections. Cut squid into 1½-inch-square pieces.
2. Mix ginger, scallions, dry sherry, and salt. Marinate squid in mixture 20 minutes; drain.
3. Dredge the squid pieces well in the cornstarch to coat. (Do not dredge squid ahead of time.) Heat 3 cups oil in wok to 375°. Add a portion of the squid and deep-fry 3 minutes until golden. Remove; drain. Deep-fry the remaining squid pieces and remove.
4. Reheat the oil to 400°. Add all the squid pieces and deep-fry briefly until golden brown and crisp. Remove; drain. Serve with Szechuan peppercorn salt.

Tip: To clean squid, pull the head and body of the squid apart. Cut off the tentacles just below the eyes. Remove the transparent quill from the inside of the body sac. Rinse the body sac well. Peel and discard the purple membrane covering it. Pull off the back flaps from the body sac.

Advance Preparation: Squid may be fried once 1 hour prior to the second frying.

Makes 6 to 8 servings.

Basic Fish Balls

Delicate fish balls are served in many ways and are an important part of the Chinese meal. This is a basic recipe to be used in a variety of recipes. Fish balls can be used in a soup, Shanghai Fish Balls in Broth, as a main course in Hot and Sour Fish Balls, and as an appetizer in Fried Fish Dumplings (see Index).

¾ **pound fish fillets (rock cod,
sea bass, pickerel, haddock,
or any white-fleshed fish)
finely chopped to a paste**
1 **egg white, lightly beaten**
2 **tablespoons dry sherry**
2 **teaspoons Chinese sesame oil**
2 **teaspoons water**

1 **tablespoon scallion, white
part only, minced**
1 **tablespoon cornstarch**
1 **teaspoon peeled, minced
ginger**
Salt
6 **cups chicken broth**

1. Put the finely chopped fish through a food mill to remove any filaments. (This is unnecessary if using a food processor.)
2. Combine the fish with the remaining ingredients, except broth, to form a smooth paste. Mix the fish paste vigorously in 1 direction only for about 5 minutes until stiff. (If using the food processor, do not overprocess.)
3. Prepare 6 cups broth and simmer it. Have a bowl of ice water beside it. With wet hands dipped in the cold water, form the paste into balls about 1 inch in diameter. Do not roll them between the palms as the texture will not be light. Repeat the process until all fish balls are formed.
4. Drop the fish balls into the simmering broth 1 at a time. When all have been added, increase the heat to moderately high. Cook, stirring gently for 3 to 5 minutes or until they rise to surface. Transfer the balls as they are cooked with a skimmer to a plate.

Advance Preparation: Cooked fish balls may be refrigerated for 1 day. Reheat by simmering in broth until heated through.

Makes 3 to 4 servings or 6 to 8 dim sum servings.

Deep-Fried Fish Balls

This is an interesting appetizer which is served with soy-vinegar dip, plum sauce, or Szechuan peppercorn salt. The combination of the light fish inside and the crisp outer crust is very appealing.

1 **recipe Fish Balls (see Index)**   **3 to 4 cups oil**

1. Prepare fish balls. When forming balls, moisten the hand with oil as the balls are to be deep-fat fried.
2. Deep-fry the fish balls in 3 to 4 cups oil at 350°. With a spoon, lower 1 ball at a time into the oil, never exceeding 6 balls. Fry 2 minutes, turning to brown evenly. Remove and drain. While other fish balls are frying, keep cooked balls in the oven at 200°.

Tip: Serve with Soy Vinegar Sesame Dipping Sauce, Plum Sauce, or Szechuan Peppercorn Salt (see Index).

Fish Cakes

The pleasant contrast between the browned exterior and the white interior makes the sliced fish cakes an attractive appetizer. As an appetizer they are served with a soy-chili dipping sauce. The addition of a stir-fried vegetable sauce makes them a good entrée.

¾ **pound fish fillets (sea bass, rock cod, or any white-fleshed fish)**	2 **tablespoons dry sherry**
	2 **teaspoons water**
	2 **teaspoons Chinese sesame oil**
2 **tablespoons scallion, minced**	1 **egg white, lightly beaten**
1 **tablespoon dried shrimp, soaked in water until soft and pliable, finely minced**	**Salt**
	1 **teaspoon cornstarch**
	3 **cups oil**
1 **teaspoon ginger, peeled, minced**	

1. Mince the fish and put the fish through a food mill to remove any filaments. (This is unnecessary if using a food processor.)
2. Combine the fish with the remaining ingredients, except 3 cups oil, to form a smooth paste. Mix the fish paste vigorously in 1 direction only for about 5 minutes until stiff. (If using the food processor, do not overprocess.)
3. Moisten the hands with oil to keep the paste from sticking. Form the paste into patties ¾ inch thick and 3 inches across.
4. Heat 3 cups of oil in wok to 375°. Deep-fry the cakes in the hot oil. When they are brown, remove them from the oil.
5. When the cakes are cool enough to handle, slice them into ½-inch pieces.
6. Serve cakes as a hot hors d'oeuvre with Chili Soy Dipping Sauce or Szechuan Peppercorn Salt.

Tip: The Fish Cakes may be fried ahead and reheated in a 350° oven until heated through.

Makes 3 to 4 servings.

Yangchow Fried Rice

Fried rice is a wonderful side dish for an American buffet as it may be made ahead and reheated. When done properly, it is light and delicate. Such simplicity allows a creative cook to add almost anything. The Yangchow Fried Rice is not darkened by soy sauce as is the Cantonese. Therefore, it is much more colorful.

In China, fried rice is a very simple dish created primarily to reheat leftover cold rice. It is a snack, served in the afternoon, eaten on the train (perhaps the best dish served on Chinese trains) and is rarely served as part of a regular meal. In Taiwan, there are teahouses specializing in dozens of different kinds of fried rice.

The only requirement for making good fried rice is that the rice be cold and firm so that it may be separated to prevent lumping during the fast stir-frying process.

Shrimp Mixture
4 ounces small shrimp, shelled, deveined, cut into peanut-sized pieces
½ teaspoon cornstarch
½ teaspoon dry sherry

5 tablespoons oil
⅔ cup diced cooked ham or barbecued pork or cubed Chinese sausages

3½ cups cold cooked long-grain rice (1 cup uncooked), cooked at least 1 day in advance
3 eggs, lightly beaten with ¼ teaspoon salt
½ cup frozen peas, defrosted
1 cup fresh bean sprouts
2 scallions, finely chopped
½ cup romaine lettuce, finely shredded
½ to 1 teaspoon salt

1. Combine shrimp, cornstarch, and sherry. Marinate 20 minutes.
2. Heat wok. Add 2 tablespoons of the oil. Heat and add the shrimp. Cook shrimp, stirring quickly and turning them in the oil until they turn pink, about 30 seconds. Remove to a dish.
3. Add 3 tablespoons of the oil to wok. Heat. Add the ham and cook to heat through, stirring. Add the rice, stirring rapidly and cook until thoroughly heated without browning.
4. Quickly make a well in the center of the rice and add the eggs-salt mixture, stirring constantly. When they have a soft-scrambled consistency, start incorporating the rice, stirring in a circular fashion.

5. When rice and eggs are blended, add the peas and bean sprouts. Blend well. Stir in the shrimp, scallions, and lettuce, tossing the rice thoroughly to blend all the ingredients. Season to taste with salt. Cook about 30 seconds until heated through. Serve.

Variations: To make Cantonese fried rice, known more commonly to Americans, add 2 tablespoons soy sauce or 2 tablespoons oyster-flavored sauce.

Any combination of meat or vegetables may be substituted. Try to have a nice contrast of colors and textures.

Cool fried rice and serve as a rice salad.

Tips: The cooked rice can be kept warm, covered in a serving bowl in a 250° oven for 30 minutes.

It may be reheated in the wok on the stove or in a covered heat-proof server in a 350° oven until heated through.

Makes 4 to 6 servings.

7

Ready for Reheating: Savory, Sauced Dishes

Sauces provide extra convenience for the cook in these recipes. All of these dishes can be made ahead and then reheated in their accompanying sauces just before serving. But that's where the resemblance ends! This scheduling ease lends itself to a rich and varied choice of fare.

You might select Stuffed Eggplant Slices filled with pork and then batter-fried before reheating in a chili-spiced sauce when you want to fill out a menu with a spicy dish. Or choose Five Treasure Vegetable Platter for its mild flavor and beautiful presentation of asparagus, carrots, straw mushrooms, baby corn, and fresh tomatoes. The technique used in Szechuan Dry-Cooked Green Beans offers a completely different meal accent: green beans fried in hot oil, without a batter, to brown crispness on the outside and tender freshness within.

Another Szechuan cooking method yields the irresistible moistness of Twice-Cooked Pork, which is slowly simmered a day ahead and then sliced and reheated in a tantalizing hoisin sauce-chili paste mixture. And yet a third mode of Szechuan ingenuity results in the incomparable crunchiness of Szechuan Dry-Fried Beef Shreds, an easygoing dinner entrée.

You'll find many vegetables as well as eggs, fish, and bean curd featured among these recipes; so you can pick an appropriate textural complement to any fried or steamed dish. But one teahouse favorite, Singapore Stir-Fried Noodles, a curry-perfumed treasury of tastes, could be served as a meal in itself—as long as there's enough for seconds!

Gold Coin Eggs

*This wonderful egg dish can be served as an appetizer, or for a
dim sum brunch. The chili peppers add a nice spiciness to the
sauce.*

6 jumbo eggs	**2 teaspoons rice vinegar**
1 teaspoon salt	**2 teaspoons light soy sauce**
4 tablespoons cornstarch	**1 teaspoon Chinese sesame oil**
⅓ cup oil	**¼ teaspoon salt**

Sauce Mixture	**1 to 2 dried red chili peppers**
2½ tablespoons scallions, thinly	**¾ teaspoons ginger, minced**
sliced	**1 teaspoon cornstarch dissolved**
¼ cup hot water	**in 2 tablespoons cold water**

1. Place eggs in a saucepan with salted water to cover 2 inches
   above the eggs. Simmer for 25 minutes. Turn off the heat and let
   the eggs sit for 10 minutes. Run them under cold water until
   cool. Peel.
2. Prepare sauce. Combine the scallions, hot water, vinegar, soy
   sauce, Chinese sesame oil, and salt in a bowl. Set aside.
3. Cut each egg into 5 rounds. Coat the egg rounds on each side
   and on the edges with the 4 tablespoons cornstarch.
4. Heat a 12-inch skillet. Add enough oil to the skillet to coat the
   bottom with ⅛ inch oil. Heat to 325°. Place the coins close
   together but not touching one another in the skillet. Brown the
   eggs on both sides. Remove to a serving plate. Remove all but 2
   tablespoons oil.
5. Heat the 2 tablespoons oil in the skillet. Add the chili peppers
   and ginger. Reduce the heat to low and cook until browned.
   Add the scallion mixture and cook until heated through. Add
   cornstarch dissolved in water. Cook until slightly thickened.
   Pour over the eggs and serve.

*Advance Preparation: Cook the eggs one day in advance. Slice and
brown 1 to 2 hours before serving. Prepare the sauce. At serving
time, reheat the eggs and the sauce. Pour the sauce over the eggs.*

Makes 6 servings.

Stuffed Bean Curd

The following is a very popular Chinese dish served as an appetizer or part of a buffet. It is easily prepared, economical, and delicious.

Stuffing Mixture

2 **teaspoons dried shrimp, soaked in very hot water for 30 minutes or until soft, drained, and rinsed**

6 **ounces pork, finely ground**

2 **teaspoons dry sherry**

2 **teaspoons light soy sauce**

1 **teaspoon ginger, minced**

1 **teaspoon sesame oil**

¼ **teaspoon sugar**

¼ **teaspoon salt**

¼ **teaspoon pepper**

3 **pieces fresh bean curd, cut into 3-inch squares**

2 **teaspoons water chestnut powder or cornstarch**

4 **tablespoons oil**

⅔ **cup chicken stock**

Sauce Mixture

2 **tablespoons oyster sauce**

¼ **teaspoon sugar**

2 **teaspoons cornstarch dissolved in 1½ tablespoons water**

1 **scallion, shredded**

1. Combine shrimp with remaining stuffing ingredients in a bowl until well mixed. Set aside.
2. Rinse bean curd squares gently under running water. Drain excess liquid. Pat squares dry with paper towels. Cut each square into 4 triangles. Make an incision in the longest side of each triangle. Carefully hollow out the triangles, leaving about a ⅜-inch rim. (Be careful not to pierce the walls of the pockets.) Dust the cutout pockets lightly with water chestnut powder. Stuff the triangles with the shrimp stuffing mixture, smoothing the surface of the filling with the back of a spoon dipped in cold water.
3. Make sauce mixture. Mix oyster sauce, ¼ teaspoon sugar, and cornstarch dissolved in water.
4. Heat a large, heavy skillet over moderately high heat. Swirl in 4 tablespoons oil. When the oil is hot, arrange the stuffed bean curd, filling side down, in the skillet. Fry for 2 minutes or until they are golden. Brown the other sides. Add the chicken stock. Heat to boiling; adjust the heat to low to maintain a gentle simmer. Cover. Simmer 8 minutes, turning once. Remove carefully to a hot platter.
5. Add the mixture to the skillet. Stir over moderate heat until the mixture is smooth and thickened. Pour the sauce over the bean curd; sprinkle the scallions on top.

Tip: A grapefruit knife is ideal for hollowing out the triangles.

Advance Preparation: The bean curd can be stuffed ahead and refrigerated.
   The sautéed bean curd can be kept warm for 20 minutes in a preheated 200° oven uncovered. Heat sauce at serving time. Pour over bean curd.

Makes 3 dinner or 6 dim sum servings.

Stuffed Eggplant Slices with Fish-Flavored Sauce

This marvelous spicy dish is wonderful for a buffet or a dinner. Stuffing the eggplant slices takes time, but is well worth the effort. "Fish-Flavored Sauce" is a Szechuan chili sauce originally served on fish for flavoring.

Sauce Mixture
1½ teaspoons sugar
4 tablespoons chicken broth
2 tablespons dry sherry
1 tablespoon light soy sauce
2 teaspoons Chinese black vinegar
1 teaspoon sesame oil

Fish-Flavored Sauce
2 tablespoons oil
1 tablespoon chili paste with garlic
2 teaspoons ginger, minced
2 scallions, minced
1 teaspoon cornstarch dissolved in 2 teaspoons cold water
1 recipe stuffed eggplant slices prepared and fried as directed (see Index)

1. Combine sauce ingredients. Set aside.
2. Make fish-flavored sauce. Heat wok. Add 2 tablespoons oil. Heat oil. Add chili paste with garlic. Cook 15 seconds. Add ginger and scallions. Cook 15 seconds. Add sauce mixture and cook until heated through. Add cornstarch dissolved in water. Cook until slightly thickened. Add the fried eggplant slices to the sauce. Heat thoroughly. Serve.

Tip: Substitute Worcestershire sauce for Chinese black vinegar.

Advance Preparation: Fry eggplant slices and make sauce 3 to 4 hours ahead. Reheat the sauce at serving time. Add the eggplant slices and reheat them in the sauce.

Makes 6 dinner servings or 18 dim sum servings.

Meat-Filled Omelets

This buffet dish consists of tiny omelets filled with a meat mixture. Tree ears and lily buds in a delicately flavored sauce cover the omelets. These are traditionally served during Chinese New Year. The golden egg skins provide a delicate wrapper for the fragrant meat filling. The dumplings are said to resemble golden coins. Offering them during the New Year conveys the wish for continuing prosperity.

½ **pound cucumber, pared, cut lengthwise in half, seeded**
½ **teaspoon salt**

Egg Pancakes
4 **eggs**
4 **tablespoons all-purpose flour**
1½ **teaspoons cooking oil**

Pork Filling
8 **ounces ground pork, including fat portion**
2 **tablespoons ginger, peeled, minced**
3 **scallions, chopped**
2 **tablespoons light soy sauce**
1 **tablespoon dry sherry**
1 **teaspoon Chinese sesame oil**
1 **egg white, lightly beaten**
½ **teaspoon sugar**
¼ **teaspoon salt**
1 **tablespoon cornstarch**

1 **egg, lightly beaten**

Sauce Mixture
2 **tablespoons dry sherry**
1 **tablespoon light soy sauce**
2 **teaspoons sugar**
1 **teaspoon Chinese sesame oil**
1 **cup chicken broth**

¼ **cup dried tree ears, soaked in hot water 20 minutes**
¼ **cup dried lily buds, soaked in hot water 20 minutes**
3 **tablespoons oil**
2 **scallions, shredded into 1½-inch lengths**
½ **teaspoon salt**
¼ **teaspoon ground roasted Szechuan peppercorn powder**
1 **tablespoon cornstarch dissolved in 2 tablespoons cold water**

1. Cut the cucumber into very thin slices. Place slices in a bowl and sprinkle ½ teaspoon salt over them. Mix thoroughly. Let stand 10 minutes. Drain well.
2. Mix the 4 eggs and flour to make a smooth batter. Heat a small flat frying pan over high heat. Add 1½ teaspoons oil and swirl it around until the bottom of the pan is covered. Pour a scant

tablespoon of egg batter into the frying pan, tilting the pan so that the batter covers a circle 3 inches in diameter. Cook the egg pancake until it has barely set and is still soft, but not runny. Remove it to a plate. Repeat procedure with remaining egg batter. There should be 24 thin egg pancakes.

3. Combine filling ingredients. Place 1 tablespoon pork mixture in the middle of one of the little pancakes. Moisten the edges with the beaten egg. Fold the pancake over the filling and press the edges together. Repeat procedure with remaining pancakes.
4. Combine sauce mixture ingredients. Set aside.
5. Drain and rinse the tree ears and lily buds. Tear each lily bud into 3 or 4 shreds.
6. Heat wok. Add 1 tablespoon oil. Heat oil. Add cucumber slices. Stir-fry 1 minute. Remove from wok.
7. Add 2 tablespoons oil to wok. Add tree ears, lily buds, shredded scallions, and ½ teaspoon salt. Stir-fry for 30 seconds.
8. Add the sauce mixture. Gently place the filled omelets into the cooking liquid. Heat sauce to boiling; cover the wok and cook over medium heat for 5 minutes.
9. Add the ground peppercorn powder and the cooked cucumbers to the wok. Heat.
10. Recombine the cornstarch and water and add to the wok. Heat until the sauce has turned clear. To serve, first place the omelets on the serving dish and arrange the tree ears, lily buds, and cucumbers on top of the omelets.

Tip: The omelets may be cooked prior to serving, refrigerated, and reheated in the cooking liquid at serving time.

Makes 4 dinner servings.

Twice-Cooked Pork

In this Szechuan specialty, the meat is simmered first, then stir-fried in a hot sauce wih green peppers and carrots. The pork may be cooked ahead, making the final preparation quick and easy.

1 **pound boneless pork loin, including fat**
2 **pieces ginger, the size of a quarter, crushed**
2 **large cloves garlic, peeled, crushed**

2 **tablespoons oil**
2 **medium-sized green peppers, shredded**
2 **carrots, shredded**
½ **cup bamboo shoots, shredded**

Sauce Mixture
2 **tablespoons hoisin sauce**
2 **tablespoons dry sherry**
1½ **tablespoons chili paste with garlic**
1 **tablespoon dark soy sauce**
1 **teaspoon sugar**

2 **tablespoons oil**
2 **scallions, cut into 2-inch pieces, shredded**

1. Place the meat in a pot with the ginger, garlic, and enough water to cover the meat to 1 inch above the meat. Heat to boiling; reduce heat. Simmer for 40 minutes. Drain the meat. Cover and refrigerate meat for a few hours until it is very firm.
2. When you are ready to stir-fry, cut the meat into slices, 1½ × ⅛ inch each.
3. Heat the wok. Add 2 tablespoons oil and heat. Add green peppers and carrots. Stir-fry for 2 minutes. Add bamboo shoots. Stir-fry for 30 seconds. Remove vegetables from wok.
4. Combine sauce ingredients. Set mixture aside.
5. Add 2 tablespoons oil to wok. Heat oil. Stir-fry pork until crisp and brown, about 3 minutes. As fat is rendered, pull the pork away from the middle of the wok and remove accumulated fat with a ladle. Add the cooked vegetables and scallions. Cook, stirring, until heated through. Pour in sauce mixture and stir until meat and vegetables are well coated with the sauce.

Advance Preparation: Cook pork 1 day in advance; prepare vegetables. Cook vegetables 1 to 2 hours before serving time. At serving time, stir-fry pork, add vegetables, and sauce mixture. Cook until heated through.

Makes 4 dinner servings.

Phoenix Dragon Chicken with Vegetables

The crispy chicken served on a bed of vegetables provides a pleasant contrast of tastes and textures.

1 recipe Phoenix Dragon
  Chicken prepared and fried
  as directed (see Index)
3 tablespoons oil
2 slices ginger, the size of a
  quarter, peeled, minced
1 medium-size clove garlic,
  crushed with the side of a
  cleaver, minced
½ cup bamboo shoots,
  shredded
4 water chestnuts, sliced

4 scallions, shredded into
  2-inch lengths
1 tablespoon cornstarch
  dissolved in 2 tablespoons
  cold water
1 teaspoon Chinese sesame oil

Sauce Mixture
¾ cup chicken broth
1 tablespoon dry sherry
1 tablespoon light soy sauce
Pinch ground white pepper

1. Prepare the Phoenix Dragon Chicken up to the refrying procedure (see Index).
2. Combine sauce ingredients. Set mixture aside.
3. Heat the wok. Add 3 tablespoons oil and heat. Add the ginger and garlic. Cook until fragrant, about 10 seconds. Add the bamboo shoots, water chestnuts, and scallions. Stir rapidly for 30 seconds. Add the sauce mixture. When the liquid comes to a boil, stir in the dissolved cornstarch to thicken the sauce. Add the Chinese sesame oil and stir.
4. Reheat the deep-frying oil from the Phoenix Dragon Chicken to 350°. When the sauce is completed, refry all the chicken together for 1 minute, turning constantly until very crisp and brown. Remove and drain on paper towels. Slice the chicken crosswise diagonally into ½-inch pieces.
5. Reheat the sauce. Spread the vegetable sauce on a platter as a bed for the sliced chicken. Place the chicken on top of the vegetables. Serve.

Advance Preparation: Fry the chicken earlier in the day. Prepare the vegetable sauce. Reheat at serving time.

Makes 6 to 8 dinner servings.

Red-Cooked Pine Nut Chicken

The sweet pine nuts are used as a flavoring as well as serving to give a nice consistency to the ground pork topping of the chicken. This dish is ideal for entertaining as it does not have to be served immediately. It may be used as an appetizer or a main course.

Batter
2 **tablespoons cornstarch, dissolved in 3 tablespoons water**
1 **egg yolk, lightly beaten**

4 **boneless chicken breasts, skin on, cut into 24 square pieces**
¼ **cup cornstarch**
½ **pound ground pork**
½ **cup pine nuts**
½ **teaspoon sugar**
½ **teaspoon salt**
1 **scallion, minced**

2 **slices ginger, the size of a quarter, peeled, minced**
1 **egg, lightly beaten**

Sauce Mixture
⅓ **cup chicken broth**
4 **tablespoons dark soy sauce**
4 **tablespoons dry sherry**
1¼ **tablespoons sugar**
½ **teaspoon Szechuan peppercorn powder**

2 **tablespoons oil**
½ **pound spinach**
4 **tablespoons oil**

1. Mix cornstarch dissolved in water and egg yolk. Pour half the batter over the chicken pieces, smoothing with your fingers, then turn the pieces and coat the other side. Save the other half for the final coating. Sprinkle the meat side of the chicken with ¼ cup cornstarch lightly. Combine sauce ingredients. Set aside.
2. Mix pork, pine nuts, sugar, salt, scallion, ginger, and egg. Divide the pork mixture into 24 portions. Pat and smooth the mixture onto the meat side of the chicken pieces and dip the mounded pieces in the remaining coating. Repeat until all pieces are coated and covered.
3. Heat 2 tablespoons oil in a large heavy skillet. Reduce heat to medium. Add half the chicken pieces, pork covered side down, and fry them for 1½ to 2 minutes. Remove them and fry the remaining pieces. Push the pieces in the pan to one side and put the first batch back in the skillet, pork side up. All the pieces should be in 1 layer.
4. Pour the sauce mixture over the pieces and baste the top for a

few seconds. Cover and let the chicken simmer gently over low heat for 15 minutes. Turn the pieces over, baste, and cook for another 10 minutes.

5. Stir-fry the spinach in 2 tablespoons hot oil until wilted. Arrange the spinach around the edge of a serving platter.

6. Remove the chicken to the serving platter, pork side up. Place in the center of the platter. Pour the sauce over the chicken.

Advance Preparation: Recipe can be prepared several hours in advance. Reheat in sauce at serving time. Then pour sauce mixture over chicken.

Makes 6 to 10 servings.

Stuffed Chicken Wings

These chicken wings are crisp on the outside and moist inside. Stuffing a chicken wing may seem like a difficult task. However, once you try the recipe, it will prove easy to make and delightful to taste.

12 chicken wings
12 strips bamboo shoots, 2 × ¼ × ¼ inch
12 strips Smithfield ham, 2 × ¼ × ¼ inch
12 strips scallions, 2 × ¼ × ¼ inch

Chicken Wing Marinade
2 tablespoons light soy sauce
1 teaspoon sugar
1 teaspoon dry sherry

Sauce Mixture
1 tablespoon light soy sauce
½ teaspoon salt
½ teaspoon sugar

2 teaspoons cornstarch dissolved in 2 tablespoons cold water
3 tablespoons oil
6 dried Chinese black mushrooms, soaked in hot water until spongy, stems removed, cut into wedges
½ cup bamboo shoots, cut into thin slices
1 scallion, shredded into 1½-inch lengths
2 ounces snow peas, shredded into 1½-inch lengths
½ cup reserved chicken broth
½ teaspoon Chinese sesame oil

1. Cut the wings apart at both joints. Use the middle section of each wing only. (The large sections may be used for fried Chicken Lollipops (see Index).
2. Heat 2 cups water to boiling. Add the chicken and simmer for 4 minutes to firm up the meat. Reserve the broth. Sever the tendon at both ends of each piece, about ½ inch from the end. Gently, with your fingers, push out the bones inside each piece. Immediately place 1 strip each of bamboo shoots, ham, and scallion in the cavity left by removing the bones. Repeat procedure with all the wings. Combine marinade ingredients. Marinate wings in mixture for 15 minutes. (If you have trouble boning as directed, make a slice lengthwise down the middle of the back side of the wing. Lift out the smaller bone. Carefully reach into the cavity and remove the larger bone. Stuff the

cavity. Tie the stuffed wing with a scallion previously soaked in water until pliable.)
3. Combine sauce ingredients. Set aside. Combine cornstarch and water. Set aside.
4. Heat wok. Add 3 tablespoons oil. Stir-fry the wings gently 3 to 4 minutes. Add the mushrooms, bamboo shoots, scallions, and snow peas. Add sauce mixture and stir. Add the reserved chicken broth and cook for 2 minutes. Recombine the cornstarch and add. Cook until translucent. Add the sesame oil. Stir. Remove wings and serve.

Tip: Stuff chicken wings in advance and refrigerate.

Makes 3 to 4 dinner servings.

Szechuan Dry-Fried Beef Shreds

This is one of the most famous Szechuanese dishes of all. I fondly remember my Szechuan chef whenever I prepare it. His version of this dish is totally unlike any other in flavor and texture.

In a properly prepared dry-fried beef, the meat has literally dried out and become hard and crunchy. This is a good dish for a dinner party as it can be made in advance and reheated quickly just before serving.

1 pound flank steak, cut against the grain into matchstick strips, 1½ inches long

Beef Marinade
2 tablespoons dark soy sauce
½ teaspoon sugar
2 tablespoons dry sherry

Sauce Mixture
1 tablespoon dark soy sauce
1 teaspoon dry sherry
1 teaspoon sugar

2 cups oil

1 teaspoon scallion, minced
1 teaspoon ginger, minced
2 teaspoons hot chili paste
1 cup carrot, cut into matchstick-size shreds
1 cup celery, cut into matchstick-size shreds
3 scallions cut into 1½ inch shreds

1 teaspoon Chinese sesame oil
½ teaspoon Chinese black vinegar
⅓ teaspoon Szechuan peppercorn salt
3 tablespoons oil

1. Mix soy sauce, sugar, and sherry. Marinate beef strips in marinade 30 minutes.
2. Prepare sauce. Mix 1 tablespoon soy sauce, the dry sherry, and 1 teaspoon sugar. Set sauce mixture aside.
3. Heat wok; add 2 cups oil. Heat oil to 375°. Add the beef shreds and fry, stirring constantly over high heat for 5 to 10 minutes or until the beef is coffee-colored and very dry. Remove and drain.
4. Heat wok. Add 3 tablespoons oil; heat until very hot. Add minced scallion and ginger and stir-fry for 5 seconds until fragrant. Add the hot chili paste and stir for a few seconds. Add the carrot shreds. Stir-fry over high heat until the carrot is tender. Add the celery and scallions. Cook for 1 minute until the celery shreds are slightly cooked but still crunchy. Add the beef

shreds and the sauce mixture. Cook until heated through. Add the sesame oil and vinegar; toss lightly. Transfer to a serving platter and sprinkle with Szechuan peppercorn salt.

Advance Preparation: Prepare the recipe several hours in advance, to the point of adding the sauce mixture. At serving time, heat the meat, add the sauce and heat. Add the sesame oil and vinegar. Stir-fry the ingredients for 30 seconds to penetrate all the pieces of beef. Sprinkle with peppercorn salt. Serve.

Tip: The beef is easier to slice when partially frozen.

Makes 4 servings as a main course.

Stuffed Green Peppers

A tasty sauce combined with the delicate flavoring of the pork and shrimp filling makes this a delightful dish. The peppers may be served as a hot appetizer or as part of a Chinese dinner.

Pork Filling
6 ounces pork, minced
2 ounces raw shrimp, shelled, chopped
8 water chestnuts, minced
1 egg white
3 tablespoons dry sherry
1 tablespoon light soy sauce
½ teaspoon salt
½ teaspoon sugar
1 tablespoon cornstarch

Sauce Mixture
1 cup chicken broth
1 tablespoon hoisin sauce
1 tablespoon dark soy sauce
1 tablespoon dry sherry
1 teaspoon sugar

4 large green peppers, seeded, cut into pieces 2 × 1½ inches
Cornstarch
6 tablespoons oil
1 tablespoon salted black beans, rinsed, drained well, chopped
2 cloves garlic, chopped
2 slices ginger, the size of a quarter, chopped
¼ teaspoon red pepper flakes (optional)
1 tablespoon cornstarch dissolved in 2 tablespoons water

1. Combine pork, shrimp, water chestnuts, egg white, sherry, light soy sauce, salt, sugar, and cornstarch. Mix lightly. Combine sauce ingredients. Set aside.
2. Sprinkle the cavity of each green pepper piece lightly with cornstarch. Fill the cavity with the pork filling and smooth the surface with the back of a spoon.
3. Heat a skillet. Add 6 tablespoons oil. Place the peppers meat side down in the skillet. Fry for 2 minutes or until golden brown. Remove peppers from the skillet. Remove all but 2 tablespoons of oil from the skillet. Add the black beans, garlic, ginger, and red pepper flakes to the skillet. Cook until garlic and ginger are lightly browned. Add the sauce mixture and the green peppers, meat side up. Cover and simmer for 8 minutes over low heat. Recombine the cornstarch and water and add to the skillet.

Cook until thickened. Remove peppers to a serving plate; pour the sauce mixture over the peppers.

Advance Preparation: Stuff the peppers several hours ahead. Refrigerate. Cook as above.
The peppers may be cooked ahead and rewarmed in the sauce at serving time or may be kept warm in a preheated 200° oven for 5 to 10 minutes after cooking.

Makes 3 to 4 dinner servings or 6 to 8 dim sum servings.

Shrimp Balls in Ginger Sauce

The ginger sauce here is a marvelous complement to the delicate shrimp balls.

1 recipe Steamed Shrimp Balls, prepared as directed (see Index)
3 cups oil

Sauce Mixture
5 tablespoons red wine vinegar
1 tablespoon dark soy sauce
1½ tablespoons light brown sugar
1 tablespoon ginger, shredded
1 teaspoon garlic, minced

1. Prepare Steamed Shrimp Balls.
2. Combine sauce ingredients. Heat the mixture over medium heat, stirring until the mixture almost comes to a boil. Pour the sauce over the Steamed Shrimp Balls. Serve.

Makes 4 dinner servings or 12 dim sum servings.

Shrimp Balls with Snow Peas

The following recipe makes an attractive, delicately flavored dish, turning shrimp balls into a main course item.

1 recipe Steamed Shrimp Balls, prepared as directed (see Index)
2 tablespoons oil
4 Chinese dried black mushrooms, soaked in hot water until spongy
4 ounces fresh snow peas, strings removed
⅓ cup water chestnuts, sliced

Sauce Mixture
½ cup chicken broth
1 tablespoon dry sherry
½ teaspoon sugar
Salt
⅛ teaspoon white pepper
1 tablespoon cornstarch dissolved in 2 tablespoons cold water
1 tablespoon Chinese sesame oil

1. Prepare Steamed Shrimp Balls.
2. Heat wok. Add oil. Heat. Add mushrooms, snow peas, and water chestnuts. Stir-fry 1 to 2 minutes. Remove from wok.
3. Prepare sauce. Mix chicken broth, sherry, sugar, salt, and pepper. Add the mixture to wok. Heat to boiling. Add the Shrimp Balls. Cover wok and let simmer 2 minutes or until Shrimp Balls are heated through. (Simmer longer if Shrimp Balls are frozen.)
4. Return vegetables to wok; stir to mix. Recombine cornstarch mixture and pour into wok, stirring until the sauce becomes translucent. Add the sesame oil. Stir and serve.

Makes 2 to 3 dinner servings.

Hot and Sour Fish Balls

This is an attractive dish with an unusual blend of tastes and textures—the spicy sauce, the delicate fish dumplings, and the crispy vegetables topped with pine nuts make this most interesting.

1 recipe Steamed Fish Balls, prepared as directed (see Index)

4 tablespoons oil

¼ cup pine nuts, fried

½ cup bamboo shoots, sliced

1 medium sweet red pepper, seeded, cut into 1-inch cubes

2 scallions, shredded into 1½-inch shreds

4 ounces snow peas

¼ cup water chestnuts, sliced

1 tablespoon Chinese sesame oil

Sauce Mixture

¾ cup chicken broth

4 tablespoons red wine vinegar

3 tablespoons honey

1 tablespoon light soy sauce

1 tablespoon chili sauce

1 clove garlic, minced

1 tablespoon cornstarch dissolved in 2 tablespoons water

1. Make fish balls. Steam on an oiled heat-proof plate over medium heat for 10 minutes. When forming the balls, have a bowl of ice water beside the balls. Dip hands in the ice water when forming the balls.
2. Heat wok. Add 2 tablespoons of the oil. Stir-fry the pine nuts until golden. Remove and set aside.
3. Mix chicken broth, vinegar, honey, soy sauce, chili sauce, and garlic. Heat the mixture to boiling over high heat.
4. Add the fish balls and heat the sauce to boiling. Add the bamboo shoots, red pepper, scallions, snow peas, and water chestnuts. Cook, stirring, for 30 seconds. Recombine the cornstarch dissolved in water; add to the sauce mixture. Stir until the sauce thickens. Heat to boiling again. Add sesame oil. Stir. Sprinkle with roasted pine nuts. Serve.

Tip: Fish dumplings may be steamed early in the day or the day before if wrapped well and refrigerated. Reheat by steaming.

Makes 3 to 4 servings.

Szechuan Dry-Cooked Green Beans

This is a typical Szechuan dry-fry dish. The beans should be brown and blistery on the outside but crisp and tender inside. Select beans that are fresh and not too mature. If possible, use Chinese yard-long green beans.

2 **cups oil**
1½ **pounds green beans, rinsed,
    dried, tough ends removed**

Sauce Mixture
2 **tablespoons dry sherry**
2 **tablespoons water**
1½ **tablespoons light soy sauce**
1 **tablespoon Chinese sesame
    oil or hot chili oil**

½ **pound ground pork**
½ **tablespoon dried shrimp,
    soaked in hot water to cover
    30 minutes, drained, finely
    minced**
2 **tablespoons Szechuan
    preserved mustard greens,
    rinsed with water to remove
    pepperiness, finely minced**

1. Heat the oil in wok to 375°. Deep-fry the beans in 2 to 3 batches until they develop brown blisters and shrivel slightly. Remove. Drain.
2. Combine sauce ingredients. Set mixture aside.
3. Remove all but 2 tablespoons oil from wok. Add the pork and stir-fry, breaking it up until it begins to brown. Add the minced shrimp and preserved mustard greens; stir well for 30 seconds. Add the string beans, stirring to mix for 15 seconds. Add the sauce mixture and stir vigorously until the liquid is absorbed by the ingredients. Serve.

Tips: Because the preserved mustard greens may vary in pungency, the amount of soy sauce in this recipe may be adjusted to taste.

Advance Preparation: The first frying may be done several hours in advance. Do the final stir-fry before serving.

Makes 4 servings.

Eggplant Szechuan Style

Eggplant and chopped meat is a combination of food that appears in many cuisines. The affinity of the two is brilliantly shown in this Szechuan dish. It is easy to make and can be prepared in advance in large quantities.

Pork Mixture
4 ounces ground pork
1 tablespoon dark soy sauce
2 teaspoons Chinese sesame oil

1 tablespoon hot bean paste
1 tablespoon ginger, chopped
1 tablespoon garlic, chopped
2 teaspoons scallions, chopped
1 teaspoon dry sherry

Sauce Mixture
1 teaspoon light soy sauce
1 teaspoon dry sherry
(sauce continued in next column)

1 teaspoon red wine vinegar
¼ teaspoon Chinese sesame oil
2 teaspoons sugar
½ teaspoon salt

8 tablespoons oil
1 pound baby eggplant, peeled, cut into strips 2 × ½ inches
⅓ cup chicken broth
2 scallions, sliced
1 teaspoon cornstarch dissolved in 2 teaspoons water

1. Combine ground pork, dark soy sauce, and sesame oil. Let marinate for 15 minutes.
2. Combine hot bean paste, ginger, garlic, scallions, and sherry. Set aside. Combine sauce ingredients. Set mixture aside.
3. Heat 6 tablespoons oil in wok. Add eggplant and stir-fry for 4 to 5 minutes or until tender. Stir continuously to avoid burning because the eggplant will quickly soak up the oil. Remove the eggplant and set aside.
4. Heat 2 tablespoons of the oil in wok. Add hot bean paste mixture. Stir until blended. Add the pork mixture. Stir-fry for 1 minute or until it turns grayish. Add the eggplant and the sauce mixture and stir-fry for 1 minute. Add ⅓ cup chicken broth. When broth comes to a boil, reduce heat to low; cover and let eggplant simmer for 15 minutes until it has become soft and has absorbed the flavors of the meat sauce. Add the scallions. Stir. Recombine the cornstarch and add to the eggplant. Cook, stirring until thickened slightly.

Tip: Add more hot bean paste if you like the dish spicier.

Advance Preparation: Prepare 4 to 5 hours ahead. Reheat on top of the stove at serving time.   Makes 3 to 4 servings.

Five Treasure Vegetable Platter

One of the most attractive vegetable dishes is this combination of vegetables in which you may use your own creativity. Be sure to have complementary colors of the vegetables arranged in a decorative pattern on a platter. I prefer to serve the vegetables at room temperature, giving me plenty of time to arrange the food presentation. I then reheat the hot sauce and pour it over the vegetables at serving time. This recipe may easily be doubled.

1 **pound asparagus, stems peeled, tough tips removed**	*Sauce Mixture*
1 **pound baby carrots, peeled, trimmed**	2 **cups chicken broth**
	1 **tablespoon dry sherry**
1 **15-ounce can straw mushrooms, drained**	1 **tablespoon light soy sauce**
	1 **teaspoon sugar**
1 **15-ounce can baby corn**	2 **tablespoons cornstarch dissolved in 4 tablespoons cold water**
3 **tomatoes**	
	½ **teaspoon Chinese sesame oil**

1. Separately blanch asparagus and carrots in boiling water 4 minutes or until barely tender; drain; rinse under cold water. Drain mushrooms; blanch in boiling water 15 seconds. Blanch corn in boiling water 15 seconds. Drain; rinse under cold water. Blanch tomatoes in boiling water 1 minute. Peel skins. Cut tomatoes into quarters and remove seeds.
2. Prepare sauce. Mix chicken broth, sherry, soy sauce, and sugar. Heat. Reheat the vegetables in the sauce mixture, adding each vegetable individually. Reheat the mushrooms. Drain. Place in the center of the platter. Reheat the corn, carrots, asparagus, and tomatoes separately. Place other vegetables in groups in a pinwheel design around the edge of the mushrooms.
3. Heat the sauce mixture to boiling. Add the cornstarch mixture and stir until thickened. Add the sesame oil. Stir. Pour the sauce over the vegetables.

Variations: Any vegetable may be substituted for the vegetables listed. Bok choy is a wonderful green vegetable. Cook bok choy 1 minute or until wilted. Cut into 2-inch pieces. The vegetables may be steamed instead of blanched.

Advance Preparation: Cook the vegetables ahead. Prepare the sauce. Reheat the vegetables individually in the broth or by steaming. At serving time, reheat the sauce mixture. Pour hot sauce over the vegetables.

Makes 8 servings.

Pork with Bean Thread Noodles

The combination of the flavors of the ginger and the hoisin sauce along with the slippery texture of the bean threads is especially pleasing. This easy-to-make dish is good hot, cold, or at room temperature.

4 ounces pork, shredded
1 tablespoon light soy sauce
1 teaspoon dry sherry
1 teaspoon cornstarch
2 tablespoons oil
1 teaspoon ginger, minced
4 ounces bean threads, soaked in hot water 20 minutes or until soft, drained well, cut into 2-inch lengths

1 teaspoon Chinese sesame oil
3 scallions, chopped

Sauce Mixture
½ cup chicken stock
1 tablespoon hoisin sauce
1 tablespoon dry sherry
1 tablespoon dark soy sauce
1 teaspoon sugar

1. Combine pork, soy sauce, sherry, and cornstarch. Let marinate for 20 minutes. Combine sauce ingredients. Set mixture aside.
2. Heat wok. Add 2 tablespoons oil and heat. Add ginger and stir until fragrant. Add pork mixture and stir-fry until the pork turns grayish in color.
3. Add the bean threads and the sauce mixture. Stir. Simmer over low heat for 8 minutes until most of the sauce is absorbed. Add the sesame oil. Stir. Garnish with scallions. Serve.

Tips: This dish can be reheated in a wok or covered, in a 300° oven.
   For a spicy taste, add 3 ounces Szechuan preserved vegetable or preserved mustard green, minced.

Makes 4 servings.

Singapore Stir-Fried Noodles

"Singapore" signals that this is a dish seasoned with curry. This is one of the favorite Chinese noodle dishes in teahouses in China and the United States. It is a meal in itself.

½ **pound dried rice sticks, soaked in very warm water for 15 minutes or until soft, drained**

Shrimp Mixture
½ **pound shrimp, shelled, deveined, cleaned, dried**
¼ **teaspoon baking soda**
½ **egg white**
1 **teaspoon dry sherry**

Sauce Mixture
¼ **teaspoon cayenne pepper**
¾ **teaspoon sugar**
⅓ **cup chicken broth**
1 **tablespoon dark soy sauce**
1 **tablespoon light soy sauce**
1 **tablespoon dry sherry**

6 **tablespoons oil**

2 **eggs, lightly beaten**
1 **red bell pepper, shredded into long thin strips**
2 **stalks celery, strings removed, thinly sliced**
1 **teaspoon garlic, minced**
1 **teaspoon ginger, minced**
4 **scallions, shredded into 1½-inch lengths**
½ **pound Chinese Barbecued Pork, cut into matchstick strips**
6 **Chinese dried black mushrooms, soaked in hot water until spongy, stems removed, shredded**
1 to 2 **tablespoons curry powder or to taste**
2 **tablespoons Chinese sesame oil**
2 **cups fresh bean sprouts**

1. Mix shrimp, baking soda, egg white, and sherry. Let marinate 20 minutes.
2. Combine sauce ingredients. Set mixture aside.
3. Heat wok or skillet over medium heat. Add 1 tablespoon of the oil. When oil is hot, swirl in eggs and spread into a large pancake. Turn pancake when it is set. Cook briefly on the other side. Remove from wok. Cool. Cut pancake into thin strips.
4. Heat wok over high heat. Add 2 tablespoons of the oil. Heat. Add red pepper and celery. Stir-fry 30 seconds. Remove. Add 4 tablespoons oil. When oil is hot, add the garlic and ginger and stir-fry for 10 seconds. Add half of the scallions, the Barbecued Pork, and the mushrooms. Stir-fry for 30 seconds. Remove the

pork mixture. Add the shrimp mixture and stir until it turns pink. Return the pork mixture to the wok. Add the celery, bell pepper, and the sauce mixture. Cook until the mixture is heated through. Remove the mixture from the wok to a bowl.

5. Add 2 tablespoons sesame oil and heat. Add the curry powder, stirring to mix with the oil a few seconds. Do not burn the curry. Add the noodles and toss to coat and heat them. When they are hot, add the cooked mixture. Toss together to mix. Add the bean sprouts. Toss and stir until thoroughly heated. Add the remaining scallions and garnish with the egg strips.

Variations: Substitute ham for the barbecued pork. Substitute zucchini for celery.

Makes 4 dinner servings.

8

Steamed Dim Sum and Other Juicy Morsels

Steamed dumplings, buns, and other juicy morsels are more than just popular teahouse snacks. They are absolutely habit forming! So it's fortunate that they cook quickly, store well in the refrigerator or the freezer, and reheat beautifully in the steamer. After all, when you want Shao-Mai or Har Gow—the translucent, dough-wrapped dumplings that spurt juices with each bite—nothing else will do! If you crave a meat-filled bun for breakfast, lunch, or tea-break, you should be able to indulge as the Chinese do—even though they are more likely to purchase the treat. And when guests arrive, expected or otherwise, it's nice to have the speedy steamer ready for filling with any of the delicious tidbits, such as Pearl Balls, that can be served as appetizers or entrées.

Traditionally reserved for subtly flavored and delicate-to-handle foods, steaming produces some surprisingly dramatic presentations. Lotus Leaf Rice is like a great gift packet of glutinous rice, chicken, vegetables, sausage, and shrimp—the wrapping is not for eating but only for the final steaming and table ceremony. The colors of Steamed Stuffed Black Mushrooms with Shrimp on Broccoli banner the flavor contrast of the deep-toned mushrooms and the pale shrimp filling. The Chinese symbol of bounty, a whole fish, and an exemplar of seasoning mystique come together in Steamed Fish with Black Beans. And because steaming yields a custard-like texture in eggs, I find that even simple Steamed Eggs with Crab can make a meal memorable, especially at brunch time.

146

Pearl Balls

These are delicately flavored meatballs covered with a pearly coating of glutinous rice. This is a very pretty dish for company, as an appetizer or as part of the main course.

1 pound lean pork, coarsely ground
4 Chinese dried black mushrooms, soaked in hot water until spongy, stems removed, minced
6 water chestnuts, minced
1 tablespoon dried shrimp, soaked in hot water to soften, minced
2 tablespoons ginger, minced
2 scallions, finely chopped
1 egg

1 tablespoon light soy sauce
1 tablespoon dry sherry
2 teaspoons Chinese sesame oil
1 tablespoon cornstarch
1 teaspoon sugar
½ teaspoon salt
⅛ teaspoon pepper
1 cup glutinous rice (sweet rice), soaked in cold water for 4 hours
Soy Vinegar Sesame Dipping Sauce (see Index)

1. Mix all ingredients together except rice and Soy Vinegar Sesame Dip. Shape mixture into balls about 1 inch in diameter (about 40 meatballs).
2. Roll meatballs in rice until well coated. Arrange meatballs on a heat-proof plate with ½-inch space between to allow for expansion of rice. Place in steamer or on steaming rack of wok and steam over water for 30 minutes. Serve hot with Soy Vinegar Sesame Dip.

Variation: Substitute beef for the pork. Omit dried shrimp.

Tips: Pearl Balls can be kept warm in a steamer for 10 to 15 minutes with the heat turned off.
If the rice falls off, the Pearl Balls have been overcooked.

Advance Preparation: Pearl Balls may be made a day in advance. When preparing ahead, steam for 20 minutes, refrigerate, then steam for 15 minutes, or until heated through just before serving.

Makes 4 to 6 dinner servings, or 8 to 12 dim sum servings.

Shao-Mai (Open-Faced Steamed Dumplings)

Steamed dumplings are eaten all over China in teahouses, as snacks or lunch, or as a main course in a Chinese meal. They make wonderful hors d'oeuvres and can be frozen.

1 recipe hot water dough or 36 thin won ton skins

Filling Mixture
½ pound pork, ground
½ pound shrimp, shelled, deveined, cleaned, diced into ¼-inch pieces
6 water chestnuts, minced
3 Chinese dried black mushrooms, soaked in hot water until spongy, stems removed, minced

3 scallions, minced
1½ tablespoons ginger, minced
1½ tablespoons light soy sauce
2 teaspoons Chinese sesame oil
1 teaspoon dry sherry
1 teaspoon sugar
½ teaspoon salt
⅛ teaspoon white pepper

36 frozen peas (optional)
Soy Vinegar Sesame Dipping Sauce (see Index)

1. Combine the pork, shrimp, water chestnuts, mushrooms, scallions, ginger, soy sauce, sesame oil, sherry, sugar, salt, and white pepper. Mix well with hands. Do not overmix.
2. Make 1 recipe of hot water dough (see Peking Pan-Fried Dumplings in Index) or cut won ton skins into 3-inch circles. Place 1 tablespoon of the pork-shrimp mixture in the center of each circle. Gather the edges around the filling to form pleats. Lightly squeeze the center of the dumpling. With a spoon, smooth the meat surface. Place a pea in the center of the meat. Set the dumpling on a table and tap it on the table to make the bottom flat. Repeat procedure until all the dumplings are formed.

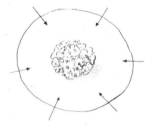

3. Oil the bottom of a heat-proof platter or steamer. Place dumplings on it, leaving a ½-inch space between the dumplings. Cover and steam them over medium-high heat for 20 minutes. Serve hot with Soy Vinegar Sesame Dipping Sauce.

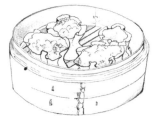

Variations: Minced chicken breast may be combined with the shrimp.

Ground beef may be used with curry as a seasoning. If using beef, omit the shrimp. The traditional Chinese recipe uses pork.

Tip: Won ton wrappers purchased in Oriental markets are thinner and more tender than in American supermarkets. Commercially purchased Gyoza wrappers may be substituted.

Advance Preparation: The dumplings may be frozen for 2 months or may be cooked 1 day ahead, refrigerated and reheated by steaming for 5 to 10 minutes. Some flavor will be lost if cooked ahead, however.

Makes 36 dumplings.

Four Happiness Shao-Mai

A decorative party form of Shao-Mai, these take some time to prepare, but make a very attractive presentation.

1. Make filling and wrappers for Shao Mai (see previous recipe). Place 1 tablespoon filling in the center of the dough. Bring the opposite edges together and pinch them to hold. Make loops like a four-leaf clover. Fill each loop with one of the following: grated carrot; black mushrooms; chopped, hard-cooked egg yolk; and chopped scallions.
2. Steam as in regular Shao Mai.

Makes 36 dumplings.

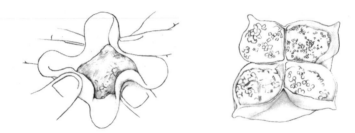

Basic Yeast Dough

The following recipe is similar to the Western yeast bread dough. Chinese buns are steamed because the traditional Chinese kitchen does not have an oven. The lengthy rising period and the added baking powder produce a light, fluffy product.

This basic dough is used for plain steamed buns and buns stuffed with savory fillings, which can be salty or sweet.

1 teaspoon active dry yeast
¼ cup lukewarm water (110° to 115°)
1 tablespoon sugar
1 cup lukewarm water

3½ cups all-purpose flour, unsifted
1½ tablespoons lard, melted, cooled
1 teaspoon baking powder

1. Sprinkle yeast over ¼ cup lukewarm water, then sprinkle the sugar over the yeast. Let sit for 5 minutes or until yeast bubbles up and doubles in volume.
2. Stir the yeast mixture and 1 cup water into the flour. Add the lard and form the dough into a ball.
3. Turn the dough onto a floured surface; knead dough, pushing and turning with the heel of your hand for 5 to 10 minutes. Dust it with flour if it becomes too sticky. The kneading is complete when the dough is smooth and springy. Form the dough into a ball.
4. Transfer the dough to a bowl at least twice the size of the dough and cover with a towel. Let dough rise in a warm place such as the back of a stove or an unlit oven (78° to 82°) until double in bulk. (This will take from 1 to 2 hours depending upon the yeast and surrounding temperature.)
5. Remove the dough to a lightly floured surface. Flatten it with the palm of your hand to make an oblong shape. Add the baking powder and knead for 3 to 5 minutes until the baking powder is well incorporated and the dough is smooth, satiny, and firm. The dough is now ready for shaping.

Tip: Frozen bread dough may be used as a substitute for this basic yeast dough.

Makes enough dough for 16 to 18 stuffed buns.

Plain Buns

The Northerners eat buns in place of rice. They can be frozen and reheated without thawing. (They are particularly good to soak up the juices in Red-Cooked Beef Stew.)

**1 recipe basic yeast dough (see   16 2-inch squares parchment or
   previous page)   wax paper**

1. Prepare dough.
2. Divide the dough in half. Shape each half into a cylinder about 1 inch in diameter. Cut the cylinder into eighths and put a piece of parchment paper under each portion.
3. Set the buns on the steamer or steamer tray 2 inches apart. Let rise 30 minutes or until double in size. The buns should be puffed and feel light. (If the air is damp and cool, this rising may take longer.)
4. Heat water to a vigorous boil in a steamer. Steam the buns over high heat for 15 minutes. Turn off the heat and wait for the steam to subside before uncovering. The drastic change of temperature will cause the buns to wrinkle on the surface if the cover is removed immediately.

Tip: The steamed buns will keep, well wrapped, in the refrigerator for 5 days and for weeks in the freezer. To reheat, steam for 10 to 15 minutes until they are heated throughout.

Makes 16 buns.

Flower Rolls

Here, basic Chinese yeast dough is shaped to resemble a flower just opening. In elegant Chinese restaurants, you can get steamed buns in the form of ducks and all manner of flowers, fans, and spirals.

**1 recipe basic yeast dough (see   12 3-inch squares parchment or
   Index)   wax paper**

1. Prepare dough.
2. Divide the dough in half. On a floured surface, roll each half into a rectangular sheet about 12 × 8 inches. Brush the rectangles with sesame oil. Tightly roll the sheets of dough lengthwise like jelly rolls, each 1½ inches in diameter. Cut each roll crosswise with a sharp knife into twelve 1-inch pieces.
3. Press 1 piece on top of another firmly. Then press a chopstick crosswise hard down the middle of the top piece. The rolled ends of the top piece will lift up and "flower." Repeat with the other pieces until all 12 flower rolls are formed. Arrange the rolls 1½ inches apart on steamer trays lined with parchment paper. Cover with a tea towel. Let them rise 20 minutes or until doubled in size.
4. Steam the buns for 15 to 20 minutes until the buns are puffed and springy.

Advance Preparation: Flower rolls can be steamed several hours in advance. Let stand at room temperature and resteam 10 minutes before serving.

Steamed rolls can be refrigerated 1 week or frozen for 2 months.

Makes 12 rolls.

Fried Flower Rolls

Prepare Flower Rolls as above. After rolls are steamed, fry a few at a time in 4 cups oil heated to 350° until golden brown on both sides. Drain and serve immediately.

Variation: Brush the dough sheets with sesame oil. Sprinkle 1 tablespoon minced cooked Smithfield ham or baked ham and 1 tablespoon scallion finely chopped, over each sheet. Roll up jelly-roll fashion. Let rise and steam.

Makes 12 rolls.

Barbecued Pork-Filled Buns

(Char Shiu Bao)

All over China, meat-filled buns are popular snacks. They are sold by street vendors, eaten as snacks at home, and have various fillings. They keep well and reheat easily, making them good buffet fare. They make excellent picnic food. They may be completely cooked, frozen, and resteamed to heat through at serving time.

1 **recipe Chinese yeast dough (see Index)**

Sauce Mixture
2 **tablespoons oyster-flavored sauce**
1 **tablespoon ketchup**
1 **tablespoon light soy sauce**
1 **tablespoon Chinese sesame oil**
2 **teaspoons hoisin sauce**
3 **tablespoons sugar**
¼ **teaspoon pepper**

Filling Mixture
2 **tablespoons lard**
2 **teaspoons ginger, chopped**
½ **pound Chinese barbecued pork, cut into a ¼-inch dice**
2 **tablespoons scallions, chopped**

1½ **tablespoons cornstarch dissolved in 3 tablespoons cold water**
16 **2-inch squares parchment or waxed paper**

1. Prepare dough. Combine sauce ingredients. Set mixture aside.
2. Heat wok. Add lard. Heat. Add ginger and pork. Cook, stirring to heat thoroughly, about 30 seconds. Add the scallions. Stir 10 seconds. Add the sauce mixture. Cook, stirring, until heated through. Recombine the cornstarch mixture and add it, stirring until thickened. Let cool. Then chill thoroughly.
3. Divide the yeast dough in half. Roll each into a cylinder 1½ inches in diameter on a lightly floured surface. Cut the cylinder into 8 equal portions. Flatten each portion with the palm of your hand. Roll each piece into a 3½-inch circle, making the center thicker than the rim.
4. Place a disk in your hand and place 1 heaping tablespoon of the filling in the center of each round. With your fingers, gather the edge of the dough up and around the filling in folds. Bring the

folds to the top and the center of the bun. Close the top by twisting the folds together. Place the bun, folded side up, on a 2-inch square of parchment paper about 1½ inches apart on steamer trays. Let the buns rise, covered with tea towels, for 20 minutes in a warm place.
5. Steam over high heat for 15 to 20 minutes or until the buns are puffed and springy.

Variation: To make Soup Buns, add ⅓ cup finely cubed jellied meat stock to the filling. During the steaming, this melts into a gravy.

Advance Preparation: The cooked buns keep well refrigerated for 2 to 3 days, or frozen for 2 to 3 months. Reheat by steaming 15 minutes or until hot throughout. It is not necessary to defrost buns before steaming.

Makes 16 buns.

Meat and Vegetable-Filled Buns

These buns are a family staple. They are served for breakfast, lunch, snacks, or dinner. They can be frozen after being completely cooked and resteamed later to heat through.

1 **recipe Chinese Yeast Dough (see Index)**

Pork Mixture
½ **pound ground pork or beef**
1 **tablespoon light soy sauce**
1 **tablespoon dry sherry**
2 **teaspoons cornstarch**

3 **tablespoons oil**
3 **medium dried Chinese black mushrooms, soaked in water until spongy, stems removed, chopped**
1 **piece ginger, the size of a quarter, minced**
1 **teaspoon scallion, minced**

8 **ounces bok choy or celery cabbage, washed, cooked in boiling water 1½ minutes, rinsed with cold water, drained, squeezed dry, coarsely chopped**
16 **2-inch squares parchment or waxed paper**

Sauce Mixture
1 **tablespoon light soy sauce**
¼ **teaspoon salt**
1 **teaspoon sugar**
1 **tablespoon Chinese sesame oil**
2 **teaspoons cornstarch, dissolved in 2 tablespoons cold water**

1. Prepare dough. Mix pork, soy sauce, sherry, and cornstarch. Let marinate 20 minutes. Combine sauce ingredients. Set mixture aside.
2. Heat wok. Add oil and heat. Add the ginger and scallion and stir-fry until lightly browned, approximately 10 seconds. Add the pork mixture, stirring to break up lumps. Add the black mushrooms and bok choy. Stir. Add the sauce mixture and stir to flavor all the ingredients. Let cool completely before filling the dough.
3. To fill and steam buns, follow the directions in steps 3, 4, and 5 for Barbecue Pork Buns recipe (see Index).

Variation: Substitute 1-ounce package frozen, chopped spinach for the bok choy. Defrost. Squeeze out excess moisture completely.

Makes 16 buns.

Stuffed Cabbage Rolls

Steamed miniature cabbage rolls stuffed with pork and topped with a delicate sauce.

14 leaves Chinese cabbage   **1 teaspoon salt**

Pork Mixture   *Sauce Mixture*
⅔ pound ground pork   **1 cup chicken stock**
6 water chestnuts, minced   **3 tablespoons dry sherry**
2 scallions, chopped   **1½ tablespoons light soy sauce**
1 teaspoon ginger, minced   **½ teaspoon Chinese sesame oil**
1 teaspoon garlic, minced   **Dash pepper**
¼ teaspoon Chinese sesame oil   **1 tablespoon cornstarch**
1 tablespoon light soy sauce   **dissolved in 2 tablespoons**
1 teaspoon dry sherry   **cold water**
1 tablespoon cornstarch

1. Place cabbage leaves in boiling water and parboil for 1 minute or until pliable. Remove and drain. Rinse immediately with cold water. Cut the stem of each leaf to 4 inches. Remove tough end of stem.
2. Mix pork, water chestnuts, scallions, ginger, garlic, and sesame oil. Mix well. Add 1 tablespoon light soy sauce, sherry, cornstarch, and the salt. Mix well.
3. Place 1½ tablespoons of the pork mixture on 1 end of stem. Roll to enclose mixture. Repeat on remaining leaves. Steam over medium heat 10 minutes. Remove to serving dish.
4. Make sauce: Mix chicken stock, sherry, soy sauce, sesame oil, and pepper. Heat mixture. When mixture comes to boil, recombine cornstarch and water, then add; heat until thickened. Stir sauce and pour over cabbage rolls.

Advance Preparation: Cabbage rolls can be cooked ahead. Just before serving, reheat by steaming. Reheat sauce. Pour over the rolls.

Makes 4 dinner servings or 8 dim sum servings.

Lotus Leaf Rice

Lotus leaves grow in profusion in picturesque West Lake, Hang Chow. The lotus leaf is not for eating, but what it does for the food it enwraps is remarkable. This is a very special buffet dish made even more attractive when served in a bamboo steamer. With a green vegetable, this can be a meal in itself.

2 **cups glutinous or sweet rice, rinsed until clear, soaked in cold water for 4 hours or until plump**
4 **tablespoons oil**
8 **Chinese dried black mushrooms, soaked in hot water until spongy, stems removed, cut into ¼-inch cubes**
½ **cup carrots, cut into ¼-inch cubes**
¼ **cup water chestnuts, cut into ¼-inch cubes**
2 **scallions, cut into ¼-inch slices**
4 **ounces Chinese pork sausage, cut into ¼-inch cubes**
¼ **cup gingko nuts**
2 **dried lotus leaves, soaked in warm water until soft and pliable**

Chicken Mixture
1 **chicken breast, boned, skinned, cut into ½-inch cubes**
½ **egg white, lightly beaten**
1 **teaspoon cornstarch**
¼ **teaspoon sugar**
Dash white pepper

Shrimp Mixture
½ **pound shrimp, shelled, cleaned, cut into peanut-sized pieces**
½ **egg white, lightly beaten**
1 **teaspoon dry sherry**
2 **teaspoons cornstarch**

Sauce Mixture
2 **tablespooons oyster-flavored sauce**
1½ **tablespoons light soy sauce**
1 **tablespoon Chinese sesame oil**
2½ **teaspoons dry sherry**
¼ **teaspoon sugar**

1. Steam soaked rice on cheesecloth for 15 minutes or until plump.
2. Mix chicken, egg white, cornstarch, sugar, and white pepper. Let marinate 15 minutes.
3. Mix shrimp, egg white, sherry, and cornstarch. Set aside. Combine sauce ingredients. Set mixture aside.
4. Heat wok over high heat. Add 2 tablespoons of the oil. Heat. Add chicken. Stir-fry for 1 minute. Remove from wok.

5. Add 2 tablespoons of the oil to wok, and heat until hot. Add the mushrooms, carrots, water chestnuts, scallions, and sausage. Stir-fry the mixture for 1 minute or until it is fragrant. Add the shrimp mixture. Stir and cook until shrimp turns pink and is almost done. Add the cooked chicken and gingko nuts. Stir in the sauce mixture. Mix well. Add the steamed glutinous rice and mix well.
6. Spread out 1 lotus leaf. Place the rice mixture on the leaf. Place the other leaf on top. Tie with a string as you would a round package.

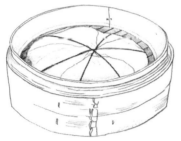

7. Steam the lotus package over high heat for 30 minutes. Serve hot. To open, cut leaf from the top in a circular fashion at the table. The leaves are not to be eaten.

Variation: Bamboo leaves may be substituted for the lotus leaves. Unsalted dry roasted peanuts may be substituted for the gingko nuts.

Advance Preparation: This dish may be prepared a day ahead. Steam when serving or steam 2 to 3 hours ahead and warm at serving time.

Makes 8 servings.

Spiced Rice Coated Spareribs

Rice is combined with sweet yams and spareribs, giving a crunchy texture to this Hunanese dish. The Chinese use rice instead of bread crumbs for texture.

Rib Mixture
- 1 **pound lean spareribs, fat trimmed, separated, cut into 1- to 1½-inch lengths (have your butcher do this)**
- 1 **tablespoon light soy sauce**
- 1 **tablespoon dark soy sauce**
- 1 **tablespoon hot bean paste**
- 1 **tablespoon dry sherry**
- 1 to 2 **teaspoons hot chili oil (optional)**
- 1 **tablespoon scallion, minced**

- 2 **teaspoons ginger, minced**
- 2 **teaspoons garlic, minced**
- 1 **teaspoon sugar**
- ½ **teaspoon black pepper**

- ¾ **cup glutinous rice**
- 1 **pound fresh small yams, peeled, cut into ¼-inch shreds**
- 1½ **tablespoons honey dissolved in 2 tablespoons boiling water**

1. Combine ribs, soy sauces, bean paste, sherry, hot chili oil, scallion, ginger, garlic, sugar, and pepper. Let marinate for 1 hour.
2. Heat a skillet over medium heat until hot. Add the rice and roast until golden brown, shaking the skillet frequently. Set aside to cool. When cool, crush the rice in a blender, food processor, or with a rolling pin.
3. Coat the yams with honey and water mixture. Toss until well mixed.
4. Line the bottom of a heat-proof dish with the yams. Pour the rice crumbs over the ribs and toss thoroughly to coat each rib. Arrange the ribs evenly over the yams. Place the dish on a rack in a steamer. Cover and steam on medium heat over water for 1½ hours, making sure to replenish the water as necessary. Serve immediately.

Tips: Steam the ribs in a serving dish and remove directly to the table.

The cooked ribs will stay warm in the steamer for 10 to 15 minutes with the heat off.

Makes 4 to 6 dinner servings or 8 dim sum servings.

Shredded Egg Balls

These mildly flavored meatballs wrapped in shredded egg sheets and served on a bed of spinach are most attractive for a buffet.

Pork Filling
¾ **pound pork, ground**
2 **teaspoons dried shrimp, soaked in warm water for 45 minutes, drained, minced**
6 **dried Chinese black mushrooms, soaked in warm water until soft and spongy, drained, stems removed, minced**
4 **tablespoons scallions, minced**
2 **teaspoons ginger, peeled, minced**
1 **tablespoon light soy sauce**
1 **teaspoon Chinese sesame oil**
2 **teaspoons cornstarch**
½ **teaspoon salt**
¼ **teaspoon sugar**
¼ **teaspoon black pepper**

Sauce Mixture
½ **cup chicken broth**
1 **tablespoon dry sherry**
½ **teaspoon Chinese sesame oil**
⅛ **teaspoon white pepper or to taste**
1 **teaspoon cornstarch dissolved in 1 tablespoon cold water**

Egg Sheets
1 **tablespoon oil**
3 **eggs, lightly beaten with 1 tablespoon water and ½ teaspoon salt**

2 **tablespoons oil**
10 **ounces fresh spinach, trimmed, washed, dried**

1. Combine pork filling ingredients lightly in a bowl. Form mixture into 12 balls. Set aside. Combine sauce ingredients in a small saucepan. Set aside.
2. Heat pan until medium hot. Coat the surface of the pan lightly with oil. Add half the eggs and tilt the pan so that the egg spreads evenly and thinly over the bottom of the pan. Cook over medium heat until the egg sheet is firm. Remove from the pan and brown lightly on the opposite side. Remove to a cutting board. Cool. Cook remaining egg. Shred finely into 1½-inch shreds.
3. Coat the meatballs as much as possible with the shredded egg. Arrange meatballs on a lightly oiled heat-proof plate. Place any remaining egg sheets on top of the meatballs. Place in a steamer or steam in wok for 20 minutes.
4. Heat sauce ingredients over moderate heat, stirring until thickened.
5. Heat wok. Add 2 tablespoons oil. Heat. Add spinach and stir-fry it until it is limp. Arrange the spinach around the edge of a

ng plate. Place the egg balls in the center of the platter.
r sauce over them.

Variation: Omit dried shrimp.

Advance Preparation: Steam ahead. Reheat by steaming at serving time. Heat sauce. Pour over the egg balls.

Makes 4 dinner servings.

Steamed Eggs with Crab

This simple dish is delicate and nourishing. It may be served as a first course, for a brunch or as a main course. The combination of the sweet crabmeat and the rich eggs is delightful.

4 **eggs, lightly beaten**	½ **teaspoon salt**
1 **cup chicken broth, heated,**	⅛ **teaspoon white pepper**
but not boiling	4 **ounces fresh or frozen**
1 **tablespoon dry sherry**	**crabmeat, flaked**
1 **teaspoon oil**	2 **scallions, sliced**
1 **teaspoon light soy sauce**	**Soy sauce and Chinese sesame**
¼ **teaspoon sugar**	**oil to taste**

Combine the eggs, broth, sherry, oil, soy sauce, sugar, salt, and white pepper and pour into a shallow heat-proof dish. Arrange crab and scallions over egg mixture. Place in a steamer and steam over low heat until the eggs are custardlike, 20 to 30 minutes. They should be semisolid. Sprinkle lightly with soy sauce and sesame oil. Serve in the steaming dish.

Variations: Omit crab.
   Substitute ½ cup roast pork, minced; ¼ cup smoked ham, minced; 2 to 3 bacon strips, minced; ½ cup chicken, minced; ½ cup clams; ½ cup shrimp. Combine any meat with vegetables (½ cup celery, chopped, fresh mushrooms, or spinach, chopped).

Tips: The texture will be custardlike only if the air content is kept to a minimum. Do not overbeat the eggs. Steaming must be done over low heat. Too much heat causes the eggs to separate and form holes in the surface of the custard.
   Do not use canned crab.

Advance Preparation: Combine in a serving dish 1 to 2 hours ahead. A shallow soufflé dish or pie plate is ideal. Steam at serving time.
                                                      Makes 4 servings.

Steamed Shrimp in Mustard Sauce

The natural sweetness of the shrimp is emphasized by the spicy mustard sauce. The shrimp may be served hot or cold.

1½ pounds very small shrimp, with shells
4 scallions, flattened with the side of the cleaver
4 pieces ginger, sliced the size of a quarter, smashed with the cleaver
1 tablespoon dry sherry
½ teaspoon salt

Sauce Mixture
2 tablespoons dry mustard combined with 3 tablespoons warm water
2 tablespoons light soy sauce
1 tablespoon dry sherry
1 tablespoon Chinese sesame oil
½ teaspoon sugar

1 tablespoon fresh coriander, finely chopped

1. Cut the shrimp along the back about ½ inch into the shrimp. Remove the black vein; dry. Mix scallions, ginger, dry sherry, and salt. Marinate the shrimp in mixture 30 minutes. Discard the scallions and ginger.
2. Combine sauce ingredients. Set aside mixture.
3. Arrange the shrimp on a heat-proof plate and steam them for 3 minutes. Remove the steamer from the heat and let the shrimp stand covered for 30 seconds. Recombine the sauce mixture. Pour over the shrimp, tossing gently to mix well. Sprinkle with coriander and serve. To serve cold, refrigerate at this point.

Makes 4 dinner servings or 12 dim sum servings.

Steamed Stuffed Black Mushrooms with Shrimp on Broccoli

The rich flavor of the dried black mushrooms contrasts superbly with the delicate shrimp. This is a very pretty dish served on a bed of broccoli.

24 Chinese dried black mushrooms (1½ to 2 inches in diameter), soaked in hot water until spongy, stems removed

Mushroom marinade
1 scallion, minced
1 tablespoon Chinese sesame oil
1 tablespoon dry sherry
½ tablespoon light soy sauce
2 teaspoons ginger, minced
¼ teaspoon sugar

Sauce Mixture
1 cup chicken broth
1 teaspoon dry sherry
1 teaspoon light soy sauce
½ teaspoon sesame oil
¼ teaspoon sugar

Shrimp Stuffing
¾ pound large shrimp, shelled, deveined, finely chopped
1 ounce pork fat or bacon fat, minced to a fine paste
½ egg white, lightly beaten
1 teaspoon dry sherry
1 teaspoon Chinese sesame oil
1 teaspoon cornstarch
½ teaspoon salt
½ teaspoon sugar
¼ teaspoon white pepper

24 flat-leaf parsley leaves
2 tablespoons cooked ham, finely chopped
¾ pound fresh broccoli, cut into bite-size pieces, (peel the broccoli stems)
1 tablespoon cornstarch dissolved in 2 tablespoons water

1. Squeeze all water from mushrooms. Combine marinade ingredients. Marinate mushrooms in mixture 15 minutes. Combine the sauce mixture in a small saucepan.
2. Lightly squeeze marinade from mushrooms. Reserve marinade and strain.
3. Combine shrimp stuffing ingredients lightly. Spoon 1½ to 2 teaspoons of the shrimp mixture onto each mushroom cap. Spread over the top of the mushroom. If there is any remaining shrimp mixture, make round balls and place them around the mushrooms. Press a piece of parsley and some chopped ham on

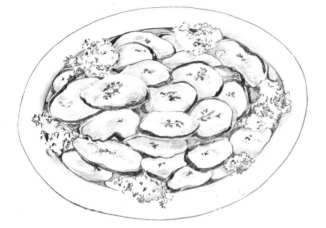

the top of each stuffed mushroom. Place on a greased heat-proof plate. Cover and steam over high heat for 5 minutes. Turn off heat. Cover to keep hot.

4. While steaming the stuffed mushrooms, heat 3 quarts of water to boiling. Blanch broccoli in water for 1 minute. Pour into a colander. Drain. Arrange the vegetables around the edge of the serving platter with the broccoli flowerets placed around the outside edge. Place cooked stuffed mushrooms in the center. Cover to retain heat.

5. Cook the sauce. Add the remaining mushroom marinade. Heat to a gentle boil. Stir in the cornstarch and water. When sauce thickens, pour evenly on the stuffed mushrooms. Serve hot.

Tip: If extra large mushrooms are used, you will need to make extra marinade.

Advance Preparation: This may be steamed ahead and reheated just before serving. You may prepare the shrimp mixture early in the day and stuff the mushrooms. Cover with plastic wrap and refrigerate until steaming.

Makes 6 dinner servings or 12 dim sum servings.

Steamed Shrimp Dumplings (Har Gow)

These delicately flavored shrimp dumplings in a slightly translucent dough are a dim sum parlor favorite. The delicate transparent skin made of wheat starch complements the crisp, lightly seasoned filling.

Dough
1 **cup wheat starch**
⅔ **cup tapioca starch**
2 **teaspoons oil**
1 **cup plus 2 tablespoons boiling water**

Filling Mixture
¾ **pound raw shrimp, shelled, deveined, washed, drained, dried, minced**
6 **water chestnuts, minced**
(filling mixture continued in next column)

2 **tablespoons pork fat, minced**
1 **teaspoon scallion, minced**
½ **teaspoon ginger, minced**
2 **teaspoons Chinese sesame oil**
2 **teaspoons dry sherry**
½ **egg white, lightly beaten**
½ **tablespoon cornstarch**
½ **teaspoon sugar**
½ **teaspoon salt**
¼ **teaspoon white pepper**

Soy Vinegar Sesame Dip

1. Combine the wheat starch, tapioca starch, and oil in a heat-proof bowl. Add the boiling water and stir, blending to make a crumbly dough. Let the dough stand until it is cool enough to handle and knead for 2 minutes or until it is smooth.
2. Divide the dough into 4 parts and roll each part into a roll about ½ inch in diameter. Cut each part of the dough into 12 sections about ¾ inch long. Using a lightly greased cleaver or an oiled tortilla press, flatten each piece into a very thin 3-inch circle. Cover them with a tea towel.
3. Combine filling ingredients. Put about 1 tablespoon of the filling in the center of each dough circle. Gather up the edges forming pleats to enclose the filling. Fold the wrapper according to the directions for Peking Pan-Fried Dumplings (see Index).

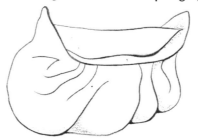

5. Arrange the dumplings on an oiled plate or in a steamer basket lined with oiled cheesecloth. Cover and steam over high heat for 8 minutes. Serve hot with a Soy-Vinegar Sesame Dipping Sauce.

Tip: The water must be boiling. Otherwise the starch will not get cooked and the dough will fall apart. The wrappers may be difficult to make at first, but after a little practice, you will be delighted with your efforts.

Advance Preparation: Cooked Har Gow may be refrigerated 1 to 2 days or frozen 2 to 3 weeks. Reheat by steaming 10 minutes if in refrigerator or 20 minutes if frozen.

Makes 6 to 8 dim sum servings.

Steamed Fish with Black Beans

Few seasonings complement the delicate flavor of fresh fish as well as fermented black beans. Topped with scallions and ginger, this dish is equally pleasing to the eye and the palate.

1 whole fish (sea bass, whitefish, pike, trout) about 1½ to 2 pounds, cleaned, scaled, with head and tail left on	2 tablespoons dry sherry
	½ teaspoon sugar
	3 slices ginger, shredded
	4 scallions, shredded into 2-inch lengths
2 tablespoons fermented black beans	½ red bell pepper, shredded into 2-inch lengths (optional)
2 cloves garlic	3 tablespoons peanut oil
2 tablespoons light soy sauce	1 tablespoon Chinese sesame oil

1. Score the fish crosswise cutting diagonally into the flesh making 3 or 4 equal diagonal cuts deep to the backbone but not through.
2. Rinse black beans with water. Drain. Coarsely chop black beans and garlic together. (Do not make a paste or beans will become bitter.)
3. Mix soy sauce, sherry, and sugar. Place fish on a heat-proof plate in an upright position. Pour the soy sauce mixture over the fish and rub into the fish well. Scatter the black beans, garlic, shredded ginger, scallions, and red bell pepper over the fish.
4. Place fish in a steamer large enough to hold the fish upright. If a large enough steamer is not available, cut the fish in half and reconstruct when serving. Steam the fish about 10 minutes per pound over high heat until the fish is no longer translucent.
5. When fish is done, remove the plate from the steamer. A thin sauce will have formed on the plate. Heat the oil and sesame oil in a small saucepan almost to the smoking point and pour the mixture over the fish to produce a sheen and add richness and flavor.
6. Fillet fish at the table. Start just below the head and make a horizontal cut down the backbone to the tail using the back of 2 spoons. Lift off pieces of the fish from one side, then the other side. Serve with the sauce.

Makes 2 to 3 servings.

Fish Rolls with Scallion Sauce

These delicious fish rolls, wrapped in an egg wrapper and steamed, can be prepared a day ahead.

1 **recipe Egg Pancakes, prepared as directed (see Index)**

Sauce Mixture
¾ **cup chicken broth**
¾ **tablespoon dry sherry**
2 **teaspoons sesame oil**
2 **teaspoons cornstarch dissolved in 1½ tablespoons water**
⅓ **cup scallions, sliced**

1 **egg yolk**

Fish Mixture
½ **pound sole fillets, cut into ¼ × 1 inch pieces**
1 **scallion, minced**
½ **egg white, lightly beaten**
1 **tablespoon oil**
1 **teaspoon dry sherry**
2 **teaspoons Chinese sesame oil**
½ **tablespoon ginger, minced**
2 **teaspoons cornstarch**
¼ **teaspoon salt**
Dash white pepper

1. Make Egg Pancakes. Cut each pancake into quarters to make 4 wedges.
2. Combine fish mixture ingredients.
3. Lay egg wrapper wedges light side up on a board. Place 1 tablespoon fish mixture in the center and place some of the egg yolk on the corners. Starting at the wide end, roll the wrapper a third of the way, tucking the sides in around the filling and continue rolling toward the point of the wrapper. When all the wrappers are filled, arrange the fish rolls on a lightly greased heat-proof dish. Steam over water for 10 minutes on medium heat. Remove to a serving plate.
3. While steaming the fish rolls, prepare sauce. Mix broth, ¾ teaspoon sherry, and 2 teaspoons sesame oil. Heat the broth mixture to boiling. Add the cornstarch and water. Cook, stirring until the sauce boils and is translucent. Add ⅓ cup scallions. Pour over the fish rolls. Serve.

Advance Preparation: Prepare pancakes. Stack, cover with plastic wrap. Refrigerate. Bring to room temperature. Pancakes will crack if rolled when too cold.

Combine the fish mixture and make the sauce mixture. Assemble a few hours before steaming. Refrigerate. At serving time, steam fish rolls. Reheat sauce mixture. Pour over cooked fish rolls.

Makes 2 to 3 dinner servings or 6 to 8 dim sum servings.

Three-Flavor Bean Curd

This is a most attractive steamed delicacy, which will please the eye as well as the taste buds. Mushrooms, ham, bamboo shoots, carrots, and snow peas are placed in a spokelike pattern in a dish with a bean curd filling. A delicate sauce is poured over the finished dish.

6 3-inch squares of bean curd, rinsed, drained
5 cups chicken broth
2 tablespoons dry sherry
1 teaspoon salt
1 tablespoon dried shrimp, soaked in hot water for 45 minutes, drained, minced
¼ cup large Chinese black mushrooms, soaked, drained, stems removed, shredded into long shreds
¼ cup cooked ham, shredded
¼ cup bamboo shoots, shredded
¼ cup cooked carrot, shredded

¼ cup snow peas, shredded lengthwise on the diagonal
1 tablespoon oil
1 pound fresh spinach, washed, trimmed, dried
1 tablespoon dry sherry
½ teaspoon salt

Sauce
1½ cups reserved chicken broth
Dash white pepper
1 tablespoon cornstarch dissolved in 2 tablespoons water
1½ teaspoons Chinese sesame oil

1. Cut off hard edge of bean curd; arrange on a tea towel. Top with a second tea towel and a 2-pound weight. Weight the bean curd for 2 hours to force out the excess liquid and compress the curd. Cut horizontally into very thin slices. Cut the slices into very thin shreds.
2. Mix chicken broth, sherry, and ½ teaspoon salt. Add the bean curd shreds to the chicken broth mixture in a pan. Simmer for 20 minutes. Drain in a colander, reserving the chicken broth.
3. Arrange the shrimp and ¼ cup of the shredded bean curd in the center of a 1½-quart oven-proof bowl 6 inches in diameter. Arrange the mushrooms, ham, bamboo shoots, carrot, and snow peas in descending order in a spokelike fashion around the shrimp and up the side of the bowl. Pour the cooked bean curd on top, being careful not to disturb the design. Ladle ½ cup of the reserved broth over the shreds to pack them into the bowl. Steam over high heat for 1 hour. Remove. Carefully drain off the

liquid, reserving it. Invert a large, shallow serving dish over the bowl and invert the bean curd mixture onto the center of the dish. Keep warm.

4. Heat wok over high heat. Add 1 tablespoon oil and heat until hot. Add the spinach, sherry, and remaining ½ teaspoon salt; stir-fry the spinach until it is limp. Arrange the spinach around the edge of the serving dish.

5. Combine 1½ cups reserved chicken broth, white pepper, and cornstarch mixture in a pan. Heat mixture. Simmer, stirring for 1 minute or until thickened. Add the sesame oil. Stir. Pour sauce over the molded bean curd. Serve.

Advance Preparation: May be steamed 2 hours in advance. Reheat by steaming at serving time.

Makes 8 servings.

Steamed Chicken and Bean Curd

This mildly flavored bean curd dish can be served hot or at room temperature. The chicken and bacon impart a savory flavor to the bean curd which has a smooth creamy texture.

8 ounces bean curd, mashed
⅔ cup chicken broth
2 egg whites
1½ teaspoons cornstarch
¾ teaspoon salt
½ teaspoon Chinese sesame oil
¼ teaspoon white pepper
1 whole chicken breast, boned, skinned, coarsely chopped
¼ pound bacon, coarsely chopped

4 medium fresh mushrooms, cut into ¼-inch slices

Sauce Mixture
½ cup chicken broth
1 tablespoon dry sherry
½ teaspoon Chinese sesame oil
1 scallion, sliced
Dash white pepper
1 teaspoon cornstarch dissolved in 1 tablespoon water

1. Mix bean curd, broth, egg whites, cornstarch, salt, sesame oil, and white pepper.
2. Combine the chicken, bacon, and bean curd mixture in a blender or food processor. Blend until the mixture is smooth.
3. Arrange the mushroom slices in a circular pattern around the edge of a lightly oiled 9-inch pie plate in a decorative manner. Place the bean curd mixture on top of the mushrooms and spread evenly. Steam over boiling water for 10 minutes or until a knife inserted in the center of the custard comes out clean. Drain off any excess drippings.
4. Make the sauce: Mix broth, sherry, sesame oil, scallion, and dash pepper. Cook mixture, stirring over medium high heat until the sauce boils. Recombine and add the cornstarch mixture and stir until translucent.
5. To serve, invert the cooked custard on a serving plate and pour the sauce over the custard.

Advance Preparation: The custard mixture may be refrigerated in the pie plate for several hours. The sauce may be made ahead. Steam at serving time and reheat sauce.

Makes 4 to 6 servings.

9

Dim Sum Complements: Quick Stir-Frys

Dim sum and stir-fried dishes usually are considered separate categories of Chinese cooking. But for American dining purposes, it makes a great deal of sense sometimes to mate them at mealtime. So I am including an assortment of stir-fried combinations here for those occasions when you want something fast, hot, and nourishing to accompany dumplings or noodles and other steamed, deep-fried, or room temperature dishes.

Choose from these recipes according to the balance of ingredients and piquancy you want to feature in the menu. Szechuan Spicy Pork with Peanuts, Spicy Tangerine Chicken, and Szechuan Shrimp are some of the hot options. Chicken with Snow Peas, Black Mushrooms, and Bamboo Shoots and Steak Kow in Oyster Sauce are mild enough for all palates. For brunch appeal, don't overlook Crab with Bean Threads which combines scrambled eggs with a bonus for the cook, since unlike many stir-frys, it gains flavor as it cooks.

Often, a vegetable is all that is needed to round out a meal. So here you will find an abundant harvest, ranging in spiciness from mild Creamed Chinese Cabbage to Hot and Sour Zucchini. Stir-Fried Zucchini, Water Chestnuts, and Black Mushrooms with Cherry Tomatoes is especially pretty to present and may be served cold as a buffet or picnic salad.

Spicy Pork with Peanuts

This dish, typical of the Szechuan region, goes together quickly. The flavors are robust and the contrast in tastes and textures unbeatable. Rice and vegetables should be served with the pork. The recipe may be served immediately or prepared ahead and served at room temperature.

1 pound boneless pork loin or butt, diced into ¼-inch cubes
1 tablespoon dark soy sauce
1 tablespoon Chinese sesame oil
1 tablespoon cornstarch

3 cups oil
¼ cup raw peanuts
2 to 4 dried chili peppers
2 slices ginger, peeled, minced
4 scallions, thinly sliced

Sauce Mixture
1½ tablespoons dark soy sauce
1½ tablespoons dry sherry
1 tablespoon chili paste with garlic
1 tablespoon red wine vinegar
1 teaspoon Chinese sesame oil
2 teaspoons sugar
Pinch salt
1 teaspoon cornstarch mixed with 1 tablespoon cold water

1. Mix pork, soy sauce, sesame oil, and cornstarch. Marinate pork mixture 20 minutes. Combine sauce mixture. Set aside.
2. Heat 3 cups oil to 375° in a wok. Fry peanuts in a strainer until golden brown. Remove. Set aside. Stir marinated meat and drop in batches into the hot oil. Stir gently to separate the pieces. Cook 1 to 2 minutes until pork is completely cooked. Remove. Drain. Set aside.
3. Remove all but 2 tablespoons oil from wok. Heat oil. Add the chili peppers pressing on side of wok until they are darkened. Add the ginger and scallions. Stir-fry for 10 seconds until fragrant. Increase the heat to high; add the meat. Stir-fry for 2 minutes.
4. Add the sauce mixture to the meat, stirring to evenly coat the meat. Heat through. Pour it into a serving dish and sprinkle with peanuts. This may be served hot or at room temperature. (The flavors should be quite spicy, but not so spicy you cannot taste the pork.)

Advance Preparation: First frying of pork may be done hours ahead. Cover and refrigerate. Bring to room temperature before the final cooking. When making several stir-fry dishes, make this dish first. The hotness of the spices allows it to be easily served at room temperature.

Makes 3 to 4 servings.

Curried Chicken with Tomatoes and Green Peppers

The Chinese took Indian curry and made it their own. The superiority of Chinese soy sauces and the ability of the Chinese to bring out the best flavor of ingredients makes this dish a superb combination.

Chicken Mixture
2 **chicken breasts, boned, skinned, cut into ½-inch pieces**

Marinade
1 **tablespoon light soy sauce**
1 **tablespoon dry sherry**
1 **tablespoon cornstarch**

1½ **tablespoons dark brown sugar**
2 **medium tomatoes, cut into wedges**
4 **tablespoons oil**
1 **green pepper, cut into 1-inch cubes**
1 **medium onion, cut into 1-inch wedges**
2 to 3 **tablespoons curry powder**
4 **tablespoons tomato ketchup**
1 **tablespoon light soy sauce**

1. Mix chicken, soy sauce, sherry, and cornstarch. Marinate chicken mixture 20 minutes. Sprinkle brown sugar over the tomato wedges.
2. Heat wok. Add 2 tablespoons of the oil. Heat. Add green pepper and onion. Stir-fry for 1 minute. Remove from wok and set aside.
3. Add 2 tablespoons of the oil to wok. Heat. Stir in the curry powder and toss vigorously a few times to let the flavors release. Add the chicken and stir-fry the chicken until it is firm and white and cooked through.
4. Add the green pepper and onion to the wok. Stir until heated through. Add the ketchup and soy sauce; heat until the sauce bubbles. Add the tomato wedges. Stir until heated through. Mix well. Serve.

Variation: 1 pound flank steak may be substituted for the chicken. Use dark soy sauce instead of light soy sauce if using beef.

Makes 4 servings.

Chicken with Snow Peas, Black Mushrooms, and Bamboo Shoots

This basic stir-fry with snow peas and black mushrooms is a perfect complement to the chicken. You will want to serve this over and over. It is always a favorite.

Chicken Mixture
1 **chicken breast, boned, cut into 1-inch cubes**
2 **egg whites, lightly beaten**
2 **teaspoons dry sherry**
2 **teaspoons cornstarch**

Sauce Mixture
2 **tablespoons dry sherry**
1 **tablespoon light soy sauce**
1 **tablespoon dark soy sauce**
2 **teaspoons sugar**
2 **teaspoons cornstarch dissolved in 2 tablespoons cold water**

4 **tablespoons oil**
¼ **pound snow peas, strings removed**
8 to 10 **large Chinese dried black mushrooms, soaked in hot water until spongy, stems removed**
6 **ounces bamboo shoots, sliced**

1. Mix chicken, egg white, sherry, and cornstarch. Marinate chicken in mixture for 20 minutes. Combine sauce mixture. Set aside.
2. Heat wok. Add 2 tablespoons oil. Heat. Add snow peas, black mushrooms, and bamboo shoots. Stir-fry about 2 minutes, until snow peas turn jade green in color. Remove from wok.
3. In 2 tablespoons hot oil, stir-fry chicken about 2 minutes until chicken is firm and white. Return the vegetables to the wok. Stir. Recombine sauce mixture. Add sauce to the wok, stirring constantly until a clear glaze appears.

Makes 3 to 4 servings.

Plum Chicken on Snow

Delicate chicken complemented by the crunchy snow peas, bamboo shoots, and black mushrooms and served on bean threads makes an eye-catching dish.

Chicken Mixture
2 chicken breasts, boned, cut into ½-inch pieces
1 tablespoon light soy sauce
1 tablespoon dry sherry
1 tablespoon cornstarch

Sauce Mixture
⅓ cup chicken broth
2 tablespoons plum sauce
1 tablespoon light soy sauce

3 cups oil

1½ ounces bean threads
⅓ cup almonds, blanched
4 ounces snow peas
6 to 8 Chinese dried black mushrooms, soaked in hot water until spongy, drained, stems removed
½ cup bamboo shoots, sliced
1 teaspoon garlic, minced
1 teaspoon ginger, minced
2 scallions, shredded into 1½-inch lengths

1. Mix chicken, soy sauce, sherry, and cornstarch. Marinate chicken mixture for 20 minutes. Combine sauce mixture. Set aside. Heat 3 cups oil in wok. When oil is hot (375°), separate bean threads and drop into hot oil. Cook 5 seconds until puffed. Remove. Drain. Cook almonds in hot oil for 15 seconds or until lightly browned. Remove and drain.
2. Remove all but 2 tablespoons oil from wok. Heat oil. Add snow peas and black mushrooms. Stir-fry for 1 minute. Add bamboo shoots. Stir-fry 45 seconds. Remove.
3. Add 2 tablespoons oil to wok. Heat. Add ginger and garlic. Cook until slightly brown. Add chicken and stir-fry until done. Add vegetables and scallions. Stir. Add sauce mixture and heat through.
4. Place bean threads on serving plate. Place chicken mixture on top of bean threads and garnish with almonds. Serve immediately.

Makes 3 to 4 servings.

Kung Pao Chicken

This dish was named for a high ranking Chinese official Ting Kung Pao. It is a very popular dish in the Szechuan area of China where the inhabitants love hot food. If your palate does not match Ting Kung Pao's, reduce the chili peppers.

Chicken Mixture
2 large, boned, skinned chicken breasts, cut into ½-inch cubes
½ egg white, lightly beaten
¼ teaspoon salt
¼ teaspoon sugar
2 teaspoons cornstarch

Sauce Mixture
2 tablespoons bean sauce
1 tablespoon hoisin sauce
1 tablespoon chili paste with garlic

(sauce continued in next column)

1 tablespoon dry sherry
1 tablespoon red wine vinegar
1½ teaspoons sugar

2 cups oil
1 cup raw unsalted peanuts
4 to 8 dried chili peppers
4 cloves garlic, peeled, flattened with the side of a cleaver
2 scallions, cut into ¼-inch slices

1. Mix chicken, egg white, salt, sugar, and cornstarch. Let marinate 20 minutes. Combine sauce ingredients. Set aside.
2. Heat 2 cups oil in wok to 350°. Deep-fry peanuts until light golden brown. (Be careful not to burn them as they will continue to cook after being removed from the heat.)
3. Reheat the oil in wok. Add the chicken mixture in batches. Stir to separate the pieces. Briskly blanch the chicken pieces in the oil until they turn white. Do not brown. Remove with skimmer.
4. Pour all but 2 tablespoons oil from the wok. Heat the oil. Add the dried peppers and cook over low heat pressing against the side of the wok, until dark. Add the garlic, chicken, and scallions; stir. Add the bean sauce mixture. Cook 1 minute. Add the peanuts, stir, and serve.

Tips: When making many stir-fried dishes, make this dish first. This may easily be served at room temperature because its flavor is so hot.

The hotness may be adjusted to your taste: 4 red peppers are medium hot, 6 are hot, and 8 to 10 are devastating.

Makes 2 to 3 main-course servings.

Spicy Tangerine Chicken

Four distinctive Szechuan ingredients—dried tangerine peel, chili paste with garlic, dried chili peppers and Szechuan peppercorns, make this a rich and complex dish. This is delicious hot or room temperature.

Sauce Mixture
2 tablespoons orange or tangerine juice
2 tablespoons dark soy sauce
1 tablespoon hoisin sauce
¾ teaspoon sugar
½ teaspoon chili paste with garlic

2 tablespoons oil
2 carrots, shredded into 1½-inch lengths
4 scallions, shredded into 1½-inch lengths
2 tablespoons Chinese sesame oil

4 dried chili peppers (or to taste)
1 tablespoon ginger, minced
1 teaspoon Szechuan peppercorn powder
2 pieces dried tangerine peel (total 3 inches wide), soaked in hot water 15 minutes or until soft, cut into ⅛-inch shreds
1 pound chicken breasts, boned, skinned, cut into ½-inch cubes
1 teaspoon salt
1 teaspoon white vinegar

1. Combine sauce ingredients. Set aside.
2. Heat a wok until hot. Add oil. Heat. Add carrots and scallions. Stir-fry 1 minute. Remove. Add sesame oil. Heat. Add chili peppers. Stir, pressing against the side of the wok until darkened. Add ginger, Szechuan peppercorn powder and tangerine peel. Add the chicken and the salt. Stir-fry for about 2 minutes until the meat loses its pink color. Add sauce mixture. Stir to mix. Reduce the heat to low. Stir. Cover and let the dish simmer for 10 minutes until most of the sauce has cooked into the meat.
3. Increase the heat to high. Add the carrots and scallions and stir until the dish is evenly colored. Add the vinegar. Stir-fry for 15 seconds. Pour into a hot serving dish or refrigerate and serve cold or at room temperature.

Variations: Deep-fry 1 cup raw, unsalted peanuts in 1 cup oil until lightly browned. Add to chicken just before serving.
  If unavailable, use the peel of one thin-skinned valencia-type orange, avoiding the white pulp. Let dry overnight. Shred before stir-frying.

Makes 3 servings.

Steak Kow in Oyster Sauce

This is a traditional Chinese stir-fry, which is easy to prepare.

Flank Steak Mixture
1 pound flank steak, cut against the grain into pieces 2 inches × 1 inch long and ⅛-inch thick
1 tablespoon dark soy sauce
1 teaspoon Chinese sesame oil
1 tablespoon cornstarch
¼ teaspoon sugar
5 tablespoons oil

Sauce Mixture
4 tablespoons oyster-flavored sauce
½ teaspoon sugar
2 tablespoons dry sherry

5 tablespoons oil

¼ pound snow peas, remove strings
1 teaspoon ginger, finely minced
1 teaspoon garlic, minced
5 scallions, cut into 1½-inch lengths

1. Mix beef, soy sauce, sesame oil, cornstarch, and sugar. Let marinate 20 minutes.
2. Combine sauce ingredients.
3. Heat wok. Add 2 tablespoons oil. Heat. Add snow peas. Stir-fry for 1 minute or until jade green in color. Remove and set aside.
4. Heat wok. Add 3 tablespoons oil. Heat. Add ginger and garlic. Cook until fragrant. Add steak. Stir-fry about 3 to 4 minutes, or until steak is done. Stir. Stir in oyster sauce mixture. Cook and stir until it begins to bubble. Add snow peas and scallions. Stir-fry until heated through. Serve.

Variations: Substitute ½ pound fresh broccoli for the snow peas. Peel stems, roll cut stems, separate flowerets.

Substitute ¾ pound fresh asparagus, cut into 1½-inch diagonal pieces, for the snow peas.

Makes 4 servings.

Mongolian Beef

This well-known spicy beef dish is served on puffy fried bean thread noodles. It is sure to be a favorite.

Flank Steak Mixture
1 **pound flank steak, trimmed, cut across the grain into strips 1½ × 1 × ¼ inch**
1 **egg, lightly beaten**
1 **tablespoon dark soy sauce**
2 **tablespoons cornstarch**

Sauce Mixture
1 **tablespoon light soy sauce**

1 **tablespoon dry sherry**
1 **teaspoon sugar**

2 **cups oil**
2 **ounces bean threads**

2 **to 4 dried chili peppers**
2 **teaspoons ginger, shredded**
3 **scallions, shredded into 1½-inch lengths**
1 **teaspoon Chinese sesame oil**

1. Combine beef, egg, dark soy sauce, and cornstarch. Let marinate 30 minutes. Prepare sauce. Mix light soy sauce, sherry, and sugar. Set aside.
2. Heat oil in wok to 375°. Add the bean threads in batches and cook until puffed (about 3 seconds). Remove and place on a serving platter.
3. Heat oil and fry the beef in 2 batches, stirring for 1 to 2 minutes or until pieces separate and change color. Transfer it with a skimmer to a plate when it is done.
4. Remove all but 2 tablespoons oil from wok. Heat to medium heat. Add the dried chili peppers and cook until darkened. Add the ginger. Stir for 5 seconds or until fragrant. Add the beef and the scallions; stir-fry for 30 seconds. Recombine and add the sauce mixture and stir until heated through. Add the sesame oil. Toss lightly and place on top of the fried bean threads, leaving a border of the bean thread exposed.

Variation: Serve in Chinese Pancakes. Omit the bean threads.

Advance Preparation: Cook beef ahead. At serving time, stir-fry the chili pepper and ginger. Add the beef and scallions. Add the sauce mixture. Stir until heated through.

Makes 3 to 4 servings.

Szechuan Shrimp

A hot dish of charred chili peppers, shrimp, and crunchy peanuts, this recipe is full of spirit. Although a stir-fry, it can be done ahead and served at room temperature.

Shrimp Mixture
1 **pound shrimp, shelled, deveined, butterflied**
1 **egg white**
1½ **tablespoons cornstarch**
2 **teaspoons dry sherry**

Sauce Mixture
4 **tablespoons ketchup**
2 **tablespoons chicken broth**
1 **tablespoon dry sherry**
1 **tablespoon light brown sugar**
1 **tablespoon rice vinegar**

(sauce continued in next column)

1 **tablespoon dark soy sauce**
Salt to taste

3 **cups oil**
½ **cup raw peanuts, deep-fried in oil until golden**
4 to 8 **dried chili peppers**
3 **slices ginger, the size of a quarter, peeled, minced**
4 **ounces water chestnuts, sliced**
2 **scallions, shredded into 1½-inch lengths**

1. Mix shrimp, egg white, cornstarch, and sherry. Let marinate 20 minutes. Combine sauce ingredients. Set aside.
2. Heat 3 cups oil in wok. Add peanuts; reduce heat to low. Deep-fry the peanuts until they are golden. Drain on paper towels.
3. Reheat the oil in the wok to 375°. Add the marinated shrimp in batches to prevent the oil temperature from dropping. Deep-fry the shrimp until they turn whitish pink (about 1 minute). Remove and drain.
4. Remove all but 2 tablespoons oil from the wok. Heat the oil. Turn the heat to low. Add the peppers and press them into the oil until darkened.
5. Add the ginger and stir until fragrant. Increase the heat to high, add the shrimp and water chestnuts. Stir. Recombine the sauce mixture and pour over the shrimp. Stir to coat the shrimp and cook until the shrimp is heated through. Add the scallions and the peanuts. Place the shrimp on a serving dish. Serve.

Tip: The hotness may be adjusted to your taste—4 chili peppers are medium-hot, 6 are hot, and 7 to 8 are devastating.

Advance Preparation: Fry the shrimp and peanuts hours in advance. Combine the dish at serving time.

Makes 4 servings.

Hot and Sour Cabbage

This dish is delicious either hot or cold. The combination of the fragrant Szechuan peppercorns and the fresh ginger gives the cabbage a distinctive flavor.

1 small head green cabbage (about 1 pound)	**½ teaspoon salt**
	2 to 4 dried chili peppers
Sauce Mixture	**¼ teaspoon Szechuan peppercorns**
2 tablespoons light soy sauce	
2 tablespoons cider vinegar	**1 teaspoon ginger, finely chopped**
1 tablespoon dry sherry	
2 tablespoons sugar	**3 tablespoons oil**

1. Cut off the base of the cabbage and remove the tough outer leaves. Quarter the cabbage and cut out the core. Cut the leaves into pieces about 1-inch square. Wash the leaves and drain.
2. Combine sauce ingredients. Set mixture aside.
3. Heat wok to moderate heat. Add the oil. Heat to low. Add the chili peppers, peppercorns, and ginger. Press and turn the chili peppers in the oil until they are deep red. Do not let them blacken as they will darken the cabbage. Increase the heat to high. Add the cabbage and stir-fry for 2 minutes. Add the sauce mixture. Cook for 30 seconds. Serve.

Advance Preparation: Prepare recipe completely in advance; refrigerate.

Makes 4 to 6 servings.

Creamed Chinese Cabbage

Creamed Chinese Cabbage is typical of Shanghai style cooking. The sauce is light and translucent. Chopped ham adds an interesting flavor to this mild, delicate dish.

Sauce Mixture
¾ cup chicken stock
1 teaspoon salt
¼ teaspoon sugar
Dash white pepper

2 tablespoons rendered
chicken fat

1 pound Chinese cabbage, trim
wilted leaves and root end of
the cabbage, wash, cut into
pieces 2 × 1 inch each
1½ tablespoons cornstarch
dissolved in ¼ cup cold milk
⅛ pound cooked Smithfield
ham, chopped (optional)

1. Combine sauce ingredients. Set mixture aside.
2. Heat wok. Add chicken fat. Heat until melted. Add the cabbage and stir-fry 1 minute or until the cabbage is coated with the fat. Add the sauce mixture. Stir. Heat to boiling. Cover. Reduce heat to low; simmer for 10 minutes or until tender. With a slotted spoon, transfer cabbage to a heated platter. Heat the cooking liquid to boiling. Recombine the cornstarch mixture and add it to the wok. Stir until thickened. Pour over the cabbage; garnish cabbage with the ham.

Makes 4 servings.

Stir-Fried Spinach

Any leafy, green vegetable may be prepared in this manner.

2 tablespoons oil
1 large clove garlic, smashed
with the side of the cleaver
1 slice ginger, the size of a
quarter, smashed
1 pound fresh spinach, washed,
drained, tough portions of
stem removed

1 teaspoon Chinese sesame oil

Sauce Mixture
2 teaspoons light soy sauce
1 tablespoon dry sherry
½ teaspoon vinegar
2 teaspoons sugar

1. Combine sauce mixture. Set aside.
2. Heat wok. Add oil. Heat. Add garlic and ginger. Stir-fry 10 seconds. Add spinach and stir-fry for 1 minute or until wilted.
3. Add the sauce mixture to wok. Stir. Add the sesame oil. Stir and serve.

Makes 2 to 3 servings.

Stir-Fried Zucchini, Water Chestnuts, and Black Mushrooms with Cherry Tomatoes

The following is an easy-to-fix, colorful vegetable dish which is wonderful with Chinese or American meals. Serve hot or chilled.

2 tablespoons oil
1 teaspoon ginger, shredded
1 teaspoon garlic, minced
2 pounds zucchini, sliced
   diagonally
8 Chinese dried black
   mushrooms, soaked in hot
   water until spongy, stems
   removed
6 ounces water chestnuts,
   drained, sliced

6 scallions, shredded into 1½-
   inch lengths
12 cherry tomatoes, halved

Sauce Mixture
2 tablespoons light soy sauce
1 tablespoon dry sherry
1 teaspoon Chinese sesame oil
1 teaspoon hot chili oil
   (optional)
1 teaspoon sugar

1. Combine sauce ingredients. Set mixture aside.
2. Heat wok. Add 2 tablespoons oil and heat. Add garlic and ginger; cook until lightly browned. Add zucchini and mushrooms. Stir-fry for 1 minute. Add water chestnuts and scallions. Stir-fry for 45 seconds. Recombine and add sauce mixture. Stir. Cook until heated through. Add cherry tomatoes. Cook until warm; stir. Serve. Do not allow cherry tomatoes to overcook.

Variations: Substitute shredded red pepper for the cherry tomatoes.

Substitute ¼ pound fresh mushrooms, sliced, for the black mushrooms. Stir-fry with zucchini when cooking.

Makes 4 servings.

Hot and Sour Zucchini

This Szechuanese vegetable is very spicy, sour, and hot, yet fresh tasting. It may also be served at room temperature.

4 tablespoons Chinese sesame oil
2 to 4 dried chili peppers
½ teaspoon Szechuan peppercorns
1 tablespoon ginger, minced
1 tablespoon scallion, minced
1 pound zucchini, washed, sliced into ¼-inch rounds, sprinkled with salt, let stand

10 minutes, rinsed, and patted dry

Sauce Mixture
2 tablespoons Chinese red vinegar or red wine vinegar
2 teaspoons light soy sauce
1 tablespoon sugar

1. Combine sauce ingredients. Set aside.
2. Heat 4 tablespoons sesame oil in wok. Add the dried chili peppers and Szechuan peppercorns. Stir-fry until the peppers are slightly brown.
3. Add the ginger, scallion, and zucchini to wok. Stir-fry for about 1½ minutes. Mix in the sauce mixture. Stir for 30 seconds. Remove and serve.

Advance Preparation: Prepare 3 to 4 hours ahead. Serve chilled or at room temperature.

Makes 4 servings.

Stir-Fry Lettuce with Straw Mushrooms

A very attractive, delicate dish, it is easily served to a large group.

Sauce Mixture
1 tablespoon dry sherry
½ teaspoon salt
½ teaspoon Chinese sesame oil

Chicken Broth Mixture
½ cup chicken broth
2 tablespoons light soy sauce
1 tablespoon oyster-flavored sauce
1 teaspoon sugar
½ teaspoon Chinese sesame oil
1 teaspoon cornstarch dissolved in 2 teaspoons water

3 tablespoons oil
1½ pounds leaf lettuce, trimmed, washed, dried, leaves cut into 1-inch pieces
2 teaspoons ginger, peeled, minced
1 tablespoon scallion, minced
30 ounce can straw mushrooms, blanched in boiling water 15 seconds, drained, rinsed under cold water

1. Prepare sauce mixture. Mix sherry, salt, and sesame oil. Set aside. Prepare chicken broth mixture. Mix chicken broth, soy sauce, oyster-flavored sauce, sugar, sesame oil, and cornstarch. Set aside.
2. Heat wok. Add 2 tablespoons oil. Heat. Add lettuce. Stir-fry 10 seconds. Add the sauce mixture. Stir-fry 30 seconds or until lettuce is partially wilted. Transfer to a serving platter and place the lettuce around the edge of the platter.
3. Heat wok. Add 1 tablespoon oil. Heat. Add ginger and scallion. Stir-fry 10 seconds or until fragrant. Stir the broth mixture and add to the wok. Add the mushrooms. Heat the liquid to boiling, stirring. Simmer for 2 minutes or until the sauce is thickened. Transfer the mushrooms to the center of the platter. Serve.

Makes 6 to 8 servings.

Bamboo Shoots in Hoisin Sauce

The crisp bamboo shoots and the jade-green spinach are an excellent accompaniment to delicate main dishes such as steamed fish.

4 cups bamboo shoots, cut into slices, 2 × ⅛ inch
2 cups oil
1 teaspoon cornstarch dissolved in 2 tablespoons water
1 teaspoon Chinese sesame oil
⅔ pound fresh spinach, washed, dried, hard stems removed

Sauce Mixture
3 tablespoons hoisin sauce
2 tablespoons chicken stock
1 tablespoon dry sherry
1 teaspoon salt
½ teaspoon sugar

1. Cut bamboo shoots into slices and dry with a towel. Combine sauce ingredients. Set aside.
2. Heat 2 cups oil in wok to 375°. Deep-fry bamboo shoots, a few at a time, stirring, for about 3 minutes to soften and extract their water. Drain.
3. Remove all but 1 tablespoon oil from wok. Add sauce mixture and mix well. Return the bamboo shoots to the wok and stir rapidly. Let cook in the sauce for 15 seconds. Recombine the cornstarch and add it to the sauce and cook until a glaze forms. Add 1 teaspoon sesame oil. Remove and place in the center of a serving dish.
4. Heat 2 tablespoons oil in wok. Add the spinach and ½ teaspoon salt. Toss lightly over high heat for 1 minute until wilted. Arrange the spinach on the opposite ends of a serving platter around the bamboo shoots. Serve immediately.

Variation: Add 1 teaspoon hot chili oil.

Makes 4 servings.

Crab with Bean Threads

The following is a delicate, but tasty, dish using just those basics of Chinese flavorings, ginger, sherry, and scallions. This is good hot, at room temperature, or cold. It is excellent for a brunch or to accompany a dinner.

Sauce Mixture
1 tablespoon light soy sauce
1 teaspoon salt
½ teaspoon sugar
⅛ teaspoon white pepper or to taste

3 eggs, lightly beaten
2 ounces bean threads, soaked in warm water for 30 minutes, drained, cut into 1½-inch strips

2 ounces bamboo shoots, finely shredded
4 scallions, shredded into 1½-inch lengths
½ cup frozen peas, defrosted
4 tablespoons oil
1 tablespoon ginger, peeled, finely chopped
6 ounces fresh or frozen crabmeat, flaked
1½ tablespoons Chinese sesame oil

1. Combine sauce ingredients. Set aside.
2. Combine the eggs, bean threads, bamboo shoots, scallions, peas, and the sauce mixture in a bowl.
3. Heat wok over high heat until hot. Add 2 tablespoons oil. Heat. Add the ginger and crab and cook about 45 seconds, stirring to mix well. Remove from wok.
4. Add 2 tablespoons oil to wok. Heat. Add the egg mixture. Stir-fry until semiscrambled consistency. Add the crab mixture. Mix gently until heated throughout. Add 1½ tablespoons sesame oil. Mix and serve.

Variation: For a more delicate dish, omit the peas.

Tip: Do not use canned crabmeat.

Advance Preparation: Prepare ahead completely. Reheat at serving time or serve at room temperature.

Makes 3 to 4 servings.

10

Wrap-Ups and Roll-Ups

You can round up diners, set out wrappers, and let everyone roll their own packet-size portions of the delectable recipes in this chapter. Call it a "wrap and roll party," if you wish. Or just call it a Chinese custom that happens to offer a great deal of fun!

The tradition combines two elements: dishes of shredded or otherwise finely cut ingredients and Chinese pancakes or other wrappers. The serving rite is simplicity itself: diners place a heaping tablespoon or so of the filling on a wrapper, fold in the sides, roll up the wrapper and eat the packets with their fingers—and help themselves again and again! Moo Shu Pork is probably the best-known wrap-up dish, but the theme extends to fillings as crisp and refreshing as Cold Szechuan Mixed Vegetable Salad and as light as Crab in Lettuce Packages.

Ants Climbing a Tree—named with typical Chinese imagery for its bits of pork and cellophane noodles resembling tree bark—is hearty enough to turn into a whole wrapped supper. Minced Pork and Bean Threads in Lettuce Packages presents the most wonderful textural array of fried bean thread noodles, chopped walnuts, water chestnuts, ground pork, and rich sauce—all pocketed in cool, crisp lettuce leaves. Minced Beef, Northern Style and Spicy Chicken in Lettuce Packages provide a change of pace from pork—a distinction especially apt when you want to enjoy the informality of serving nothing but roll-up fare. I should add that all of these recipes can be served as appetizers as well as entrées. So when you're looking for a dish that will launch any kind of party in style, remember that wrapping and rolling are definite conversation starters.

Treat the wrappers as a matter of convenience, and feel free to mix or match them with any of the fillings. Chinese Pancakes are irresistible, easy to make, and can be kept frozen for impromptu entertaining. But it is perfectly legitimate to substitute flour (not corn!) tortillas or pita bread, which closely resembles a northern Chinese bread. You might stock up on spring roll wrappers when you visit a Chinese market and freeze them for future wrap-ups. However, Egg Wrappers are more delicate, like crepes, and can be made ahead and refrigerated. Lettuce leaves are, of course, the most carefree alternative—as well as the one most likely to please calorie-counters. (For details of how to schedule preparations for a Wrap-Up Party, see Chapter 16.)

Chinese Pancakes (Peking Doilies)

Chinese pancakes are used frequently. They traditionally serve as wrappers for Peking Duck and Moo Shu Pork. Many of the recipes in this book can be made as pancake fillings. Almost any dish consisting of shredded ingredients can be eaten inside a pancake.

2 cups sifted all-purpose flour　　**3 tablespoons Chinese sesame**
¼ teaspoon salt　　　　　　　　　**seed oil**
About ¾ cup boiling water

1. Place flour and salt in a mixing bowl. Gradually stir in the boiling water. Place on a lightly floured board. Knead until the mixture is smooth and silky, about 5 to 8 minutes. Cover and let rest for 30 minutes. Knead the dough again lightly. The dough should be slightly on the dry side, but not so dry it will crack. Roll dough into a long sausage about 1½-inch in diameter. Divide the dough into 16 pieces of equal size. Roll into small balls. Flatten 2 balls with the palm of your hand, making 2 small round pancakes, 1½ inches in diameter. Brush sesame seed oil on 1 side of pancake. Place a second pancake on it to make a small sandwich. Roll the 2 together with a rolling pin, rotating to keep the circle as uniform as possible. The pancake should be as thin as possible and about 6 to 7 inches in diameter.
2. Heat an ungreased heavy skillet on top of the stove. Cook 1 pair of pancakes over low heat for about 2 minutes or until small bubbles form. Turn over and cook the other side. Remove from the pan and separate into 2 very thin pancakes. Continue until all are cooked. They should be a very light beige color and the bottom should be speckled with small, light brown spots.
3. To serve, steam the pancakes over medium-low heat for 3 to 5 minutes or reheat in foil in a 250° oven for 10 minutes or until they are hot.
4. To eat, spread a pancake on a plate. Place a rounded spoonful of the filling in the center of the pancake. Fold one side over, fold the pancake up from the bottom and then fold the other side over at a 90-degree angle. Roll up the pancake and eat with your fingers.

Variations: Shanghai spring roll wrappers, moo shu pork wrappers, flour tortillas, pita bread, or lettuce leaves for the pancakes.

Advance Preparation: These pancakes can be frozen easily. Make plenty of them as they are time consuming. When ready to use, defrost them at room temperature for about an hour. Steam them for 3 to 5 minutes until soft and warm.　　　　Makes 16 pancakes.

Egg Wrappers

Egg Wrappers are made from a batter similar to crepes. They make an interesting variation of the spring roll wrapper and will hold up better than spring rolls on a buffet table. They can be made ahead and served cold. The wrappers can be filled and shaped into dumplings for soups or wrapped in a spiral and deep-fried for a crunchy light appetizer. Egg wrappers may be prepared 1 to 2 days in advance.

4 **eggs, beaten**   **Pinch of salt**
4 **tablespoons flour**   1 **tablespoon oil**
1 **tablespoon sesame oil**

1. Mix eggs, flour, sesame oil, and salt until smooth with no lumps using a chopstick or a blender.
2. Heat a heavy 7-inch skillet or wok until very hot. Add the 1 tablespoon oil; swirl and pour the oil into a small heat-proof dish. Reduce the heat to low under the skillet. Pour in about 2 tablespoons batter into the pan. Tilt the pan to spread the eggs over the entire bottom. When the batter is set, peel the wrapper off and turn it over with your fingers. Cook a few seconds. Remove from the pan. Let dry; stack with parchment paper or aluminum foil between wrappers. Store in the refrigerator in a plastic bag.
3. Bring wrappers to room temperature before using. The wrappers will tear more easily when cold.

Makes 10 to 12 wrappers.

Egg Pancakes

Egg Pancakes or sheets can be shredded and used as a decorative topping for a dish or can be rolled into a pancake for use as a delicate wrapper for an appetizer.

3 **eggs, lightly beaten**
$\frac{1}{8}$ **teaspoon salt**
1 **tablespoon oil**

1. Mix eggs and salt.
2. Follow the directions for Egg Wrappers. When using as a wrapper for an appetizer, do not make the wrapper too thin or it will tear.

Makes 2 cups egg shreds or 3 egg pancakes.

Minced Pork with Bean Threads in Lettuce Packages

This dish is a treasure. It is an attractive presentation, easily made, and wonderful for a buffet or as a snack for a crowd.

Pork Mixture
3/4 pound pork, ground
1 egg, lightly beaten
1 1/2 tablespoons dark soy sauce
1 teaspoon cornstarch

Sauce Mixture
2 tablespoons oyster-flavored sauce
1 tablespoon light soy sauce
1 tablespoon dry sherry
1 teaspoon Chinese sesame oil
1 teaspoon sugar
1/4 teaspoon cayenne pepper

1 head Boston or romaine lettuce, cored, leaves detached, washed, dried

2 cups oil
1 ounce bean threads
1/3 cup walnuts
1 teaspoon garlic, minced
1 cup water chestnuts, coarsely chopped
6 to 8 Chinese dried black mushrooms, soaked in hot water until spongy, stems removed, chopped
1/2 cup bamboo shoots, shredded
1 cup bean sprouts
2 teaspoons cornstarch combined with 2 tablespoons water
2 scallions, sliced
1/2 cup plum sauce

1. Combine pork, egg, dark soy, and cornstarch. Let marinate 20 minutes. Combine sauce ingredients. Set mixture aside.
2. Arrange lettuce around the edge of a large serving platter.
3. Heat 2 cups of oil to 375°. Deep-fry the bean threads until puffed, about 4 to 5 seconds. Drain and place in the center of the lettuce. Deep-fry walnuts. Remove, drain, chop.
4. Remove all but 2 tablespoons oil from wok. Heat. Add garlic and stir-fry 5 seconds until light brown. Add pork mixture. Stir-fry until grayish. Add water chestnuts, black mushrooms, bamboo shoots, and bean sprouts. Stir-fry for 1 minute. Add sauce mixture. Stir until heated through. Add cornstarch mixture. Cook until thickened slightly. Place on top of bean thread. Garnish with scallions and chopped walnuts.
5. To serve, place 1 teaspoon plum sauce on a lettuce leaf. Add 2 to 3 tablespoons of pork mixture and some bean threads. Fold the end up and the other 2 sides in to the center forming a lettuce package. This is finger food!

Advance Preparation: Fry bean threads and walnuts. Stir-fry pork and reheat at serving time. Assemble just before serving.

Makes 4 dinner servings or 8 dim sum servings.

Pork Shreds in Hoisin Sauce

In this attractive Northern dish, the hoisin sauce predominates, giving a rich flavor.

1 **head iceberg or Boston lettuce**

Pork Mixture
½ **pound pork, shredded into 1 × ¼ inch shreds**
2 **teaspoons light soy sauce**
2 **teaspoons dry sherry**
2 **teaspoons cornstarch**

Sauce Mixture
1½ **tablespoons hoisin sauce**
1 **tablespoon dry sherry**
1 **tablespoon dark soy sauce**
1 **teaspoon Chinese sesame oil**
1 **teaspoon sugar**

4 **tablespoons oil**
1 **teaspoon ginger, minced**
6 **ounces bamboo shoots, coarsely chopped**
1 **medium carrot, coarsely chopped**
2 **scallions, chopped**

1. Core lettuce. Separate into leaves. Chill in refrigerator.
2. Combine pork, soy, sherry, and cornstarch. Marinate for 20 minutes. Combine sauce mixture ingredients. Set mixture aside.
3. Heat wok over high heat. Add 2 tablespoons oil and heat. Add ginger and press into the oil until slightly brown. Add carrots, bamboo shoots, and scallions. Stir-fry 1 minute. Remove from wok.
4. Heat 2 tablespoons oil in wok. Add pork shreds and stir-fry for 2 minutes or until pork is grayish in color.
5. Add vegetables. Stir until heated through. Recombine sauce mixture and add to wok. Stir until thoroughly combined.
6. Arrange lettuce around the edge of a platter. Place pork in the center. Let each guest place a spoonful or two of pork mixture on the lettuce, folding it before eating.

Variation: Use shredded beef or chicken in place of the pork.

Tip: Chinese pancakes or pita bread may be used instead of the lettuce. This may also be served as a main course.

Advance Preparation: Cook ahead. Rewarm on the stove top or in a 350° oven.

Makes 3 to 4 dinner servings, or 8 servings with other entrees.

Moo Shu Pork

In Chinese, moo shu means "yellow cassia blossoms." The tiny pieces of scrambled eggs mingled in with the shredded meat and vegetables resemble the blossoms of the cassia flower. This is a traditional northern dish served particularly around Peking. Serve with Chinese pancakes.

12 Chinese pancakes

Pork Mixture
½ pound fresh lean pork, cut into matchstick shreds
2 teaspoons light soy sauce
1 teaspoon dry sherry
2 teaspoons cornstarch

Sauce Mixture
1 tablespoon light soy sauce
1 tablespoon dry sherry
1 teaspoon sugar

4 tablespoons oil
20 pieces dried tiger lily buds, soaked in hot water 30 minutes

4 Chinese dried black mushrooms, soaked in hot water until spongy, stems removed, drained, shredded
¼ cup dried cloud ears, soaked in hot water 30 minutes, drained, shredded
½ cup bamboo shoots, shredded into matchstick shreds
4 eggs, lightly beaten
½ cup chicken broth
1 teaspoon Chinese sesame oil
Hoisin sauce
2 scallions, shredded into 1½-inch lengths

1. Make Chinese Pancakes (see Index).
2. Combine pork, soy, sherry, and cornstarch. Let marinate 20 minutes. Combine sauce ingredients. Set aside.
3. Heat wok. Add 2 tablespoons oil and heat. Add pork. Cook, stirring, 2 minutes, until pork strips turn grayish. Add sauce mixture. Stir. Add tiger lilies, mushrooms, cloud ears, and bamboo shoots. Cook, stirring, for 1 minute. Remove from wok.
4. Wipe out wok. Add 2 tablespoons oil. Add the eggs and cook to the scrambled stage, stirring to the hard scrambled stage. Return the pork mixture to the pan. Add the chicken broth and cook about 1 minute, stirring to blend. Add the scallions and stir. Stir in 1 teaspoon sesame oil and mix. Pour into a serving dish.
5. Heat the pancakes in a steamer for 5 minutes.
6. To serve, place one pancake flat on a dish. Spread a little hoisin

sauce on the pancake. Spoon a generous amount of filling on the pancake. Garnish with scallions. Roll up to enclose the filling, folding one end over. Eat from opposite end.

Advance Preparation: Cook ahead completely. Warm up at serving time. For optimum results, cook eggs 1 hour in advance. Combine with pork at serving time. Steam pancakes 5 minutes before serving.

Makes 4 dinner servings or 8 appetizer servings.

Spicy Chicken in Lettuce Packages

Spicy chili paste combined with delicate chicken and crunchy vegetables in an unexpected combination of flavors makes this a marvelous dish. It may be served wrapped in lettuce or as a meal.

Chicken Mixture

2 large chicken breasts, boned, skinned, shredded
1 egg white
1 teaspoon light soy sauce
1 teaspoon dry sherry
2 tablespoons cornstarch

Sauce Mixture

2 teaspoons light soy sauce
2 tablespoons dry sherry
2 tablespoons chili paste with garlic
1 teaspoon sugar
½ teaspoon Chinese sesame oil
1 tablespoon cornstarch combined with 2 tablespoons water

1 head Boston or romaine lettuce, leaves detached, washed, dried
2 long green chilies, minced
12 water chestnuts, shredded
½ cup celery, shredded
½ cup carrots, shredded
1 cup oil
½ cup raw peanuts
1 teaspoon ginger, minced
1 teaspoon garlic, minced
½ cup bean sprouts
2 scallions, shredded into 1½-inch lengths

1. Partially freeze chicken breasts. Flatten with cleaver. Cut breasts into very thin slices horizontally. Shred. Marinate chicken in egg white, soy sauce, sherry, and cornstarch for 20 minutes.
2. Core lettuce; separate into leaves. Chill in refrigerator. Combine sauce ingredients. Set mixture aside.
3. Core chilies. Split in half and mince. Combine chilies, water chestnuts, celery, and carrots.
4. In 1 cup hot oil, fry peanuts until golden brown. Remove and drain. Chop peanuts. Remove all but 3 tablespoons oil from wok. Heat oil. When hot, add the chicken, stirring constantly to separate the shreds. Cook for about 1½ minutes and drain. Set aside.
5. Heat 2 tablespoons oil in wok. Add ginger and garlic, press into the oil, and stir-fry about 10 seconds. Add chilies, water chestnuts, celery, and carrots. Stir-fry 30 seconds. Add bean sprouts. Stir until heated through. Add cooked chicken and scallions. Stir in sauce mixture. Cook until thickened slightly, stirring until heated through.

6. Arrange lettuce around the edge of a platter. Place chicken in the center. Sprinkle with chopped peanuts. Let each guest place a spoonful of chicken on the lettuce, folding it before eating.

Variations: Serve on fried rice sticks. Serve with Chinese pancakes.

Advance Preparation: Cook ahead completely. Reheat at serving time.

Makes 4 dinner servings or 8 appetizer servings.

Minced Beef, Northern Style

A delicious spicy dish which may be served as a main course or wrapped in lettuce leaves or Chinese Pancakes. Spoon minced beef into the center of the lettuce leaf or pancake and fold into a package and eat with your hands.

Beef Mixture
1 **pound flank steak, shredded into matchstick-size pieces**
1 **egg, slightly beaten**
1 **tablespoon dark soy sauce**
1 **tablespoon cornstarch**

Sauce Mixture
1 **tablespoon light soy sauce**
½ **teaspoon sugar**
1 **tablespoon dry sherry**
1 **tablespoon Chinese sesame oil**
1 **tablespoon cornstarch dissolved in 2 tablespoons cold water**

1 **head iceberg or Boston lettuce**
4 **tablespoons oil**
8 **water chestnuts, shredded**
2 **medium carrots, peeled, shredded**
6 **snow peas, shredded**
2 **scallions, shredded**
2 **dried chili peppers or to taste**
2 **teaspoons ginger, minced**
1 **teaspoon garlic, minced**
1 **tablespoon Chinese sesame oil**
2 **tablespoons chopped roasted peanuts**

1. Marinate flank steak in egg, soy, and cornstarch. Prepare sauce mixture. Set aside.
2. Core lettuce. Separate into leaves. Wash, dry, and refrigerate.
3. Heat wok; heat 2 tablespoons oil. Stir-fry water chestnuts, carrots, snow peas, and scallions for 1 minute. Remove from wok.
4. Heat wok. Add 2 tablespoons oil and heat oil. Add chili peppers, pressing into the oil and cook until brown. Add minced ginger and garlic. Cook until slightly brown. Add beef mixture to wok. Stir until beef loses its red color.
5. Add vegetables to the wok. Recombine sauce mixture and pour sauce into wok, stirring until sauce thickens. Add sesame oil. Stir and serve. Arrange lettuce around the edge of a platter. Place beef mixture in the center. Garnish with peanuts. Let each guest place a spoonful of beef mixture on the lettuce, folding it before eating.

Advance Preparation: Beef can be cooked ahead and reheated at a low temperature on top of the stove.

Variation: Celery, chopped, may be substituted for the snow peas.

Makes 3 to 4 dinner servings or 8 appetizer servings.

Ants Climbing a Tree

This famous Szechuan combination acquired its name from the cellophane noodles colored reddish brown with hot bean sauce, soy sauce, and meat juices. They are said to resemble bark of a tree and the chopped pork to suggest climbing ants. It is highly spiced and easily prepared and makes a marvelous informal meal. This is also good for a buffet table as it can be served warm and is equally enjoyable when wrapped in a lettuce leaf.

Pork Mixture
½ **pound pork, ground**
1 **tablespoon dark soy sauce**
2 **teaspoons Chinese sesame oil**

Sauce Mixture
2 **tablespoons dry sherry**
1 **tablespoon light soy sauce**
1 **tablespoon dark soy sauce**

2 **tablespoons oil**
1 **scallion, finely sliced**
1½ **teaspoons garlic, minced**

1 **tablespoon ginger, peeled, minced**
1 **tablespoon hot bean sauce**
4 **ounces dried bean threads, soaked in boiling water 15 minutes or until soft, drained**
½ **cup chicken broth**
2 **scallions, sliced**
½ **to 1 teaspoon salt, depending upon the saltinesss of the hot bean sauce**
Freshly ground black pepper

1. Combine pork, soy, and the sesame oil. Combine sauce ingredients. Set mixture aside.
2. Heat wok. Add 2 tablespoons oil and heat. Add finely sliced scallions, garlic, ginger, and hot bean sauce. Stir-fry 10 seconds Add the pork. Stir-fry until the pork is done, about 2 minutes, making sure the pork is chopped up into small pieces. Add the sauce mixture. Stir-fry for 30 seconds. Add the bean threads to the pan and cook 1 minute, turning occasionally and breaking up the noodles with the spatula as you are cooking. Add the stock and the scallions; cook 5 minutes until the liquid has cooked down slightly. Taste for salt. Sprinkle with black pepper. Serve.

Variation: Add 6 dried Chinese black mushrooms, soaked in water until spongy, chopped. Stir-fry with the pork. Serve in lettuce packages or as a noodle dish.

Advance Preparation: Make ahead. Reheat on medium heat until thoroughly heated through. Serve hot or room temperature.

Makes 4 dinner servings or 8 dim sum servings.

Crab in Lettuce Packages

Delicate crab combined with lightly seasoned vegetables makes a marvelous filling for crispy lettuce.

8 **leaves romaine lettuce or Boston lettuce**

Sauce Mixture
1 **tablespoon dry sherry**
1 **tablespoon light soy sauce**
½ **teaspoon Chinese sesame oil**
Salt to taste
Dash white pepper

2 **cups oil**
1 **ounce bean threads, deep-fried**

1 **slice ginger, minced**
6 **ounces crabmeat, fresh or frozen, flaked**
2 **carrots, shredded into 1½-inch shreds**
½ **green pepper, shredded into 1½-inch shreds**
2 **scallions, shredded into 1½-inch shreds**
½ **cup bamboo shoots, shredded into 1½-inch shreds**
⅓ **cup water chestnuts, shredded**

1. Wash and remove the ends of the lettuce leaves and arrange in a circular manner around the edge of a serving platter. Combine sauce ingredients. Set mixture aside.
2. Heat wok. Add 2 cups oil. Heat to 375°. Drop in the bean threads. Cook until fluffy, about 5 seconds. Remove to a serving platter.
3. Remove all but 2 tablespoons oil from the wok. Add the crab and ginger. Stir-fry for 30 seconds. Remove. Add 2 tablespoons oil. Heat oil. Add the carrots and green pepper. Stir-fry for 1 minute. Add the scallions, bamboo shoots, and water chestnuts. Stir-fry for 1 minute more. Add the crab and stir. Add the sauce mixture and cook until heated through. Remove from the wok and place the crab mixture on the bean threads in the center of the platter. Surround with lettuce leaves.
4. To eat, place hot portions of the crabmeat mixture on individual lettuce leaves and roll up. Eat with hands.

Tip: Do not use canned crab.

Makes 4 dinner servings or 8 dim sum servings.

Szechuan Mixed Vegetable Salad

Carrots, cucumbers, and cellophane noodles are combined in this raw salad. Serve in a Chinese Pancake, in a lettuce leaf, or as a salad.

The shredding is time consuming unless you have a food processor. However, everything can be done in advance, as this is to be served cold or at room temperature. The longer the salad stands, the more it will absorb the flavors of the sauce.

2 carrots, shredded into 1½-inch lengths

2 cucumbers, seeds removed, shredded into 1½-inch lengths, drained

2 scallions, shredded into 1½-inch lengths

2 cloves garlic, finely minced

2 ounces cellophane noodles, soaked in hot water for 15 minutes or until soft, drained, cut into 1½-inch pieces

Sauce Mixture
2 tablespoons light soy sauce
1 tablespoon Chinese sesame oil
1 tablespoon rice vinegar
1 to 2 teaspoons hot chili oil
1 teaspoon salt
½ teaspoon Szechuan peppercorn powder

1. Place carrots, cucumbers, scallions, and garlic in a bowl. Add cellophane noodles.
2. Combine sauce ingredients. Add to vegetable-noodle mixture; mix well. Chill. Serve.

Makes 4 dinner servings or 8 dim sum servings.

11

From Teahouse to Your House: One-Dish Bounty

Filling, one-dish preparations and casseroles are as popular in China as they are here. The teahouses are like noodle sanctuaries, offering all-day solace in the form of heaping bowls of Barbecued Pork Lo Mein and Szechuan Red-Cooked Beef Noodles. At home the multiple comforts of meat and vegetables might be found in Chicken Steamed with Chinese Sausages or Red-Cooked Beef Stew. Convenience is the key for both settings: all segments of the meal are served together, and often the whole potful can be held a day or two and reheated with no loss of savor.

Oddly enough, it's not so much the convenience as the incomparable temptation of these recipes that has made them staples in my home. Red-Cooked Pork and Red-Cooked Beef Stew are wonderful for family meals and informal parties, but I prepare them whenever I crave the kitchen aroma of meat slowly simmering in a treasury of spices. The desire for fried noodles is just as compelling, but the appeasement comes much quicker; both the noodles and their whole-meal complement of either beef and bok choy or shrimp and chicken can be fried in minutes.

When presentation is a priority, I turn again and again to three completely different "combination platters." Lion's Head balances a buffet beautifully with its satisfying juxtaposition of oversized meatball "lion heads" and celery cabbage "lion manes." By contrast, Chicken in a Bird's Nest is a lighter dish, but it too provides a self-contained focal point, with mild chicken and vegetables seated in a "nest" of fried, shredded potatoes. And sometimes the best combination is Peking Noodles with Meat Sauce, for this bounty provides not only dinner but also entertainment as guests toss their own mixtures of noodles, meat sauce, and many vegetables. (For details of how to schedule preparations for a One-Dish Dinner, see Chapter 16.)

Peking Noodles with Meat Sauce

A popular one-dish meal in China, this is served cold in the summer and hot in the winter. Everything may be prepared ahead, making this recipe excellent for informal entertaining. The ingredients are placed in the center of the table and each guest mixes the noodles, meat sauce, and vegetables according to his or her taste. Spaghetti with a Chinese twist!

12 ounces fresh lo mein noodles or 8 ounces dried vermicelli

2 tablespoons Chinese sesame oil

2 cups fresh bean sprouts

2 tablespoons oil

1 tablespoon garlic, minced

¾ pound pork, ground

8 large water chestnuts, chopped coarsely

2 scallions, shredded into 1½-inch lengths

2 cucumbers, pared, cut in half, seeded, shredded into 1½-inch lengths

Sauce Mixture

½ cup chicken broth

4 tablespoons brown bean sauce

3 tablespoons hoisin sauce

2 tablespoons dry sherry

1 teaspoon sugar

1 tablespoon cornstarch dissolved in 2 tablespoons cold water

1. Cook noodles in 3 quarts boiling water until al dente. Remove and drain. Toss with sesame oil. Set aside. Combine sauce ingredients. Set mixture aside.
2. Heat 1½ quarts water to boiling. Immerse bean sprouts in water for 45 seconds. Drain. Refresh with cold water. Drain. Set aside.
3. Heat wok. Add 2 tablespoons oil and heat. Add garlic; cook until lightly browned. Add pork and stir-fry for 2 to 3 minutes. Add water chestnuts and scallions. Cook for 30 seconds.
4. Add sauce mixture to wok. Stir to mix. Heat sauce to boiling, stirring. When sauce is smooth and thick, pour it into a bowl.
5. To serve, place noodles, cucumber shreds, bean sprouts, and sauce in separate bowls on the table. Each person fills his bowl half full of noodles and adds the vegetables and sauce mixture to taste, mixing well before eating.

Advance Preparation: The sauce may be cooked 2 days ahead. Refrigerate.

Cook the noodles al dente 1 day ahead. Toss with 1 tablespoon sesame oil. Put in plastic bag. Refrigerate. Serve cold or reheat by plunging noodles into a large pot of boiling water and heat to warm through. Do not overcook.

The vegetables may be cut up half a day in advance.

Makes 4 servings.

Barbecued Pork Lo Mein

Barbecued Pork Lo Mein makes an excellent lunch or midnight supper. This also may be served with a meal in place of rice. The barbecued pork may be omitted for a simpler dish. In Chinese, mein means "noodles" and lo means "mixing."

8 ounces Chinese lo mein noodles	8 ounces Chinese Barbecued Pork, shredded (see Index)
2 tablespoons Chinese sesame oil	½ cup chicken broth
2 tablespoons oil	*Sauce Mixture*
1 teaspoon ginger, minced	2 tablespoons oyster-flavored sauce
2 cups bok choy or Chinese cabbage, cut into ½-inch pieces	1 tablespoon dark soy sauce
	½ teaspoon sugar
1½ cups fresh bean sprouts	Dash pepper

1. In 4 quarts boiling water, cook the noodles until they have reached the al dente stage. Drain. Toss with the sesame oil. Set aside.
2. Combine sauce ingredients. Set mixture aside.
3. Heat wok. Add 2 tablespoons oil and heat. Add the ginger. Stir for 10 seconds or until fragrant. Add the bok choy, bean sprouts, and pork. Stir-fry for 2 minutes. Add the chicken broth. When the chicken broth is hot, add the noodles and mix with the pork and vegetables. Cover and cook for 2 minutes. Add the oyster sauce mixture. Stir well. Serve.

Variations: Roast beef, roast lamb, cooked shrimp, or chicken may be substituted for the barbecued pork. Substitute any fresh vegetable or combination of vegetables in season. Use vegetables with colors and textures which complement each other. Use up leftovers in this dish. Very fine spaghettini may be substituted for lo mein noodles.

Tip: To keep warm, heat in a 150° oven for an hour.

Advance Preparation: The noodles can be cooked, rinsed, and tossed with the sesame oil a day ahead. The barbecued pork can be made in advance or purchased. Cut the vegetables ahead and wrap in plastic wrap.

The completed dish may be prepared ½ hour in advance and kept warm in a 250° oven or reheated in a wok.

Makes 4 to 6 servings.

Flank Steak with Rice Sticks

A mildly flavored family dish, the following recipe uses basic Chinese ingredients—bok choy, bean sprouts, and black mushrooms combined with beef and rice sticks.

Beef Mixture
1 **large egg**
1 **tablespoon dark soy sauce**
1 **tablespoon cornstarch**
¾ **pound flank steak**

Sauce Mixture
2 **tablespoons light soy sauce**
1 **cup chicken broth**
1 **teaspoon salt**
½ **teaspoon sugar**
Dash white pepper
¼ **to ½ teaspoon cayenne pepper (optional)**

5 **tablespoons oil**
1 **teaspoon ginger, minced**
6 **dried Chinese black mushrooms, soaked in hot water for 20 minutes, drained, stems removed, shredded**
4 **cups bok choy, cut into 1½-inch pieces**
4 **ounces rice sticks, soaked in hot water for 10 minutes or until soft, drained, cut into 2-inch lengths**
2 **cups fresh bean sprouts**
1 **tablespoon Chinese sesame oil**

1. Partially freeze flank steak for 30 minutes to firm meat for easier slicing. Slice the meat horizontally into 2-inch strips. Cut strips against the grain into ⅛-inch slices. Mix egg, dark soy sauce, and cornstarch. Marinate beef in mixture 20 minutes.
2. Combine sauce ingredients. Set mixture aside.
3. Heat wok. Add 3 tablespoons of the oil and heat. Stir-fry the meat for 2 minutes or until browned. Remove and set aside.
4. Add 2 tablespoons oil to wok. Heat oil. Add the ginger. Stir until fragrant. Add black mushrooms and bok choy and stir-fry 1 minute. Add the sauce mixture. Stir until heated through. Add rice sticks. Cook until the liquid is almost absorbed. Add the steak, bean sprouts, and sesame oil. Mix thoroughly. Serve.

Variation: Substitute pork for the beef.
Substitute fresh mushrooms for the Chinese black mushrooms.

Advance Preparation: Make ahead. Reheat in the wok.

Makes 4 servings.

Fried Noodle Cake

In the noodle cake, the two sides of the noodle are brown and crisp, while the inside stays moist and soft.

12 ounces fresh thin Chinese
  egg noodles
5 tablespoons oil

1. Blanch fresh egg noodles in boiling water for 2 minutes. If using dried noodles, cook until "al dente" stage. Remove. Drain well.
2. Scatter the noodles on a pan, tossing to dry and untangle the noodles.
3. Heat a heavy skillet or wok and add oil. Heat until smoking. Slide the noodles into the pan and cook them, shaking the pan to prevent sticking for about 5 minutes. When golden brown, turn the noodles over, keeping the noodles together in a "cake." Cook the other side until golden. Add more oil if the noodles seem to be sticking. To serve, slide them on a platter and use as a base for any dish with sauce.

Tip: Substitute dried vermicelli for fresh egg noodles.

Advance Preparation: If doing ahead, toss noodles with 1 table-spoon sesame oil and refrigerate in a plastic bag until ready to use. This may be done a day ahead. If any moisture has collected, be sure to dry the noodles before frying them. The noodles may be kept warm in a 200° oven for 15 to 20 minutes.

Makes 4 servings.

Fried Noodles with Beef and Bok Choy

This wonderful noodle dish is topped with beef and bok choy and is a one-dish meal or a traditional ending to a dim sum meal. The noodle cake is crisp on the outside and moist on the inside, making an interesting combination of textures.

Beef Mixture
½ **pound flank steak, cut into strips 2 × ⅛ inch each**
1 **tablespoon light soy sauce**
2 **teaspoons dry sherry**
2 **teaspoons cornstarch**
½ **teaspoon brown sugar**

Sauce Mixture
½ **cup chicken stock**
2 **tablespoons oyster-flavored sauce**
1 **tablespoon light soy sauce**
1 **tablespoon dry sherry**
1 **teaspoon sugar**

½ **pound long, thin fresh Chinese egg noodles, cooked al dente, drained well**
5 **tablespoons oil**
2 **cups oil**
1 **pound bok choy, cut into 2-inch sections**
1 **small red pepper, shredded into 2-inch lengths**
1 **tablespoon cornstarch dissolved in 2 tablespoons cold water**

1. Combine beef, soy sauce, sherry, cornstarch, and the brown sugar. Let marinate 20 minutes. Combine sauce ingredients. Set mixture aside.
2. Scatter noodles on a pan, tossing to dry and untangle.
3. Heat wok. Add 5 tablespoons oil. Heat until smoking. Slide the noodles into the pan and cook them, shaking the pan to prevent sticking, for almost 5 minutes. When golden brown, turn the noodles over, keeping them together in a "cake." Cook the other side until golden. Add more oil if they seem to be sticking. Remove to a serving platter. Keep warm in a 200° oven.
4. Heat wok. Add 2 cups oil. Heat to 350°. Stir marinated meat and add half the meat to the wok, stirring to separate the pieces. Cook about 15 seconds; remove the meat. Cook the remaining beef. Remove and set aside.
5. Remove all but 2 tablespoons oil from the wok. Heat the oil. When it is hot, add the bok choy and red pepper and stir-fry 1 minute.
6. Add the cooked beef to wok and stir to heat through. Add the sauce mixture. When sauce is hot, thicken with the dissolved cornstarch and water. Stir until heated through and translucent. Serve over the fried noodle cake.   Makes 4 servings.

Fried Noodles with Chicken and Shrimp

Chicken and shrimp make a delightful topping for fried noodles in this one-dish meal.

Shrimp Mixture
½ **pound shrimp**
½ **egg white**
1 **tablespoon dry sherry**
1 **slice ginger, the size of a quarter, smashed**
1 **teaspoon cornstarch**

Chicken Mixture
2 **chicken breasts, boned, shredded into ¼-inch shreds**
1 **tablespoon light soy sauce**
1 **tablespoon dry sherry**
1 **teaspoon Chinese sesame oil**
1 **teaspoon cornstarch**

Sauce Mixture
2 **tablespoons light soy sauce**
½ **teaspoon sugar**
2 **cups chicken stock**
⅛ **teaspoon pepper**

6 **ounces broccoli, stems peeled and roll cut, flowerets separated**
3 **carrots**
12 **ounces thin Chinese fresh egg noodles, cooked "al dente," in the method of Fried Noodle Cake (see Index)**
6 **tablespoons oil**
1 **teaspoon garlic, minced**
1½ **teaspoons ginger, minced**
5 **dried Chinese black mushrooms, soaked until spongy, tough stems removed, shredded**
6 **scallions, shredded into 1½-inch lengths**
1 **cup bean sprouts**
2½ **tablespoons cornstarch dissolved in 4 tablespoons water**
1 **teaspoon Chinese sesame oil**

1. Combine shrimp mixture ingredients. Let marinate 20 minutes. Combine chicken mixture ingredients. Let marinate 20 minutes. Combine sauce ingredients. Set aside.
2. Cook broccoli in boiling water for 2 minutes. Remove. Rinse with cold water. Drain. Cook carrots in boiling water for 2½ minutes. Remove. Drain. Rinse in cold water. Cut into diagonal slices. Shred.
3. Make noodle cake as directed (see Index).
4. Remove and discard ginger from the shrimp. Heat wok. Add 2 tablespoons oil. Heat. Add shrimp. Stir-fry until they turn pink. Remove. Add 2 tablespoons oil to wok. Heat. Add chicken and stir-fry for 2 minutes or until done. Remove. Add 2 tablespoons oil to wok. Heat. Add garlic and ginger and stir-fry 10 seconds or until lightly browned. Add carrot, broccoli, and mushrooms. Stir 45 seconds. Add scallions and bean sprouts. Stir-fry 30 seconds. Add shrimp and chicken. Stir. Add sauce mixture. When heated

through, add cornstarch mixture. Cook until thickened, stirring. Add sesame oil. Mix thoroughly. Pour over the fried noodle cake and serve.

Variations: Substitute 1 pound spinach for the broccoli. Substitute ½ pound fresh mushrooms for the dried mushrooms.
    Use all chicken or all shrimp.   Makes 4 to 6 servings.

Red-Cooked Beef Stew

The following is a Chinese beef stew which is slowly braised to tenderize the meat and allow the flavors to intermingle. Chinese turnip, also known as daikon or Japanese radish adds just the right bite. This recipe can be made ahead and reheats well. Serve with steamed buns.

Sauce Mixture
6 cups boiling water
4 tablespoons light soy sauce
4 tablespoons dry sherry
2 tablespoons hoisin sauce
1½ tablespoons sugar
1 whole star anise
½ teaspoon five-spice powder

2 tablespoons oil
4 scallions, flattened with the side of a cleaver

3 slices ginger, the size of a quarter, flattened with a cleaver
2 cloves garlic, bruised with the flat side of a cleaver
2 pounds brisket, rump, loin, bottom of the round roast, fat trimmed, cut into 1½-inch cubes
1 pound Chinese turnip, peeled, roll cut

1. Combine sauce ingredients. Set mixture aside.
2. Heat wok or heavy pot. Add 2 tablespoons oil. Heat. Add the scallions, ginger, and garlic. Stir-fry for 20 seconds or until fragrant. Add the beef. Brown lightly on all sides. Add the sauce mixture. Heat the liquid to boiling. Reduce the heat to a simmer. Skim off any scum that might have formed on the top. Cover. Braise the beef for 2 hours. Add the turnip and cook for 30 minutes more until the beef and turnip are tender. Serve.

Variations: Use 2 pounds meat. Do not cut up. Omit the turnip. Cook as above. Remove to a chopping block to cool and firm. Slice crosswise into the desired thickness. Skim the fat from the sauce and serve over the meat.
    Substitute turnips or carrots and potatoes for the Chinese turnip.

Advance Preparation: Prepare 1 to 2 days ahead. Reheat at serving time.   Makes 4 to 6 servings.

Red-Cooked Pork

This is the most basic of all Chinese stews. Red-cooking, the process of braising in a soy-based liquid, lends itself nicely to pork. Its rich, dark sauce is spicy and fragrant with star anise, but it is not hot. This is a nice dish for entertaining, as the flavor improves upon standing. The recipe can be doubled and the whole dish can be prepared in advance.

5 tablespoons dark soy sauce
4 tablespoons dry sherry
2 whole star anise
$1\frac{1}{2}$ to 2 tablespoons crushed rock sugar or granulated sugar to taste
$\frac{1}{2}$ teaspoon salt
2 tablespoons oil
4 quarter-sized pieces peeled ginger, smashed with cleaver
2 cloves garlic, peeled, smashed with a cleaver

2 scallions, cut into 2-inch lengths
2 pounds boneless pork loin roast or butt, cut into 2-inch cubes
1 cup boiling water
2 medium carrots, cut into 1-inch chunks
2 medium potatoes, cut into 1-inch chunks
1 cup bamboo shoots, sliced

1. Mix dark soy, sherry, star anise, rock sugar, and salt. Set aside.
2. Heat a heavy pot over high heat until hot. Add the oil; heat. Add ginger, garlic, and scallions. Stir. Add meat. Stir until the pinkness is gone. Add the soy mixture and stir to color the meat evenly. Add the boiling water and stir. Heat to boiling, reduce heat. Simmer covered for 1 hour.
3. Add the carrots and potatoes and bamboo shoots. Add $\frac{1}{4}$ cup more water if necessary. Let the stew simmer for 30 minutes, stirring once or twice.
4. Uncover, turn heat high and let meat and vegetables bubble a few minutes to thicken the sauce. Pour into a serving dish.

Variation: The addition of Chinese pickled cabbage will heighten the flavor.

Tip: This dish tastes even better when made ahead and reheated.

Makes 6 servings.

Beef in Broth with Transparent Noodles

This casserole using beef and vegetables is good served with flower rolls or crusty bread. It is an excellent family one-dish meal.

Sauce Mixture
4 cups chicken broth
1 cup dry sherry
3 tablespoons light soy sauce
¼ teaspoon Szechuan peppercorn powder

4 tablespoons oil
2 slices ginger, the size of a quarter, crushed with the side of a cleaver
2 cloves garlic, crushed with the side of a cleaver, stems removed
2 scallions, sliced into 1-inch lengths

1 pound beef chuck, cut into 1-inch cubes
3 ounces transparent noodles, soaked in warm water 15 minutes or until soft
¼ pound mushrooms, sliced
2 medium carrots, shredded
2 cups Chinese cabbage, shredded
3 scallions, shredded into 1-inch lengths
Salt and pepper to taste
1 teaspoon Chinese sesame oil

1. Combine sauce ingredients. Set aside.
2. Heat a large heavy saucepan over high heat until hot. Add 4 tablespoons oil. Heat. Add ginger, garlic, 2 scallions, and beef cubes. Stir until meat is seared and browned on all sides. Add the sauce mixture and stir until meat is well covered. Heat to boiling. Cover; reduce heat. Simmer 1½ hours or until beef is tender. Add the noodles, mushrooms, carrots, cabbage. Return to heat and simmer 1 hour. Sprinkle with shredded scallion and season with salt, pepper, and sesame oil.

Makes 4 servings.

Noodles with Beef

These noodles are typical of the noodle dishes served in teahouses in China. This pleasant, mild combination of beef and vegetables will be welcome on a cold winter night or can be served with many dishes in a Chinese buffet.

Beef Mixture
½ **pound flank steak, cut into slices 1 × ½ × ⅛ inch each**
1½ **tablespoons dark soy sauce**
2 **teaspoons dry sherry**
1½ **teaspoons cornstarch**

Sauce Mixture
2 **tablespoons oyster-flavored sauce**
1 **tablespoon dark soy sauce**
½ **teaspoon sugar**
¼ **teaspoon salt**
1 **tablespoon dry sherry**

½ **pound fresh egg noodles**
1 **tablespoon Chinese sesame oil**
5 **tablespoons oil**
4 **Chinese dried black mushrooms, soaked in hot water until spongy, stems removed, shredded**
2 **medium carrots, shredded**
12 **ounces celery cabbage or bok choy, shredded**

1. Mix beef with dark soy, sherry, and the cornstarch. Marinate 20 minutes. Combine sauce ingredients. Set mixture aside.
2. Cook egg noodles in 6 cups water, stirring occasionally for about 2 minutes to the al dente stage. Drain and rinse in cold water. Toss with 1 tablespoon sesame oil. Set aside.
3. Heat wok. Add 1 tablespoon oil and heat. Stir-fry mushrooms and carrots for 1 minute. Add the cabbage and stir for 1 minute. Remove from wok.
4. Heat wok over high heat. Heat 2 tablespoons oil. Stir. Add beef and stir-fry until meat is browned on all sides, about 2 minutes. Remove from wok.
5. Clean and dry wok. Heat. Add 2 tablespoons oil and heat. Add noodles and toss until they are coated with oil and heated through. Add the vegetables and beef. Recombine sauce mixture. Add to noodle dish. Toss until thoroughly mixed. Serve.

Variations: Fresh mushrooms may be substituted for the Chinese mushrooms. Chicken or pork may be substituted for the beef.

Makes 3 to 4 servings.

Szechuan Red-Cooked Beef Noodles

This is a well-known spicy, meal-in-one from the Szechuan area. It is rich and tasty and the flavor improves when the meat is cooked a day ahead.

Sauce Mixture
5 tablespoons dark soy sauce
3 tablespoons dry sherry
1½ tablespoons hot bean paste
1 tablespoon sugar
1 teaspoon salt

4 tablespoons oil
1 teaspoon Szechuan peppercorns
4 scallions, cut into 1½-inch pieces

4 slices ginger, peeled, the size of a quarter, smashed
3 cloves garlic
1 pound beef chuck, cut into 1-inch cubes
6 cups chicken broth
2 whole star anise
8 ounces egg noodles
1 pound celery cabbage, shredded
1 tablespoon Chinese sesame oil

1. Combine sauce ingredients. Set aside.
2. Heat a large, 5-quart heavy saucepan until hot. Add 4 table-spoons oil. Reduce heat to medium low and add Szechuan peppercorns. Let brown until fragrant aroma is released. Scrape peppercorns out and discard. Increase heat to high, add scallions, ginger, garlic, and cubed meat. Stir until meat is seared or browned on all sides. Add the soy mixture. Stir until meat is well covered. Add 6 cups chicken broth and star anise. When it comes to a boil again, turn heat to low and simmer, covered, for 1½ to 2 hours or until meat is tender.
3. Taste and adjust seasonings with soy sauce or sugar if necessary. At this time, you may refrigerate and reheat before serving.
4. Just before serving, boil noodles; drain. Add to the hot red-cooked beef. Add shredded cabbage. Toss well. Heat mixture to boiling. Reduce heat and simmer, covered, for 15 minutes. Add sesame oil. Stir. Serve in individual soup bowls.

Tips: For those who like hotness, serve with a bowl of chili paste or hot chili oil to be added by each diner to suit his taste.

This is a family dish. If you prefer to Americanize the meal, you may add more meat and/or celery cabbage. Typically, the Chinese use more noodles.

This dish reheats well on top of the stove.

Makes 4 to 6 servings.

Lion's Head

Lion's Head is ideal for a buffet table. The large pork balls resemble the heads of lions and the cabbage served with them, their manes. This is a northern Chinese dish, which is very tasty. It has a rich sauce for rice or bread, and can be easily doubled or tripled for a crowd.

Pork Mixture
1 **pound lean pork, coarsely ground**
5 **Chinese dried black mushrooms, soaked in hot water until soft, drained, stems removed, minced**
½ **cup water chestnuts, finely minced**
1 **teaspoon ginger, minced**
2 **scallions, minced**
1 **egg, lightly beaten**
2 **tablespoons dark soy sauce**
1 **tablespoon cornstarch**
½ **teaspoon salt**
½ **teaspoon sugar**
Dash pepper

Sauce Mixture
¾ **cup chicken broth**
1 **tablespoon dry sherry**
1 **tablespoon light soy sauce**
1 **teaspoon sugar**

4 **tablespoons oil**
2 **slices peeled ginger, the size of a quarter, smashed**
1½ **pounds celery cabbage, cut into 1½-inch cubes**
½ **teaspoon salt**
1 **tablespoon cornstarch dissolved in 2 tablespoons water**

1. Mix thoroughly pork, mushrooms, water chestnuts, minced ginger, scallions, egg, soy, cornstarch, salt, sugar, and pepper. Do not overmix or meatballs will be tough. Combine sauce ingredients. Set mixture aside.
2. Heat a flat skillet. Add 4 tablespoons oil. When oil is hot, add meatballs and lower heat to medium. Brown evenly. Remove to plate.
3. Leave oil in skillet. Add 2 slices ginger and press them into the oil briefly. Add cabbage and stir. Add salt and stir 1 minute. Transfer cabbage to a 3- to 4-quart enameled casserole or a pot in which you can serve. Stir sauce mixture into cabbage and mix well. Place meatballs on top of the cabbage. Cover casserole and simmer for 1 hour until pork is done and cabbage is soft.

4. Serve in casserole or arrange cabbage on a serving platter, placing meatballs on top. Blend cornstarch and water. Add to liquids in the pot and cook, stirring to thicken. Pour sauce over the meatballs and serve.

Advance Preparation: Make 1 to 2 days ahead and reheat on top of the stove.

Makes 6 servings as a side dish.

Pine Nut Meat Patties

Meatballs subtly flavored with pine nuts and smothered with mushrooms make an extremely tasty dish. The flavors improve upon standing so the dish may be cooked well in advance. Reheat at serving time. Serve with noodles or rice to soak up the rich sauce.

Pork Mixture
1 **pound pork, including the fat portion, ground**
¾ **cup pine nuts, finely chopped**
1 **egg, lightly beaten**
1½ **tablespoons dark soy sauce**
1 **tablespoon ginger, finely minced**
1 **tablespoon scallions, minced**
1 **tablespoon dry sherry**
4 **teaspoons cornstarch**
2 **teaspoons sugar**
Salt to taste

1 **egg, lightly beaten**
4 **cups oil**
6 **scallions, shredded into 2-inch lengths**
3 **slices ginger, peeled, the size of a quarter, smashed**
3 **cups chicken broth**
1 **tablespoon sugar**
1 **pound large mushrooms, cleaned, stems removed**
4 **scallions, shredded into 2-inch lengths**

1. Make pork mixture. Combine pork, pine nuts, egg, soy sauce, ginger and scallions, sherry, cornstarch, sugar, and salt. Shape pork mixture into 8 balls of equal size.
2. Dip fingers into beaten egg. Pick up 1 meatball and toss it back and forth from one hand to the other until smooth and coated with the egg. Flatten the meat ball into a thick patty.
3. Heat 4 cups oil in wok to 350°. Add 4 meat patties and deep-fry 2 minutes on each side, spooning oil over the exposed portions if necessary. They should be golden brown. Cook the remaining patties. Remove. Transfer the patties to a casserole so that they fit tightly in 1 layer. Add 6 scallions and 3 slices ginger.
4. Add the chicken broth and sugar; heat to boiling. Cover and simmer 1¼ hours.
5. Meanwhile, reheat the oil in the wok; add half the mushrooms, cap side down. Cook, stirring, for about 5 minutes. Remove. Drain. Add the remaining mushrooms to wok and cook in the same manner.
6. Garnish the meatball casserole with the mushrooms and 4 shredded scallions. Cover and continue cooking for 30 minutes. Serve.

Advance Preparation: Make ahead completely. Reheat at serving time.   Makes 4 to 6 servings.

Red-Cooked Chicken with Chestnuts

Red cooking, the process of braising in a soy-based liquid, lends itself to chicken, eggs, beef, and pork. The sweet chestnuts contrast nicely with the fragrant chicken here. Be sure to allow time for the chestnuts to soak overnight.

This dish, which originated around Shanghai, tastes even better and has better texture when prepared ahead of time. It can be cooked a day in advance and is wonderful served with noodles and a light vegetable.

1 **cup dried shelled chestnuts, soaked in 2 cups water overnight or until soft.**
2 **tablespoons oil**
2 **slices ginger, peeled, minced**
1 **scallion, cut into 2-inch lengths**
1 **large chicken, cut into 1-inch pieces, skin intact**
¼ **cup dry sherry**
2 **tablespoons dark soy sauce**

2 **tablespoons sugar**
½ **cup bamboo shoots, sliced into 1-inch pieces**
¼ **cup dried Chinese black mushrooms, soaked in hot water until spongy, drained, stems removed**
1 **whole star anise**
1 **cup chicken broth**
2 **tablespoons hoisin sauce**

1. After soaking chestnuts overnight, place in a saucepan; add 2 cups cold water. Heat to boiling. Cook over medium heat for 20 minutes. Drain. Set aside. Remove any remaining pieces of red skin from the chestnuts with a toothpick.
2. Heat a large, heavy pot over high heat until hot; add the oil, swirl and heat for 30 seconds. Add the ginger and scallion. Add the chicken pieces and sear until the skin is yellow, tossing and turning them continuously.
3. Add the sherry, soy sauce, and sugar. Stir for 1 minute to color the chicken. Add the bamboo shoots and mushrooms. Mix well. Add the chestnuts and stir. Add the star anise and the chicken broth and heat to boiling. Cover. Reduce heat to medium-low and cook for 25 minutes. Uncover and mix. Turn heat to simmer and cook for 15 minutes. Stir in hoisin sauce and cook for another minute uncovered.

Advance Preparation: This may be frozen for several weeks and reheated on top of the stove.

Makes 4 servings.

Chicken Steamed with Chinese Sausage

Few dishes match the delicious simple flavor of chicken steamed with Chinese sausage and black mushrooms. This is a Chinese classic dish that is excellent for a buffet or a one-dish meal with rice and a stir-fried vegetable. It is extremely easy to prepare in advance.

Chicken Mixture
1 chicken (3 pounds), chopped into bite-size pieces (bone included)
2½ tablespoons dry sherry
2 tablespoons dark soy sauce
2 teaspoons Chinese sesame oil
2 tablespoons cornstarch
2 teaspoons sugar
Salt

4 Chinese pork sausages, cut diagonally into ¼-inch slices
10 Chinese dried black mushrooms, soaked in hot water until soft and spongy, drained, stems removed, halved
1 scallion, cut into 1-inch lengths
5 pieces paper-thin ginger
1 teaspoon Chinese sesame oil
1 tablespoon scallion, minced

1. Combine chicken, dry sherry, soy sauce, sesame oil, cornstarch, sugar, and salt to taste. Let marinate 30 minutes.
2. Arrange the chicken pieces in a soufflé dish or a similar heat-proof dish about 8 inches in diameter. Start with the neck and back pieces as a base and continue making layers until all the chicken is arranged.
3. Rinse and pat the sausages dry.
4. Intersperse the mushrooms, sausages, scallion, and the ginger in the chicken; steam the mixture for 1 hour or until the chicken feels firm rather than mushy when pressed. Sprinkle with the sesame oil and minced scallion. Serve.

Variation: Instead of the sausage, use slices of lemons, fermented black beans, dried fruit peel, or pickled vegetables.

Advance Preparation: Steam ahead and reheat at serving time.

Makes 4 dinner servings.

Bird's Nest

The addition of a bird's nest to most stir-fried dishes will win you praises. The shredded potato nest has a crunchy texture that will enhance any dish. It can be made several days ahead and re-warmed in the oven at serving time. Fillings for lettuce packages, given elsewhere in this book (see Chapter 10), are particularly nice with this nest.

<table>
<tr><td>¾ pound potatoes, peeled and shredded (use baking potatoes)</td><td>½ teaspoon salt
About 6 cups oil</td></tr>
<tr><td>2 tablespoons cornstarch</td><td>Shredded lettuce for garnish</td></tr>
</table>

1. Place the potato shreds in a colander and rinse lightly with cold water to remove the starch. Drain thoroughly. Wring the potato shreds with towels, squeezing out excess moisture. Blot them dry.
2. Place shreds in a bowl; toss and coat them evenly with cornstarch and salt.
3. While preparing the potatoes, heat 6 cups oil for deep-frying, 375°.
4. Dip a 5-inch slotted strainer with a long handle into the hot oil and remove. Spread the potato shreds out evenly in the strainer. Dip another 5-inch slotted strainer into the hot oil and place on top of the potato shreds. Deep-fry the potato shreds for 5 minutes on high heat. Be sure the potato nest stays completely immersed during the cooking by holding it down in the oil. Remove carefully and drain on absorbent paper. Continue making nests until all the potato is gone.
5. Serve on a bed of shredded lettuce.

Variation: Sweet potatoes or taro root, shredded, may be substituted for the white potatoes.

Tips: The fried nests can be kept in the refrigerator 3 to 4 days and in the freezer several weeks. They are very fragile and should be stored carefully.

The size of the strainer may vary. If you have 2 large strainers of equal size, you may make 1 large bird's nest.

If you are not frying the potatoes immediately, keep the shredded potatoes in cold water to prevent darkening. Drain and dry when using.

Makes 4 servings.

Chicken in a Bird's Nest

This mildly flavored chicken dish will stand alone or be even more interesting when served in a "bird's nest."

1 recipe Bird's Nest (see previous recipe)

Chicken Mixture
2 chicken breasts, skinned, boned, cut into ½-inch cubes
1 egg white
1 tablespoon light soy sauce
1 tablespoon cornstarch

Sauce Mixture
2 tablespoons light soy sauce
1 tablespoon dry sherry
1 teaspoon Chinese sesame oil
1 teaspoon sugar
Dash white pepper

4 tablespoons oil
1 teaspoon ginger, peeled, minced
1 teaspoon garlic, minced
2 carrots, shredded into 1½-inch lengths
1 green pepper, shredded into 1½-inch lengths
⅓ pound fresh mushrooms, sliced
⅓ cup water chestnuts, sliced
2 scallions, sliced
1 teaspoon cornstarch dissolved in 1 tablespoon cold water
Shredded lettuce for garnish

1. Prepare Bird's Nest.
2. Mix chicken, egg white, 1 tablespoon soy, and 1 tablespoon cornstarch. Let marinate for 20 minutes. Combine sauce ingredients. Set aside.
3. Heat 2 tablespoons oil in the wok. Add ginger and garlic and stir-fry about 10 seconds. Add carrots and green pepper. Stir-fry 1 minute. Add mushrooms, water chestnuts, and scallions. Stir-fry 1½ minutes more. Remove and set aside.
4. Heat wok. Add 2 tablespoons oil and heat. Add the chicken. Stir-fry 2 minutes until very lightly browned. Add the vegetables and stir until heated through. Add the sauce mixture and heat. When bubbling, recombine the cornstarch mixture and add to the wok. When the sauce is translucent, remove and place in the Bird's Nest. Serve with shredded lettuce placed around the bottom of the nest.

Advance Preparation: The Bird's Nest may be made ahead and frozen or kept in the refrigerator for 3 to 4 days.

The preparation of the chicken may be done several hours ahead.

Makes 4 servings.

12

Soup with Every Meal

Make it a light accompaniment or the heart of a meal, but do serve soup! It is the omnipresent beverage of Chinese meals as well as the most varied source of nourishment. A substantial bowl of Won Ton Soup can warm a whole day with its hearty portion of dumplings. A snack of Shredded Pork with Szechuan Cabbage Soup justifies a teahouse stop in mid-morning or afternoon. A light broth, garnished with pale cucumber or deep-green watercress, can signal the pace and tone of a meal that offers many dishes to sample. Whatever its ingredients, soup should never be an afterthought. Its seasonings should heighten the enjoyment of everything else you plan to serve.

Good, rich chicken broth is integral to most types of Chinese soups. The Chinese broth is quite uncomplicated but deeply flavored; its quality depends on the chicken. To turn the strained broth into a light soup, pork, poultry, and vegetables, cut into small pieces, can be added and cooked very quickly; tough vegetables such as carrots should be blanched first and shredded, so that they don't have to steep in the broth. But for thick, hearty soups, the added ingredients are simmered slowly to blend the flavors.

The serendipity in a bowl of soup can range from Shanghai Fish Dumplings in Broth to Pork-and-Shrimp Filled Won Tons. It can be as spicy, pungent, and laden with textural intrigue as Hot and Sour Soup. Or it can tantalize like molten gold with the elegance of Crabmeat Corn Soup.

223

Basic Chinese Chicken Broth

Broth is the basis for soups, sauces, and gravies. It contributes greatly to the depth and flavor of each dish.

1 **roasting chicken, fat removed, tail removed, rinsed, cut into quarters**	3 **slices ginger, peeled, the size of a quarter, flattened with the side of a cleaver**
About 3 quarts water	3 **tablespoons dry sherry**
2 **scallions**	

1. Cover the chicken in a large kettle with cold water. Heat the water to boiling and cook 5 minutes. Remove the chicken and rinse with cold water.
2. Discard the water in the kettle; rinse and clean the kettle. Add 3 quarts of fresh cold water and return the chicken to the kettle. Heat the water to boiling. Add the scallions, ginger, and sherry. Simmer the mixture, skimming any froth as it rises to the surface, for $2\frac{1}{2}$ hours. Remove the chicken from the kettle.
3. Strain the broth through a fine sieve or line a large strainer with three layers of cheesecloth. Cool the broth. Skim off any fat on the top before using.

Variations: Save the bones from chicken breasts, backs, wings, skins, and pork. Freeze them until you have enough to fill a large pot. Cover them with water and cook as above.

Tips: The broth will keep in the refrigerator for 4 to 5 days or for months in the freezer. When freezing, store in 1 or 2 cup portions.

Chicken and Watercress Soup

This is an easily prepared, light, tasty soup.

1 boned, skinless chicken
  breast, cut into pieces 1 × 1
  × ⅛ inches
½ egg white (beat egg white
  lightly, then divide in half)
6 cups chicken broth
1 teaspoon salt
¼ teaspoon sugar

⅛ teaspoon white pepper
1 teaspoon light soy sauce
12 sprigs watercress, washed,
  long stems removed, cut into
  1-inch-long pieces
½ cup water chestnuts, sliced
1 teaspoon Chinese sesame oil

1. Mix chicken and egg white.
2. Combine broth, salt, sugar, white pepper, and soy sauce in a 3-quart pot. Heat broth mixture to boiling. Add watercress and water chestnuts. Cook over medium heat until watercress turns bright green.
3. Add chicken mixture, stirring immediately with chopsticks to prevent pieces from sticking to each other. As soon as soup comes to a boil again, turn off heat. Stir in sesame oil. Serve hot.

Variations: Add ¼ cup cooked Smithfield ham or a substitute.
  Substitute 2 cups small young spinach leaves. Rinse carefully. Cook just until wilted.

Tip: Overcooking will make chicken tough.

Makes 4 to 6 servings.

Hot and Sour Soup

This classic Northern soup is ideal for cold weather. It is hearty with a spicy and pungent flavor. The soup may be served with crusty bread as a one-dish meal or with a dinner.

Pork Mixture
6 ounces pork, cut into matchstick strips
2 teaspoons Chinese sesame oil
1 teaspoon light soy sauce
1 teaspoon dry sherry
2 teaspoons cornstarch

Sauce Mixture
1 tablespoon light soy sauce
½ teaspoon sugar
½ teaspoon salt

16 dried lily buds, presoaked, tough ends removed, cut in half
2 tablespoons cloud ears, presoaked, hard eyes discarded, shredded

6 dried Chinese mushrooms, soaked until spongy, stems removed, shredded into matchstick strips
4 cups chicken stock
¼ cup bamboo shoots, shredded
1 square fresh bean curd (tofu), cut into ¼-inch cubes
2 tablespoons cornstarch dissolved in 3 tablespoons cold water
1 egg, lightly beaten
2 tablespoons Chenkong vinegar or red wine vinegar
2 teaspoons Chinese sesame oil
½ teaspoon white pepper
1 scallion, chopped

1. Mix pork, sesame oil, soy sauce, sherry, and cornstarch. Let marinate 20 minutes. Combine sauce mixture. Set aside.
2. Soak lily buds, cloud ears, and dried mushrooms separately in hot water for 30 minutes or until soft. Squeeze dry.
3. Heat chicken stock to boiling. Add pork, lily buds, cloud ears, mushrooms, bamboo shoots, and bean curd. Heat to boiling, reduce heat and simmer for 3 minutes. Stir in the sauce mixture and cornstarch mixture. Stir until soup boils gently. Slowly swirl in beaten egg. Remove from heat. Pour immediatey into a serving tureen containing the vinegar, sesame oil, and pepper. Garnish with chopped scallion.

Variation: Substitute chicken, beef, small fillets of fish, or small shrimp for the pork.

Tips: Eggs are lighter and fluffier when freshly cooked. Vinegar and pepper lose their strength from prolonged cooking. The

Chinese chefs pour the soup into the vinegar mixture in a serving tureen.

For additional spice, add hot chili oil or Szechuan preserved vegetables, minced. If fresh bean curd is not available, omit it.

Advance Preparation: Prepare everything early in the day. Cook the soup up to the addition of the vegetables (mushrooms, tree ears, lily buds, and bamboo shoots).

Makes 3 main-course servings or 6 first-course servings.

Pork and Cucumber Soup

The crispness of the cucumbers lends a nice texture to this clear soup.

4 ounces lean pork, cut into paper-thin slices, 1 inch long
1 tablespoon dry sherry
2 teaspoons light soy sauce
1 teaspoon cornstarch
4 cups chicken stock

1 medium cucumber, pared, cut in half lengthwise, seeded, halves sliced crosswise into $\frac{1}{8}$-inch slices
$\frac{1}{2}$ teaspoon Chinese sesame oil
Salt
Dash white pepper

1. Mix pork, sherry, soy, and cornstarch. Let marinate 20 minutes.
2. Heat the chicken stock to boiling. Stir in the pork mixture until the soup boils again. Add the cucumber slices. Stir 2 or 3 times. Remove from heat. Add the sesame oil. Season to taste with salt and white pepper. Serve.

Tip: Center cut pork chops are ideal for this recipe.

Makes 4 to 6 servings.

Won Ton Soup

Won tons are found in every region of China. They are sold in street stands and by the street vendors who wander about day and night with their portable kitchens; they are in every home.

As you wander around, you can see the white-capped Chinese girls wrapping the won tons in the open air restaurants and families making them out in the streets during the summer.

In the winter, and especially around Chinese New Year, groups of women gather together to make the won tons. Once the won tons are formed and arranged on trays, they are left to chill from the cold air. Then, whenever they are needed, they are boiled and then ladled into a bubbling broth. A touch of soy sauce and sesame oil would be added around Shanghai. In the Szechuan area, the seasonings would be soy sauce, sesame oil, hot chili oil, and a touch of Szechuan preserved vegetables. A meal could be ready in minutes for anyone who might drop by.

The wrappers are rarely made at home since in every neighborhood, there is a noodlemaker. Here you can purchase the wrappers in Oriental markets. Some American markets stock them; however, they tend to be thicker and not as tender. You can also make them at home. This is not the won ton soup you see in American restaurants. It is a much more substantial meal. Allow 4 to 6 won tons per person for the soup course.

1 recipe won ton filling for Pork and Shrimp Fried Won Tons (see Index)	3 cups spinach or celery cabbage, torn into shreds
25 to 30 won ton wrappers	8 to 10 cups chicken stock
	Light soy sauce and Chinese sesame oil to taste

1. Prepare won tons as in Pork and Shrimp Fried Won Tons (see Index).
2. Heat 8 to 10 cups water to boiling in a large pot. Reduce heat to medium-high. Drop in the won tons and stir gently. When the water boils again, add 1½ cups cold water; when it comes to a boil again, add another 1½ cups cold water. When it comes to a boil a third time, let it boil for about 2 minutes. The won tons are cooked when they float to the top. Adding cold water allows the won tons to cook, as well as rinsing them. The filled won tons should not be rinsed after cooking. Drain and discard the water from the pot.

3. Heat the chicken stock to simmering over medium heat; drop the won tons into it. Add the torn spinach; when the stock comes to a boil, reduce heat to medium-low and simmer for about 2 minutes. Season to taste with 1 tablespoon light soy sauce and a dash of sesame oil. Serve in a soup bowl.

Variation: Additional seasonings for the soup are hot chili oil plus a sprinkling of Szechuan minced preserved vegetable.

Advance Preparation: Won tons can be boiled early in the day, placed on a greased cooky sheet covered with plastic wrap.
   Won tons can be refrigerated 1 to 2 days or frozen. Place won tons on a pan and freeze. When frozen, wrap tightly.

Makes 8 to 10 servings.

Shrimp Ball Soup

Shrimp Ball Soup is an extremely delicate, pretty, and delicious soup.

½ recipe Steamed Shrimp Balls (see Index)	1 tablespoon dry sherry
4 cups chicken broth	1 teaspoon Chinese sesame oil
½ cucumber, cut in half, seeded, very thinly sliced	Dash white pepper
	Salt

1. Prepare Shrimp Balls.
2. Heat chicken broth to boiling. Add the shrimp balls and return the broth to boiling. Let simmer for 2 minutes. (If frozen shrimp balls are used, simmer them longer or until heated through.) Add sliced cucumber and cook for 1 minute. Sprinkle with sherry, sesame oil, white pepper, and salt to taste. Serve hot.

Variation: Watercress or spinach may be substituted for the cucumber.

Makes 4 to 6 servings.

Shanghai Fish Balls in Broth

These light fish balls make a delightful soup. They are a favorite preparation among the Chinese. The balls can be made hours ahead and refrigerated until you are ready to use them.

1 recipe Fish Balls (see Index)	½ pound fresh spinach,
6 cups chicken broth	trimmed, washed
1 tablespoon dry sherry	1 teaspoon Chinese sesame oil
Salt	

1. Make the fish balls, moistening the hands with water when forming them. Drop the balls into the simmering broth 1 at a time. When all of the balls have been added, increase the heat to moderately high. Cook the balls, stirring gently for 3 to 5 minutes or until they rise to the surface. Transfer the balls as they are cooked with a skimmer to a plate.
2. Drain all but 4 cups of the poaching liquid. Strain liquid if necessary; salt to taste. Heat to boiling. Add the spinach, dry sherry, sesame oil, and fish balls. Heat the liquid just to boiling. Ladle the soup into a heated tureen.

Variations: Substitute shrimp for the fish. Substitute watercress for the spinach. Remove 2 inches of the stems and discard. Cut the remaining watercress into 1½-inch pieces.

Tip: Fish balls are low in calories and cholesterol, but high in protein.

Makes 6 servings.

Shredded Pork with Szechuan Cabbage Soup

Szechuan preserved vegetable has an appealing salty-sour flavor which makes this soup spicy and intriguing. Pork shreds and cellophane noodles lend an added texture. This is typical of a soup served in a dim sum *noodle stand.*

Pork Mixture
¼ **pound pork, shredded**
2 **teaspoons dry sherry**
1 **teaspoon light soy sauce**
½ **teaspoon cornstarch**

Sauce Mixture
6 **cups chicken broth**
2 **teaspoons dry sherry**
¾ **cup bamboo shoots, shredded**

½ **cup Szechuan preserved vegetable**
2 **ounces bean threads, soaked in hot water to cover for 20 minutes or until soft, drained, cut into 4-inch lengths**
¼ **teaspoon white pepper**
Salt to taste
1 **teaspoon Chinese sesame oil**
2 **tablespoons scallions, minced**

1. Mix pork, sherry, soy sauce, and cornstarch. Let marinate 20 minutes.
2. Heat 6 cups chicken broth to boiling in a saucepan. Add dry sherry. Add the pork shreds and stir a few times with a chopstick. Add the bamboo shoots and preserved vegetable. Simmer for 1 minute. Add the bean threads. Stir in white pepper, salt and sesame oil. Garnish with the scallions. Serve.

Tip: The vegetable commonly called "Szechuan cabbage" is not cabbage at all but a form of radish preserved with hot chilies. On most cans it is labeled "Szechuan preserved vegetable."

Makes 6 servings.

Crabmeat Corn Soup

This is an elegant and delicious soup combining the red-white crabmeat, golden corn, and green scallions to make a wonderful presentation. The original soup was made from "field corn" available only a few days in the summer and considered a great delicacy.

2 tablespoons oil
2 tablespoons scallions, finely chopped
1 teaspoon ginger, peeled, minced
½ pound fresh or frozen crabmeat, flaked
2 cups chicken broth
17-ounce can cream-style corn
1 tablespoon dry sherry

1 to 2 tablespoons light soy sauce
1 tablespoon cornstarch dissolved in 2 tablespoons water
1 large egg beaten with ¼ teaspoon salt
Dash white pepper
1 teaspoon Chinese sesame oil
Parsley

1. Heat a medium soup pot over high heat until hot. Add 2 tablespoons oil; heat. Add the scallions and ginger. Stir rapidly for 5 seconds until flavors release. Add the crabmeat and stir for 45 seconds. Add the chicken stock and the corn. Stir until the soup comes to a boil. Add the sherry and soy sauce. Reduce heat to low and simmer 1 minute.
2. Recombine the cornstarch mixture and pour it in, stirring in a circular motion as the soup thickens. Turn off the heat and pour the egg in a wide circle over the surface. Stir gently a few times when it forms ribbons. Adjust seasonings by adding more salt or soy sauce if desired.
3. Pour into a soup tureen, sprinkle with white pepper and add sesame oil. Garnish with parsley.

Variations: Substitute minced chicken or shrimp for the crabmeat. For a sharper flavor, add cider vinegar to taste.

Makes 2 to 3 servings.

13

Sweet Snacks and Desserts

You can draw a graceful compromise between the absence of dinner-table sweets in China and the American clamor for desserts by ending a meal with just-slightly-glorified fresh fruits. Steamed Pears, stuffed with dates and walnuts, are symbolic of prosperity and redolent of honey. Oriental Oranges glisten with a light sugar syrup and glazed shreds of orange peel. But most resplendent is the Chinese Fruit Bowl, which features nothing more or less than an opulent assortment of seasonal and exotic fruits.

For the joys of sweeter, stickier treats, you have to go beyond the dinner-table norms to the Chinese pastry-shop and teahouse offerings. There you'll find many fruit and sugar versions of savory spring rolls and noodles. One of these, Date and Pine Nut Rolls, takes the shape of a firecracker; the delicious filling is divided among egg roll wrappers, the wrappers are sealed with a twist at each end, and the pastries are deep-fried to crunchiness. Fried Banana Rolls are similar, but more fragile, with a filling of bananas and peanuts and a sprinkling of flaked coconut added after frying. The simplest variation is Fried Sugar Knots, a quick snack of sugar-powdered, deep-fried egg roll wrappers.

Deep-fried, noodle-type sweets are a taste that's all too easy to acquire—or so I've found, to my dismay! Sweet, red bean paste, a favorite Chinese filling for steamed buns and dumplings, is more startling to American palates. If you like it, you can look forward to the festivity of Steamed Buns with Date Filling and Sesame Bean Paste Puffs. Complement the sweet steamed buns with light, subtle Custard Tarts for a choice of classics at teatime. The melt-away quality of the tarts makes them unusually well suited to brunches and light meals, too.

Steamed Pears

To the Chinese, pears are the symbols of prosperity. The following is an easy-to-prepare pear dessert, which can be served hot or cold.

6 **pears**
3 **tablespoons blanched walnut**
   meats, chopped
3 **tablespoons dates, chopped**

½ **teaspoon five-spice powder**
   or cinnamon
6 **tablespoons honey**

1. Cut tops off pears about 1 inch down from the top. Reserve as lids. Core each pear with a fruit corer to make a deep cavity, being careful not to pierce the bottom. Cut a slice from the bottom of the pear to make the pear stand upright, if necessary.
2. Mix the walnuts, dates, and five-spice powder. Fill the pear cavities with the mixture. Drizzle honey in each cavity and over the top of each pear.
3. Place pears upright in individual heat-proof dishes. Steam until tender, 15 to 30 minutes, depending upon the ripeness and type of pear. Serve pears hot in steaming dishes or refrigerate and serve the next day.

Advance Preparation: Prepare completely 1 to 2 days ahead. Chill. To serve hot, steam several hours ahead, resteam to heat through at serving time.

Makes 6 servings.

Oriental Oranges

This is a light, refreshing dessert—and easily prepared in advance.

6 to 8 large oranges	**¼ teaspoon cream of tartar**
2 cups water	**½ cup Cointreau**
2 cups sugar	**1 to 2 tablespoons Cognac**

1. Peel oranges as thinly as possible, being careful not to include any of the white part of the orange. Cut the peel into very fine shreds.
2. Combine the orange shreds, water, sugar, and cream of tartar in a saucepan. Heat to boiling; reduce heat. Cook at a rolling boil until the mixture is syrupy. Simmer until thick. Remove from heat. Stir in the Cointreau and Cognac. Refrigerate.
3. Finish peeling the oranges, removing all the white part. Leave the oranges whole, or slice or break into sections. Refrigerate in a plastic bag for 2 hours.
4. Spoon the chilled syrup over the oranges. Garnish with the shredded peel.

Tip: The syrup can be refrigerated 3 to 4 weeks. It is marvelous as a topping on many other foods.

Makes 6 to 8 servings.

Chinese Fruit Bowl

This colorful assortment of fruits makes a delightfully refreshing dessert.

1 **pineapple**	8 **canned loquats, drained**
1 **pint strawberries, hulled**	2 **bananas, sliced diagonally**
1 **11-ounce can lichee nuts, drained**	½ **cup syrup from preserved kumquats**
1 **11-ounce can mandarin orange sections, drained**	¾ **cup white rum**
½ **cup preserved whole kumquats, drained, syrup reserved**	2 **tablespoons chopped candied ginger (optional)**

1. With a long-bladed sharp knife, cut the pineapple into quarters through the frond. Remove pineapple in one piece from the shells. Remove the core. Slice the pineapple into wedges ½ inch thick.
2. Toss the pineapple wedges with the remaining ingredients. Refrigerate covered until well chilled, at least 2 hours.

Variations: Any fruit in season such as honeydew, watermelon, apple wedges, or fresh orange sections, may be used.
The syrup from the kumquats and the rum from the recipe may be omitted to have a fresh fruit bowl.
Serve the fruit in the pineapple for a lovely presentation.

Makes 12 to 14 servings.

Caramelized Raisin Sesame Noodles

The noodle appears in this dish coated with caramel. It is sold in individually wrapped squares in the United States, but homemade is far superior. This recipe tastes best at room temperature and keeps many days.

3 **cups flour**	1 **cup sugar**
2 **teaspoons baking powder**	½ **cup honey**
4 **eggs, lightly beaten**	½ **cup water**
½ **cup white sesame seeds**	¼ **teaspoon lemon juice**
4 **cups oil**	1 **cup raisins**

1. Combine flour and baking powder. Sift on a pastry board. Spread to form a hollow in the center. Add eggs. Blend the flour and eggs with fingers. Then knead the dough thoroughly until smooth. Let the dough rest, covered with a dampened tea towel for 15 minutes.
2. Dry-fry the sesame seeds. Heat a skillet. Add sesame seeds. Cook, stirring until light brown.
3. Divide the dough in half. Using a rolling pin, roll each half into a rectangle $\frac{1}{16}$ inch thick. Cut each rectangle into strips 2 inches wide and shred the strips into $\frac{1}{4}$-inch noodles. Place the noodles on a baking sheet and dust with flour so that they will not stick together.
4. Heat oil in wok or deep fryer to 375°. Add the noodles and fry them in 4 to 5 batches for 2 minutes or until they are puffed and golden. Remove; drain on paper towels. Place noodles in a large bowl.
5. Combine the sugar, honey, water, and lemon juice in a small heavy saucepan. Heat the mixture to boiling over moderately high heat, stirring until the sugar is dissolved and the mixture is syrupy, medium brown, and pours out as a thread. Pour mixture over the fried noodle strips. Add the sesame seeds and raisins. Mix thoroughly.
6. Transfer the mixture to an oiled pan 13 × 9 inches. Press it into a compact rectangle and let it cool. Cut the noodles into 16 pieces.

Variation: Add chopped walnuts.

Tips: To make this recipe in the food processor and pasta machine, see directions for egg noodles. (See Index.)

Additional flour may be necessary. The weather and type of flour used greatly affect the dough. More liquid is needed in dry weather than in humid weather. If the dough is too moist, add more flour.

Advance Preparation: This recipe can be prepared completely 1 to 2 days in advance.

Makes 16 pieces.

Date and Pine Nut Rolls

Sweets are offered during a meal as well as at the end. These rolls are wonderful served hot or at room temperature. They will keep several weeks in an airtight container. Sprinkle with powdered sugar before serving. They are sure to be one of your special treats!

1 pound pitted dates	**2 tablespoons lemon rind, grated**
3 tablespoons sesame seeds	**½ pound egg roll wrappers**
4 tablespoons corn syrup or honey	**3 cups vegetable oil**
6 tablespoons whole pine nuts	**Powdered sugar**

1. Mince dates with cleaver. Combine sesame seeds and corn syrup with the dates. Mix in pine nuts. Add grated lemon rind to the mixture. Mix well. Refrigerate.
2. Cut each egg roll wrapper into 6 equal sheets. Shape 1 rounded half teaspoon of chilled filling into an oblong roll and place on a piece of wrapper. Roll lengthwise. Twist about ½ inch from each end to seal. This will resemble a small firecracker.

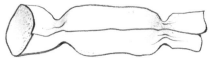

3. Heat oil in wok to 375°. Deep-fry a few rolls at a time until golden brown. Cool. Sprinkle with powdered sugar.

Note: If you wish to make your own egg roll wrappers, see Index for recipe.

Variation: Substitute walnuts for pine nuts.

Makes 72 rolls.

Steamed Buns with Date Filling

Steamed Buns with sweet bean paste and date filling are a tasty snack or dessert. A little minced orange rind or chopped walnuts are a nice variation.

¼ **cup lard**
1 **cup sweet red bean paste**
½ **pound pitted dates, finely chopped**

1 **teaspoon vanilla**
1 **recipe basic yeast dough**

1. Heat wok or skillet over moderate heat. Add the lard. When the lard is melted, add the bean paste and dates. Cook, stirring constantly, for 8 to 10 minutes. Add the vanilla. Cool the mixture. With the palm of your hands, roll the filling into balls about 1 inch in diameter.
2. Fill the buns, shaping the dough as in barbecued pork-filled buns. Arrange the buns, pinched side down, on parchment or waxed paper on steamer tray. Cover with tea towels. Let rise 20 minutes.
3. Steam buns 15 to 20 minutes or until buns are puffy and springy. Serve hot.

Note: To distinguish date buns from pork-filled buns, dip the top of a chopstick in red food coloring and stamp top of the bun with a red dot.

Advance Preparation: Cooked buns can be refrigerated for 3 to 4 days or frozen for 2 to 3 months. It is not necessary to thaw them. Resteam for 15 minutes or until thoroughly heated.

Makes 18 buns.

Sesame Bean Paste Puffs

This typical Chinese sweet pastry is served as a tasty snack or dessert.

2 pounds sweet potatoes or taro root, pared, steamed for 25 to 30 minutes or until tender	1½ cups sweet red bean paste
	¼ cup shredded coconut
	¼ cup candied orange peel, minced
5 tablespoons lard	½ teaspoon vanilla
1½ cups cornstarch, sifted	1 cup sesame seeds
2 tablespoons powdered sugar	6 cups oil

1. Mash steamed potatoes or puree in the food processor. (They should equal 3 cups.) If there is excess moisture in the potatoes, heat them over medium heat until the moisture is absorbed. Add the lard, cornstarch, and sugar to form a smooth dough.
2. Divide dough in half. Roll each half into an 18-inch-long log. Cut each log into 1-inch pieces. Flatten 1 piece of dough into a 3-inch circle. Keep the remaining pieces covered with a damp towel.
3. Mix red bean paste, coconut, orange peel, and vanilla in a bowl. Put a tablespoon of the filling in the center of the circle and gather the dough around the filling to enclose it. Roll the dumpling into a 2½-inch cylinder. Moisten the dumpling with cold water and roll it in sesame seeds, pressing the seeds in the dough so that they adhere. Repeat procedure with remaining ingredients.
4. Heat oil in wok. Add a third of the dumplings and fry them, turning, for 3 minutes. Increase the temperature and fry the dumplings 1 minute more or until they are lightly browned. Repeat procedure with remaining dumplings.

Makes 36 puffs.

Deep-Fried Sweet Sesame Balls

These are traditional sweet dim sum *served during Chinese New Year. They are sometimes referred to as "open-mouthed laughs" as they pop into an open-mouthed smile. They can be made in advance. Be careful not to handle the dough too much as the pastry will not expand in the oil.*

¾ cup sugar
¼ cup hot water
1 tablespoon baking powder
1 tablespoon oil
1 small egg, beaten well

½ tablespoon finely grated
  lemon rind
12 ounces cake flour, sifted
½ cup white sesame seeds
3 cups oil

1. Dissolve the sugar in the hot water. Cool. Add the baking powder, 1 tablespoon oil, egg, and lemon rind. Mix well with a whisk. Stir in the flour. Use both hands to toss the flour and liquid together. Do not knead. Press the loose dough lightly with your fists. Fold the dough gently and press it lightly again.
2. Place the dough on a lightly floured surface. Fold the dough very gently and press it lightly several times until the dough is combined. Wrap in plastic wrap; let dough rest for 1 hour. The dough will be slightly crumbly.
3. Press the dough gently into 1-inch-thick squares. Cut the dough into 1-inch cubes. Roll each cube into a round ball. Wet your hands and moisten each ball by rolling it between your hands gently. Roll each ball in sesame seeds to coat generously. Dry your hands. Roll the balls in the sesame seeds again to allow the sesame seeds to adhere firmly.
4. Dust the cleaver with flour. With the dull edge, cut a slit in each ball at the center.
5. Deep-fry balls, cut side down, in 3 cups oil over medium-low heat. When the balls begin to float, deep-fry until they double in size and turn golden brown. Drain on paper towels. Cool.

Tip: These balls can be stored in a tight container for several days. If they loose their crispness, heat in a 350° oven until they are crisp.

Makes 6 to 8 servings.

Sweet Potato Dumplings

The sweet potato is formed into an interesting dough in this deep-fried sweet.

2 **pounds sweet potatoes, thinly sliced**
6 **tablespoons lard**
1½ **cups sifted cornstarch**
2 **tablespoons sifted powdered sugar**
½ **cup sesame seeds**
3 **cups oil**

Filling Mixture
1½ **tablespoons sweet red bean paste**
¼ **cup shredded coconut**
¼ **cup minced candied orange peel**
½ **teaspoon vanilla**

1. Steam sliced potatoes for 25 minutes or until tender. Drain well in a strainer, removing *all* excess moisture. Puree in a food mill or food processor to equal 3 cups. If the sweet potatoes are not dry enough to make a paste, heat over medium heat until the excess moisture is absorbed. Add lard, cornstarch, and sugar to form a smooth dough. If it is too moist, knead more cornstarch into the dough.
2. Combine filling ingredients. Set aside.
3. Divide the dough in half. Roll each half into an 18-inch-long log; cut each log into 1-inch pieces. Flatten the dough in the palm of your hand into a 3-inch circle. Place 1 tablespoon bean paste mixture in the center. Gather the dough around the filling to enclose it, shaping into a cylindrical shape. Repeat procedure with remaining ingredients.
4. Moisten each dumpling with water; press the sesame seeds into the dumpling.
5. Heat 3 cups oil to 350°. Add the dumplings and deep-fry in batches until light brown and crisp, about 2 to 3 minutes. Remove, drain, and serve.

Makes 6 to 8 servings.

Fried Banana Rolls

Simple to make, Fried Banana Rolls are wonderful as a snack or as a dessert.

10 ripe bananas, sliced thinly
¾ cup dry roasted peanuts,
  chopped
20 spring roll skins

3 cups oil
1 cup powdered sugar
¾ cup sweetened flaked
  coconut

1. Place banana slices and 1 to 2 teaspoons chopped peanuts on a spring roll skin, using about half a banana for each skin. Wrap like a spring roll (see Index) and seal with an egg wash. Prepare the remaining rolls.
2. Heat oil to 375°. Deep-fry the rolls until golden brown. Drain well on paper towels. Sprinkle each roll with sugar and coconut. Serve hot.

Note: Egg roll wrappers can be substituted for the spring roll skins. However, they will not be as crisp and should be fried twice.

The rolls can be prepared, but not deep-fried, 1 day in advance. Refrigerate rolls.

Makes 20 servings.

Fried Sugar Knots

This is an easy-to-make appetizer or sweet prepared from egg roll wrappers that have been deep fried.

1 package of won ton or egg   **2 cups oil**
roll wrappers   **1 cup powdered sugar**

1. Cut each won ton wrapper into 2 rectangles. If using egg roll wrappers, cut each egg roll wrapper into quarters and then into 2 rectangles.
2. Make one ½-inch slit lengthwise in the center of each rectangle. Insert one end of the rectangle to form a twist by pulling the inserted end through and back to its original position forming a knot.

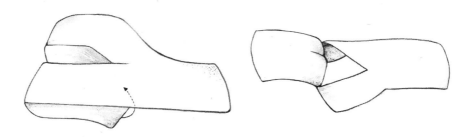

3. Heat oil to 375°. Deep-fry wrappers until golden, about 1 minute. Drain. Sift powdered sugar over both sides. Cool.

Variations: Sprinkle freshly ground Parmesan cheese and coarse salt on the fried wrappers. Serve with cocktails.

  Tear the wrappers into 1½-inch pieces and fry as above. Top with either topping. This is a faster method of achieving almost the same result.

Tip: These knots can be stored several weeks in an airtight container.

Makes 12 servings.

Custard Tarts

Custard Tarts make a marvelous snack or dessert.

½ **cup butter**	*Filling*
½ **cup lard**	3 **egg yolks**
1 **cup cake flour, sifted**	2 **eggs**
1 **cup all-purpose flour, sifted**	¾ **cup sugar**
1 **tablespoon powdered sugar**	1 **cup half-and-half**
1 **large egg, lightly beaten**	½ **cup whole milk**
2 **to 4 tablespoons ice water**	1 **teaspoon vanilla**

1. Cream butter with lard. Sift flours and powdered sugar together. Cut the butter and lard into the flour mixture until small pea shapes are formed. Add 1 egg and 2 tablespoons ice water to the flour mixture. With your hands, quickly gather the dough into a ball. Knead lightly until the mixture adheres. Add more ice water gradually, if necessary. Cover dough with plastic wrap; refrigerate 15 minutes.
2. Make filling: Beat 3 yolks and 2 eggs together thoroughly at low speed. Add sugar, half-and-half, and milk. Beat lightly just to combine. Do not overbeat. Let mixture rest 10 to 15 minutes. Skim all foam from the mixture.
3. Roll the dough into a 12-inch-long log on a lightly floured surface. Cut log into ½-inch slices to make 24 tart shells. Press each slice into a 2½-inch tart tin, making an even layer across the bottom and all the way up the side. Fill each tart shell two-thirds full with egg-milk mixture. Heat oven to 325°. Arrange the tins on a large baking sheet. Bake in the lower third of the oven for 30 to 40 minutes or just until the filling is set. Cool on a rack for 10 to 15 minutes. Loosen and unmold.

Variation: Use lemon extract instead of vanilla.

Tip: The custard should not be browned. It should be just set. If the oven is too hot, the tarts will crack.

Advance Preparation: The shells can be prepared in advance and refrigerated 2 to 3 days or frozen for 1 month. Prepare the filling and bake the day of serving the tarts.

Makes 24 tarts.

14

For Very Special Occasions

One extraordinary dish can turn buffet-style convenience into banquet-style elegance. This principle can be applied to any meal course and it does not necessarily entail elaborate preparation. Mostly, it is a matter of matching appearances with superlative taste.

The "petals" of an egg-pancake flower—detailed with the colors of shredded scallops, black mushrooms, carrots, peapods, and ham—unfold majestically in Flower Soup. The bright contours of a whole pumpkin herald a fabulous, hearty entrée of Spiced Ribs in Pumpkin. In Sweet and Sour Fish the succulence of a whole, deep-fried fish is enhanced with a sauce fine-tuned to perfect harmony.

A centerpiece as easily simmered as Red-Cooked Fresh Ham nevertheless looks magnificent, for the mound of juicy meat comes draped in a deeply colored and incredibly fragrant sauce. If you wish to invest more effort, you are certain to make a grand impression with Peking Duck. Put aside the aura of ceremony that surrounds this dish and you'll find that it's fun to make; after all, how many recipes call for you to inflate a duck and hang it in front of a window! But when you're pressed for time, you might prefer Crispy Pepper Skin Duck, a less challenging specialty that may be served, like Peking Duck, with Chinese Pancakes (see Index.)

The most effortless option is to let guests cook their own dinner—while they celebrate the rites of Mongolian Hot Pot. The tabletop pot, heated with hot coals, invites diners to dip pieces of meat and seafood in bubbling broth; afterwards, they sip the juice-enriched broth. You can reward their efforts, if you like, with a dessert of Peking Dust. This sinful mound of chestnut puree and whipped cream is a banquet exception to the Chinese custom of plain meal endings and it is sublime.

Quail Egg Pastries

The crisp exterior of the rice noodles contrasted with the quail egg inside gives a very interesting texture and makes an exceptionally attractive dish.

30 quail eggs, canned (15 ounce can)

Pork Mixture
¾ pound pork, ground
3 ounces shrimp, minced
8 water chestnuts, minced
4 Chinese dried black mushrooms, soaked in hot water until spongy, stems removed, minced
3 scallions, minced
1 tablespoon ginger, minced

2 tablespoons light soy sauce
1 tablespoon dry sherry
1 teaspoon Chinese sesame oil
2 tablespoons cornstarch
1½ teaspoons salt

3 ounces rice noodles, crumbled into small pieces
6 cups oil
Soy Vinegar Sesame Dip (see Index)

1. Blanch quail eggs in boiling water for 30 seconds. Rinse with cold water. Drain. Dry eggs with paper towels. Set aside. Combine pork, shrimp, water chestnuts, black mushrooms, scallions, and ginger. Mix lightly. Mix soy sauce, sherry, sesame oil, cornstarch, and salt. Add to pork mixture; mix well.
2. Mold 1 tablespoon of pork mixture around each egg and roll in the noodle crumbs. Heat 6 cups oil in wok to 350°. Add eggs in small batches and fry them, turning until they are golden. Drain on paper towels. Serve with Soy Vinegar Sesame Dip.

Tip: The pastries are good hot or at room temperature. Do not make more than 30 minutes in advance.

Makes 30 pastries.

Flower Soup

This recipe makes a lovely presentation on any table. The egg pancake when opened forms the shape of a flower which floats in the tasty soup. It is hearty enough for a main course with a steamed bun.

2 **eggs**
¼ **teaspoon salt**
1 **tablespoon oil**
6 **scallops, torn into shreds**
6 to 8 **Chinese dried black mushrooms, soaked in hot water 15 to 20 minutes until spongy, stems removed, shredded**
⅓ **cup carrots, shredded into 2-inch lengths**
6 **pea pods, shredded lengthwise into 2-inch lengths**
¼ **cup cooked ham, shredded into 2-inch lengths**

Filling Mixture
8 **ounces pork, minced**
2 **ounces shrimp, minced**
6 **water chestnuts, diced**
4 **Chinese dried black mushrooms, soaked in hot water until spongy, stems removed, diced**
3 **scallions, minced**
¼ **cup bamboo shoots, diced**
1 **teaspoon light soy sauce**
½ **teaspoon Chinese sesame oil**
Dash white pepper

Broth Mixture
6 **cups chicken broth**
1 **teaspoon rice vinegar**
1 **teaspoon dry sherry**
¼ **teaspoon white pepper**
1 **teaspoon Chinese sesame oil**

1. Make egg pancake: Lightly beat 2 eggs with ¼ teaspoon salt. Heat wok or skillet with 1 tablespoon oil. Swirl around pan. Discard excess oil. Add the eggs and tilt the pan so that the egg spreads evenly and thinly over the bottom of the pan. Cook over medium heat until the egg pancake is firm. Remove from the pan and lightly brown the opposite side. Remove and cool.
2. Combine filling ingredients. Set aside. Combine chicken broth, rice vinegar, dry sherry, white pepper, and sesame oil.
3. Lightly oil a 3-cup bowl. Line with the egg pancake. Place the shredded scallops in the center. Arrange the shredded mushrooms, carrots, pea pods, and ham on the egg pancake in a spokelike pattern up the sides of the bowl from the center scallops. Place the pork mixture on top and pack down lightly.

Smooth the top of the pork mixture with a spoon and place pork-filled bowl in a steamer. Steam 40 minutes over high heat. Remove.

4. Drain off excess liquid from the steaming bowl into the chicken broth mixture. Invert the steamed filled pancake into a soup tureen. Make 6 to 8 diagonal cuts in the egg pancake, stopping 1 inch from the edge of the egg pancake.

5. Heat the chicken broth mixture to boiling. Pour into the serving tureen. Open the egg petals. Serve.

Advance Preparation: The flower filling can be prepared in the morning, refrigerated, and steamed at serving time.

Makes 6 to 8 servings.

Spiced Ribs in Pumpkin

Ribs are served from a pumpkin in this dish, making an unusual and pretty offering. Pumpkin, squash, and sweet potatoes are used frequently in China. They add an interesting, subtle flavor. This is truly a buffet dish!

1 fresh whole pumpkin (about 5 pounds)
2 tablespoons scallions, sliced
2 tablespoons ground bean sauce
2 tablespoons chili paste
1½ tablespoons dry sherry
1 tablespoon dark soy sauce
1 tablespoon sugar
1 teaspoon ginger, minced
1½ pounds spareribs, cut into 1½-inch pieces, excess fat and gristle removed
¾ pound pork, shredded into thin strips, 1½ inches long
⅓ cup glutinous or sweet rice
½ teaspoon Szechuan peppercorns
1 tablespoon Chinese sesame oil

1. Cut top of the pumpkin neatly about 2 to 3 inches below the base of the handle. Remove seeds and center of the pumpkin. Rinse the inside with water and pat dry.
2. Combine scallions, the bean sauce, chili paste, sherry, soy, sugar, and ginger. Marinate the spareribs and pork in the mixture 2 to 4 hours.
3. Heat a skillet; add the glutinous rice. Toast over medium heat until golden brown, shaking pan frequently. Add Szechuan peppercorns to the hot rice and toast until they turn brown and fragrant. Remove from the heat. Crush the rice and peppercorns in a blender or food processor, or place in a plastic bag and roll with a rolling pin into a coarse powder.
4. Combine the rice mixture with the spareribs and pork. Steam over water in a heat-proof dish over high heat for 45 minutes. Remove from heat. At the same time, steam the pumpkin with the lid on in a separate pot for 15 minutes. Wrap cheesecloth around the pumpkin so that it can be easily lifted out of the steamer pot.
5. Spoon hot pork mixture into the steamed pumpkin. Cover and steam pork in the pumpkin for 20 minutes. Lift the pumpkin out of the pot gently. Stir 1 tablespoon sesame oil into the pork. Serve the pork hot from the pumpkin.

Variations: Chicken breasts may be substituted for the pork.

If pumpkin is not available, you may use acorn squash or half a large squash and put some of the mixture in each half. The pumpkin is not to be eaten. It is a serving dish.

Advance Preparation: Steam the ribs and the pumpkin in the morning. Place the ribs in the pumpkin and steam before guests arrive. It will keep warm 20 minutes in the steamer with the heat turned off, but may be rewarmed briefly at serving time.

Makes 8 servings.

Red-Cooked Fresh Ham

A classic red-cooked fresh ham will dominate any Chinese buffet and is served during the wedding feast in Szechuan.

Yet this spectacular dish is incredibly easy to make. All you do is simmer the ham with some spices for several hours. Like all long-simmered dishes, it can be made in advance and reheated just before serving. This is a good amount of meat and would equal 2 to 3 smaller dishes when you plan your meal.

A good accompaniment to the ham would be steamed flower rolls to soak up all the marvelous sauce.

½ **fresh ham, shank end (about 6 to 7 pounds)**
2 **tablespoons oil**
6 **slices ginger, the size of a quarter, smashed with the side of a cleaver**
4 **large whole scallions, cut in half**
1 **cup dark soy sauce**

1 **cup dry sherry**
6 **cups boiling water**
1 **teaspoon salt**
5 **tablespoons rock sugar, crushed**
3 **whole star anise**
4 **dried chili peppers (optional)**
1 **tablespoon Szechuan peppercorns**

1. Tie the ham in several places with a string before cooking so that it will not fall apart. Heat a large, heavy pot that will hold the meat comfortably until hot. Add oil and heat. Add the ginger and scallions. Press them in the oil. Add the ham and sear it, turning until the surface has whitened.
2. Add soy sauce and ½ cup of the sherry. Turn the ham from side to side to cover it completely. Add the boiling water, salt, 4 tablespoons of the rock sugar, star anise, dried chili peppers, and peppercorns. Stir until liquid boils again. Adjust heat to maintain a very gentle simmering; cover and simmer for 4 to 5 hours, turning the meat every hour and basting it at each turn. Add the remaining ½ cup dry sherry. Taste the sauce and adjust the flavors, adding the remaining rock sugar or to taste. Cover and simmer 30 minutes more. When the meat is tender, turn it carefully, making sure not to tear the skin and fat.
3. Increase the heat; heat the sauce to a gentle bubble and baste the meat continuously for 5 minutes to deepen the color of the meat and thicken the sauce. Remove from the heat and remove

the ham carefully to a large, deep platter. Remove the strings.
4. Skim the surface fat from the sauce. Heat to boiling. Discard the ginger, scallions, anise, chili peppers, and peppercorns. Pour the sauce over the ham. The ham should be served with plenty of rich sauce over the meat.

Variation: The meat is delicious when jelled. Chill the sauce. Remove the congealed fat. Place a slice of meat in a dish, pour the sauce over it. Add several more slices of ham and more sauce. Chill until firm. Turn out onto a serving dish. Slice thinly to serve.

Tip: It is important to use a heavy pot into which the ham fits securely. Otherwise the liquid will reduce too much.

Advance Preparation: Prepare completely 1 to 2 days ahead. Reheat at serving time.

Makes 12 servings.

Peking Duck

This is the most impressive of all the banquet dishes in Chinese cuisine. Although it requires a great deal of preparation, much of it can be done well in advance. I prefer to do two ducks at a time and invite more people because it takes little more effort to prepare than one duck. Allow one duck for every four people for a dinner.

The inflating, scalding, and drying of the duck must be done the day before. The pancakes and the scallion brushes must also be made in advance.

I quite often serve Peking Duck during the cocktail hour before a large banquet or a buffet, as there is very little last-minute preparation other than carving and serving the duck. In this way, my guests can appreciate the fine presentation of Peking Duck.

1 **duck, about 5½ to 6 pounds, with the head on if possible (available in Chinese markets or live poultry stores)**
3 **to 4 quarts water**
¼ **cup malt sugar or honey dissolved in 1 cup boiling water**
4 **slices peeled ginger, the size of a quarter**

2 **scallions, cut into 2-inch lengths**
Chinese pancakes (see Index)
12 **scallion brushes (see instructions that follow)**

Hoisin Sauce Dip
8 **tablespoons hoisin sauce**
1 **tablespoon Chinese sesame oil**

1. Wash the duck thoroughly under cold running water; pat dry with paper towels. Remove the excess fat from the cavity of the duck and discard.
2. Massage the entire body by rubbing the skin back and forth; this loosens the skin from the meat. Make sure you do not puncture the skin or you will not be able to inflate the duck with air.
3. Close the lower cavity of the duck tightly with skewers. Starting at one end of the cavity, push the point of a 5-inch skewer through the skin on one side of the opening. Bring the point of the skewer around the opposite edge of the skin (on the other side of the cavity) and pierce it fom the outside about ¾ inch below the original puncture. Continue in this fashion, pushing the head of the skewer down when necessary.
4. When the cavity is closed, secure the skewer by pushing it through a double fold of skin. The two sides of the cavity have

been braided together with a skewer. Knot it with a single knot and pull on it, further tightening the closing.

5. Pinch and pull the skin again to loosen it from the meat. In the duck's neck cavity, separate the skin from the flesh and insert a large plastic or glass straw or bamboo tube through the neck hole to the tip of the breast area. Blow into the tube as if inflating a balloon until the duck is almost one and one-half times larger, pinching and plucking at the skin to allow the air in. Tie the neck cavity closed by winding twine around the neck several times and pulling tight. Leave the twine long and use the twine for hanging the duck or use a wire hook. (A clean bicycle pump, balloon, or football pump may also be used.)

6. Heat 3 to 4 quarts of water to boiling in a large, deep pot. Add honey and water, ginger, and scallions. Hold the duck by the twine and dip it in and out of the boiling water, turning it from side to side while you ladle water over the exposed skin. Bring the water mixture back to a boil. Repeat this dipping process several times until the skin is white and acquires a dull look. Hang the duck up to dry 6 hours or longer in a draft near a window, over a shower rod or in a ventilated basement. The duck also may be hung in front of a fan or air conditioner. With a fan, the drying process takes about 1½ to 2 hours, without, 6 to 8 hours. The duck may deflate somewhat, but it will puff up in the oven later as the trapped air heats and expands.

7. Baste duck with malt sugar dissolved in boiling water. Hang it again to dry for 2 hours if using a fan, for 4 hours if not. This step should be done 1 day in advance. You may wrap and refrigerate the duck overnight and hang it to dry for a few hours the next day before the final cooking.

8. If your oven is tall, remove all the racks except the top one. Cover a large pan with aluminum foil and place it on the bottom of the oven. Heat the oven to 425°. Wrap the lower wings of the duck with aluminum foil and place a meat hook or a hook fashioned from a wire hanger securely through the neck bone above the string. Hook the duck vertically over the top rack in the center of the oven over the drip pan. Roast duck for 15 minutes. Remove the foil from the wings. Reduce heat to 375°. Roast duck for another 15 to 20 minutes until the duck is evenly browned. Remove the grease from the drip pan occasionally to prevent the grease from smoking.

If your oven is not tall enough for hanging a duck, set the duck on a V-rack, breast side up, so that it is totally exposed to the oven heat. Place the pan on the middle rack of the oven.

Roast duck at 425° for 15 minutes. Turn duck breast side down and roast for 15 minutes longer. Turn the duck again, reduce the heat to 350° and roast 1 hour. Remove the wrappings from the wing tips. Increase the heat to 375° and brown the duck for 15 to 20 minutes, removing the grease from the pan when necessary.

   Because of differing oven temperatures, be sure to *watch the duck closely.* The idea is to lightly brown the duck at the beginning, then, with lower heat, to cook it thoroughly, and finally, with high heat, to give it a deep brown color.

9. Transfer the duck to a carving board. With a small sharp knife, remove the crisp skin from the breast, sides, and back of the duck. Cut the skin into rectangles, 3 × 2 inches each, and arrange them in a single layer on a heated platter. Cut the wings and drumsticks from the duck and cut all the meat away from the breast and carcass. Slice the meat into pieces 2½ × ½ inch each.

10. Arrange the meat in the center of the platter with the wings and drumsticks placed on either end, creating a symbolic whole duck. You may place a few pieces of skin on the duck meat for garnish.

11. Mix hoisin sauce and sesame oil in a bowl. To serve duck, place the platters of duck, the heated pancakes, the scallion brushes, and the bowl of hoisin sauce in the center of the table. Each guest spreads a pancake flat on his plate, dips a scallion brush in the sauce and brushes the pancake with it. The scallion is placed in the center of the pancake with a piece of duck skin and a piece of meat on top. The pancake is folded over the scallion and the duck and tucked under. One end of the pancake is then folded over about 1 inch to enclose the filling and the whole rolled into a cylinder that can be picked up with the fingers and eaten.

Variation: Though not as crisp a duck as in the recipe above, this simplified version using a Long Island Duckling and omitting the air pumping produces a very crisp and delicious duck.

   Rinse and drain the duck. Remove the fat from the cavity and trim the excess neck skin. Insert a meat hook or a fashioned wire hook through the base of the neck bone. Proceed with the pinching and pulling of the duck skin, the scalding, drying, sugar coating, drying, roasting, and carving as in the above recipe.

Tip: A vertical roaster is ideal for this variation.

Scallion Brushes

Cut scallions to 3-inch lengths using the white portion and trim off the roots. Reserve the green ends for another use. Cut ¾-inch deep slits all around both ends of each piece of scallion, leaving about an inch of solid scallion in the center. Place scallions in ice water and refrigerate for 1 hour or longer. The shredded ends will curl, making lovely green-white frills.

Makes 4 to 6 dinner servings or 8 dim sum servings.

Crispy Pepper Skin Duck

This is a famous Szechuan specialty which was one of my Szechuan chef's favorite dishes. It is aromatic, flavorful, and very crunchy. The duck is traditionally served with steamed buns or bread or Chinese pancakes to offset the richness of the skin.

The combination of salt, Szechuan peppercorns, and five-spice powder makes a fragrant dry marinade, which serves to draw some of the moisture out of the skin, allowing the spices to penetrate the duck. The duck is then steamed to cook and firm it and is finished by deep-frying.

1 duck, 4½ to 5 pounds	6 slices ginger, crushed with
3 tablespoons coarse salt	the side of a cleaver
1 tablespoon Szechuan	1 tablespoon dark soy sauce
peppercorns, roasted,	⅓ cup flour
crushed	6 cups oil
2 teaspoons five-spice powder	Szechuan peppercorn salt
5 scallions, crushed with the	Coriander or parsley
side of a cleaver	Chinese pancakes or steamed
	buns (optional)

1. Rinse duck and dry. Discard the fat and tail. Press down hard on the duck's breastbone to snap the bone and flatten the duck.
2. Mix coarse salt, crushed peppercorns, and five-spice powder. Rub mixture all over the duck, inside and out. Refrigerate the duck, covered, 6 hours or overnight.
3. Drain off any liquid and transfer the duck to a large, wide heat-proof bowl. Place the scallions and ginger in the cavity and steam the duck over rapidly boiling water for 1½ hours, replenishing with boiling water when necessary. (Long steaming of the duck makes the duck juicy.)
4. Drain duck; remove to a plate. Discard the scallion and ginger. Blot the duck dry. Remove the surface peppercorns. Brush with soy sauce and dust with flour, tapping off the excess.
5. Heat wok. Add the oil and heat to 375°. Lower the duck in gradually and deep-fry, basting continuously with the oil, for about 3 minutes, turning once. Drain and remove the duck to a plate for 2 minutes. Reheat the oil and deep-fry the duck for 2 more minutes, basting constantly until golden brown and crisp.

Remove from the oil. Drain well. Place on a serving platter. Cut the duck through the bone into bite-size pieces. Arrange the pieces on a platter. Serve with Szechuan peppercorn salt. You may also serve the duck whole at the table, pull the meat off the bones and eat it wrapped in Chinese pancakes.

Advance Preparation: Steam the duck in the morning. Fry duck several hours in advance. Refry until completely reheated.

Makes 4 servings.

Sweet and Sour Fish

The following is a classic version of sweet and sour whole fish, which appears in many northern Chinese banquets. The fish is deep-fried and glazed with a colorful vegetable sauce.

1 **whole white-fleshed fish, 2 to 2½ pounds (sea bass, haddock, or pickerel), scaled, cleaned, dried (leave the head and tail intact)**
¼ **cup cornstarch**
¼ **cup all-purpose flour**

Fish Marinade
1½ **teaspoons ginger, peeled, minced**
1 **scallion, minced**
1 **teaspoon salt**
¼ **teaspoon ground white pepper**
1 **tablespoon dry sherry**

Sauce Mixture
3 **tablespoons ketchup**
1 **tablespoon dark soy sauce**
1 **tablespoon light soy sauce**
½ **teaspoon salt**
⅓ **cup cider vinegar**
8 **tablespoons dark brown sugar**
1 **cup chicken broth**
2 **tablespoons cornstarch dissolved in 4 tablespoons water**
1 **tablespoon Chinese sesame oil**

6 **cups oil**
1 to 2 **dried chili peppers (optional)**
1½ **tablespoons ginger, shredded**
1 **clove garlic, smashed, peeled**
4 **large Chinese dried black mushrooms, soaked in hot water until spongy, stems removed, shredded**
¼ **cup carrots, shredded**
½ **cup bamboo shoots, shredded**
½ **cup frozen peas**
Coriander or parsley

1. Combine marinade ingredients. Set aside. Holding a knife on the diagonal, make deep scores an inch apart lengthwise along the body of the fish. Turn the fish over and repeat on the other

side. Rub the marinade all over the fish inside and out and into the scores. Let the fish marinate for 20 minutes.

2. Combine the cornstarch and flour; coat the fish completely. Let it stand as you prepare the sauce, vegetables, and seasonings.

3. Heat oil in a wok until it is 350°. Slowly lower fish into the oil head first and immerse it in the oil. Ladle the hot oil over the fish. Deep-fry the fish 5 to 7 minutes or just long enough to brown lightly on each side basting and shifting occasionally. Gently remove the fish with a strainer. Set on paper towels to drain.

4. Combine sauce ingredients. Set aside. Heat 4 tablespoons oil in the wok or large saucepan. Add the dried chili peppers, ginger, and garlic. Cook 10 seconds until fragrant. Add the mushrooms, carrots, and bamboo shoots and stir rapidly for 2 minutes. Add the peas and toss for 10 seconds. Recombine the sauce mixture and add, stirring. Discard the garlic. Cook until the sauce returns to a boil and is smooth and has a glaze. Remove from the heat and cover.

5. Reheat the oil in the wok. Deep-fry the fish a second time to crisp the fish and finish the cooking process. Remove and place on a warm serving platter. Pour the sauce over the fish, placing the shredded vegetables on top. Garnish with coriander or parsley and serve.

Variation: Use 1 cup mixed pickled vegetables and rinds instead of black mushrooms, carrots, bamboo shoots, and peas.

Tips: The sauce may be made ahead. The fish may be deep-fried the first time 1 to 2 hours before serving. Refry the second time when ready to serve. Fillet fish at the table. See Steamed Fish with Black Beans for fillet directions.

Makes 4 servings.

Mongolian Hot Pot

The Mongols used firepots as a way to cook their food during the bitterly cold winter months. The gourmets of Peking transformed the simple firepot into the festive dish we have today. It is one of the most interesting and appetizing do-ahead dinners you can serve, and, by far, the best type of "fondue." The hot pot is perfect for fall and winter entertaining.

There are many types of firepots. They are made of brass, copper, or stainless steel. The traditional firepot is fueled by charcoal; and the improvised chafing dish pot is fueled by Sterno. The Sterno "firepot" is more practical; however, I prefer the traditional firepot using charcoal fuel.

Place the firepot in a pan filled with 1 inch water. Set the firepot on your table on a hot pad. Fill it with boiling chicken broth, which simmers throughout the meal. Then set out platters of raw ingredients and dishes of condiments so that each guest can create a dipping sauce to the individual's tastes. Each guest is supplied with a plate, chopsticks, or a fork, a small dipper to cook his own ingredients in the stock, a small dish for the dipping sauce, and a soup bowl and spoon.

Guests take up several pieces of meat at a time and dip them into the boiling broth. The meat cooks quickly and while it is hot, it is dipped into the dipping sauce before eating. After the meat is eaten, spinach is cooked briefly in the broth, removed with chopsticks and served to each diner. At the end of the meal when all the ingredients have been eaten, everyone fills his bowl with the tasty broth and eats it as soup.

Not only is this an easy-to-prepare, do-ahead elegant dinner, but it is low in calories, too!

2 chicken breasts, skinned,
　boned
½ pound flank steak
½ pound lean boneless pork
½ pound shrimp, shelled,
　deveined, butterflied
½ pound fillets of sole,
　flounder, or pike, cut
　crosswise into 2-inch-wide
　pieces
½ pound scallops, sliced
18 small, hard-shelled clams,
　opened, left in the half shell,
　with the meat from the
　attaching muscles loosened
½ pounds fresh squid or canned
　abalone
Watercress or coriander
8 scallions, trimmed into 2-inch
　lengths, green part included,
　made into Scallion Brushes
　(see Index)

2 pounds fresh spinach, rinsed,
　drained, ends removed
8 to 10 cups chicken broth
3 ounces cellophane noodles,
　presoaked in warm water for
　15 minutes until soft

Dipping Sauce
8 tablespoons light soy sauce
2 tablespoons Chinese sesame
　oil
½ cup dry sherry

8 eggs

Seasonings
½ cup ginger, minced
½ cup Chenkong or red wine
　vinegar
4 tablespoons chili sauce or
　chili paste
½ cup scallions, chopped

1. For easier slicing, partially freeze chicken, beef, and pork for 2 to 3 hours until it is very firm, but not solid. Slice the meat into paper-thin strips, 3 × 1 inch each.
2. Arrange the sliced chicken and meats, and all the seafood on separate platters in overlapping circles. The platter should be large enough so that the meat and seafood will not be overcrowded. Garnish with scallion brushes. Place spinach on a platter. Cover the platters and refrigerate. This may be done hours in advance.
3. Combine dipping sauce ingredients; pour into 8 individual bowls. Place the seasonings in individual cups or bowls. Place on a tray. Place a basket of eggs on the table.
4. Bring chicken broth to a boil.
5. Heat the charcoal outside in a charcoal grill until a white ash forms on the briquets. This may be done in the oven also. Oven method: Heat the broiler to its highest point. Arrange 20 charcoal briquets side by side in a baking pan lined with heavy-duty aluminum foil. Place pan under the broiler. Heat for 10 to

15 minutes until a white ash forms on the briquets. With tongs, transfer the briquets to the funnel of the fire pot. Lay an asbestos mat in the center of the table and carefully set the firepot on it. Pour boiling broth mixture into the bowl of the firepot. Set remaining broth aside.

6. Arrange all the platters of the meats and seafood on the table around the pot. Give each guest a bowl of dipping sauce. Break an egg into the bowl of dipping sauce. Beat gently with chopsticks. Place extra sauce in a bowl on the table. Pass the seasonings and let each guest season his sauce to his taste.

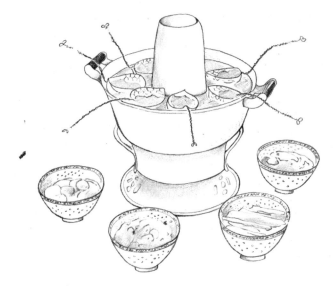

7. Each guest should choose a piece of food from the platters with chopsticks. Transfer the food to a wire strainer to cook in the simmering broth. When cooked, remove the strainer. Dip the cooked food into the dipping sauce and eat. If you do not have a strainer, use chopsticks or a long-handled fork with a heatproof handle.

8. When all the meat and seafood have been eaten, add the rest of the broth. Add the spinach and cook a few seconds until wilted. Remove with chopsticks and serve each guest. Add noodles and ladle the pleasantly flavored broth into each soup bowl to eat as a last course.

Tips: You may substitute any meat or add more of certain meat, fish, or poultry in place of the listed foods.

This dish is best served at a round table so all the guests may reach the pot.   Makes 8 generous servings, but may serve 10.

Peking Dust

This is a light, delicate dessert which is a marvelous ending to any meal.

1 cup shelled pecans	Pinch of salt
2 cups water	1 teaspoon vanilla
½ cup sugar	2½ cups heavy cream
1 cup oil	¼ cup confectioners sugar
1 pound fresh chestnuts or a 1-pound can of chestnuts	1½ teaspoons vanilla
Water to cover chestnuts	½ cup shredded glacéed orange peel (optional)
¼ cup sugar	

1. Heat pecans to boiling in 2 cups of water over high heat. Reduce heat to medium. Simmer uncovered for 1 minute. Remove pan from the heat and drain all the water. Add ½ cup sugar and stir until the pecans are evenly coated. Spread the pecans on a sheet of waxed paper; let dry 30 minutes. Heat 1 cup oil in wok to 375°. Fry the pecans 1 to 2 minutes, stirring until the nuts develop a rich, brown glaze. Transfer the nuts to a greased platter; spread apart in a single layer to cool to room temperature.
2. Score the chestnuts by making a crisscross cut on the flat side of each one. Heat water to a boil. Add the chestnuts and cook until soft, about 40 minutes. Drain and shell.
3. Mince or grind the chestnut meats into a puree. Blend in ¼ cup sugar, the salt, and 1 teaspoon vanilla.
4. In a chilled bowl, beat the heavy cream with ¼ cup sugar and 1½ teaspoons vanilla until stiff peaks form. Add 1½ cups of the whipped cream to the chestnut puree and pack into a lightly oiled 4-cup mold. Chill the mixture and the reserved whipped cream, covered, for at least 1 hour.
5. Carefully unmold onto a serving platter. Garnish mold with the reserved whipped cream and pecans. Garnish with orange peel.

Variations: Divide the chestnut mixture among 6 dessert plates, mounding and tapering it to the top. Garnish with the reserved whipped cream, pecans, and orange peel.

Add 1 to 2 tablespoons brandy to the chestnut-whipped cream mixture.

Makes 12 servings.

15

Dipping Salts and Sauces

Szechuan Peppercorn Salt

4 tablespoons coarse salt
2 teaspoons Szechuan
  peppercorns

1 teaspoon freshly ground
  black pepper

Heat salt with Szechuan peppercorns in a dry pan on low heat for a few minutes, shaking the pan until the salt turns golden and you can smell the aroma from the peppercorns. Remove and cool. Crush mixture with a rolling pin or in a food processor. Remove husks of peppercorns. Store in a covered jar. Mixture will keep for months.

Szechuan Peppercorn Powder (Flower Peppercorn Powder)

1. Heat a skillet over low heat until hot. Add 3 tablespoons Szechuan peppercorns. Stir constantly until the peppercorns turn deep brown and become aromatic. This may take about 5 minutes. Remove from heat.
2. Grind peppercorns to a powder in a blender or roll with a rolling pin between waxed paper or grind in a pepper mill. Powder will keep for months.

Five-Spice Dipping Salt

6 tablespoons coarse salt
½ teaspoon freshly ground
  pepper

½ teaspoon five-spice powder

Heat all ingredients in a dry skillet over medium-low heat. Stir or shake the skillet until the mixture is very hot. Remove from heat. Store in a covered jar.

Cinnamon Dipping Salt

6 tablespoons coarse salt

1 teaspoon ground cinnamon

Prepare as in Five-Spice Dipping Salt.

Soy Oil Dipping Sauce

3 to 4 tablespoons light soy
  sauce

1 tablespoon Chinese sesame
  oil

Combine soy sauce and oil. Serve as a dipping sauce.

Soy Vinegar Dipping Sauce

¼ cup Chinese red vinegar or
  red wine vinegar

2 tablespoons light soy sauce

Combine vinegar and soy. Serve.

Soy Vinegar Sesame Dipping Sauce

¼ cup light soy sauce
1 tablespoon Chinese red
  vinegar or red wine vinegar

½ tablespoon Chinese sesame
  oil

Combine soy, vinegar, and oil. Serve.

Hot Chili Oil (Chili Oil, Hot Oil, Red Pepper Oil, Szechuan Oil)

2 cups peanut or vegetable oil
1½ cups dried chili peppers
4 teaspoons cayenne pepper
   (optional)

Heat oil over medium heat. Test the oil by dropping 1 pepper in the oil. If the pepper turns black immediately, the oil is too hot. The pepper should sizzle gently in the oil. Add the peppers. Cover and cook gently over low heat until the oil becomes dark red and the peppers turn black. Turn off the heat and let cool about 15 minutes. Add the cayenne. The cayenne will burn if the oil is too hot. Mix well. Cover and let stand overnight. Strain through a cheesecloth. Store in a tightly closed jar. This oil will keep indefinitely although it will lose some of its hotness.

This hot oil is hotter than the bottled oil purchased in Chinese grocery stores. Use it sparingly!

Chili Soy Dipping Sauce

2 tablespoons dark soy sauce   **1 tablespoon hot chili oil**

Combine soy and oil. Serve.

Spicy Soy Vinegar Dipping Sauce for Spring Rolls, Won Tons, Dumplings, Peking Pan-Fried Dumplings

1½ tablespoons ginger, peeled,   **½ cup light soy sauce**
   finely minced   **2 tablespoons rice vinegar**
1½ tablespoons garlic, finely   **1 to 2 teaspoons hot chili oil**
   minced   **2 tablespoons sugar**

Combine all ingredients. Mix well. Will keep refrigerated for weeks.

Hoisin Dipping Sauce for Peking Duck, Moo Shu Pork

8 tablespoons hoisin sauce　　1 tablespoon Chinese sesame oil

Combine hoisin sauce and oil in a bowl.

Ginger Sauce for Shrimp

1 tablespoon light soy sauce
5 tablespoons red wine vinegar
1½ tablespoons light brown
　sugar

1 tablespoon ginger, minced
1 teaspoon garlic, minced

Combine all ingredients. Heat over medium heat until the mixture almost comes to a boil. Remove and pour sauce over the shrimp.

Mustard Sauce

2 tablespoons mustard powder
4 tablespoons water
½ teaspoon rice vinegar

½ teaspoon Chinese sesame oil
　(optional)

Mix mustard with enough water to make a thin paste. Add vinegar and sesame oil. Let stand 10 minutes; serve. Mustard will lose its strength if prepared too far in advance.

Soy Mayonnaise

1 cup mayonnaise
2 teaspoons light soy sauce
½ to 1 teaspoon rice vinegar

Lemon juice and white pepper
　to taste

Combine all ingredients. Serve cold or at room temperature.

16

Menus and Preparation Schedules

DIM SUM PARTY

Dim Sum is easy to serve and interesting for brunch or lunch. Many of the *dim sum* can be prepared ahead and frozen. If you live near a Chinese restaurant or a Chinese bakery, you may want to supplement your brunch with some of the unusual pastries you can purchase there.

Easy Dim Sum Party for Six

Pot Stickers
Barbecued Ribs
Steamed Eggs with Crab (double recipe)
Jade Salad
Fruit
Tea

ADVANCE PREPARATION

1 Month to 1 Day Before:
1. Make pot stickers. Freeze or refrigerate.
2. Prepare ribs. Freeze or refrigerate.

Morning of Party:
1. Prepare Jade Salad. Make egg pancakes.
2. Make dipping sauce for pot stickers.
3. Prepare fruit.

2 Hours Before Serving:
Assemble Steamed Eggs with Crab.

30 Minutes Before Serving:
1. Steam eggs.
2. Cook Pot Stickers.

15 to 30 Minutes Before Serving:
1. Heat wrapped ribs in the oven (400°) until heated through. They
   will take longer if frozen.
2. Place egg shreds on Jade Salad.

5 minutes Before Serving:
1. Reheat Pot Stickers. Serve.
2. Prepare tea.

*Tip: For optimum results, cook Barbecued Ribs 1 hour before
serving.*

DIM SUM PARTICIPATION PARTY FOR TEN

Prepare your fillings and wrappers in advance. Invite your guests
over to wrap the dumplings and they will be made in no time.
Everyone shares in the pleasure of making the dumplings along
with having a good time. Make sure you have mastered the
methods of wrapping the dumplings before your guests arrive, as
they will probably need to learn from you.

Be sure to have a variety of cooking methods—steaming, pan-
frying, and deep-frying—so that you can cook all of the dumplings
as they are wrapped.

A soup might also be served, such as Hot and Sour Soup. A
good time to serve this would be in the middle of the party when
everyone might need a reprieve from wrapping—or serve the soup
while the dumplings are cooking.

Hot and Sour Soup (double recipe)
Spring Rolls
Peking Pan-Fried Dumplings (Pot Stickers)
Shao Mai (Open-Faced Steamed Dumplings) (double recipe)
Barbecued Ribs (double recipe)
Chinese Fruit Bowl or Fresh Fruit

ADVANCE PREPARATION

1 to 2 Months in Advance
1. Make or purchase wrappers for Peking Pan-Fried Dumplings and Shao Mai. Purchase Spring Roll wrappers. Freeze.
2. Cook Barbecued Ribs. Wrap in aluminum foil. Freeze.

1 Day in Advance
1. Prepare fillings for Peking Pan-Fried Dumplings and Shao Mai. Cover and refrigerate.
2. Prepare filling for Spring Rolls. Cover and refrigerate. Defrost all wrappers in refrigerator.
3. Prepare soup up to the addition of the vegetables (mushrooms, tree ears, lily buds and bamboo shoots).
4. Prepare fruit for fruit bowl.

1 to 2 Hours Before Guests Arrive
1. Soak black mushrooms, tree ears, lily buds and shred bamboo shoots for soup.

Wrapping Party
1. Reheat frozen wrapped ribs in a 400° oven for 30 minutes.
2. Heat oil for Spring Rolls to 375°.
3. Heat water in wok or steamer for Shao Mai.
4. Wrap Spring Rolls, Peking Pan-Fried Dumplings and Shao Mai.
5. Fry Spring Rolls.
6. Steam Shao Mai.
7. Pan-fry Peking Pan-Fried Dumplings
8. While the Dim Sum are cooking, finish soup preparation. The soup may be served at any convenient time—first, along with the Dim Sum, as a beverage, or after the meal. Serve fruit for dessert.

A WRAP-UP PARTY

A delightful informal buffet or supper is one in which the dishes are served wrapped in a package. The wrappers can be lettuce leaves, Chinese Pancakes, Spring Roll wrappers, Moo Shu Pork wrappers, flour tortillas, or pita bread. A combination of any of these wrappers might also be used. Each guest places a heaping tablespoon or more of the filling in the wrapper, folds it into a package and eats it with his fingers—the Chinese answer to a taco! Plan to serve 4 to 5 wrappers per person for the average appetite. For an informal gathering, after a game of tennis or a show, you may serve just the wrap-ups. The addition of Pork and Cucumber Soup, however, makes the menu suitable for any dinner hour.

Except for lettuce, whichever wrappers you choose should be heated on a plate in a steamer for 5 minutes. Serve some of the wrappers and keep the remaining wrappers warm in the steamer. Heat frozen pita bread by wrapping in aluminum foil and warming in an oven at 350° for 10 to 15 minutes. To serve, cut the bread in half to yield 2 pockets; the pockets can then be stuffed with various meats and/or vegetable combinations.

For those who like very assertive flavors, set out condiment dishes of coarsely chopped peanuts, hoisin sauce, plum sauce, and hot chili oil, if you wish. However, these recipes do not need additional seasonings.

Wrap Up Party for Six

Pork and Cucumber Soup
Minced Pork with Bean Threads
Spicy Chicken
Szechuan Mixed Vegetable Salad
Date and Pine Nut Rolls

Wrap Up Party For Eight

Add Minced Beef Northern Style

ADVANCE PREPARATION
1 to 2 Weeks Ahead
1. Make Date and Pine Nut Rolls. Store in an airtight container.
2. Decide which wrappers you plan to use—Chinese Pancakes, Moo Shu Pork wrappers, Flour Tortillas, or Pita bread. Make or purchase wrappers. Freeze.

Day Before or Morning of Party
1. Cut up pork and cucumber for soup. Prepare broth.
2. Prepare Szechuan Mixed Vegetable Salad. Cover. Refrigerate.
3. Cut up chicken and vegetables for Spicy Chicken. Wrap well. Refrigerate. Prepare sauce mixture. Deep-fry peanuts.
4. Cut up vegetables for Minced Pork. Wrap tightly with plastic wrap or put in a plastic bag. Refrigerate. Prepare sauce and cornstarch mixtures. Fry bean threads. Fry walnuts. Chop walnuts.

5. Wash lettuce. Dry. Put in plastic bag. Refrigerate.
6. Defrost wrappers in the refrigerator. Keep wrappers tightly covered until used.
7. Check Date and Pine Nut Rolls. If not crisp, deep-fry briefly in hot oil to crisp. Sprinkle with powdered sugar.
8. (If serving Minced Beef) Cut up flank steak and vegetables. Cover and refrigerate. Prepare sauce mixture. Cover. Chop peanuts.

2 to 3 Hours Before Serving
1. Marinate chicken for 20 minutes. Cook Spicy Chicken.
2. Marinate pork for 20 minutes. Deep-fry bean threads. Drain. Place on serving platter. Cook Minced Pork. Place lettuce on serving platter. Cover with plastic wrap. Refrigerate.
3. Place plum sauce in serving dish.
4. (If serving Minced Beef) Marinate beef. Cook the beef and vegetables.

10 to 15 Minutes Before Serving
1. Reheat Spicy Chicken.
2. Reheat Minced Pork.
3. Heat wrappers by steaming or if using Pita bread, wrap in aluminum foil. Heat in a 350° oven.
4. Put lettuce on serving plate.
5. Heat soup. Add pork and cucumber.
6. (If serving Minced Beef) Reheat beef.

A CHINESE DINNER

Varied cooking methods, ingredients, textures, degree of spiciness, and serving temperatures make this menu a marvelous example of the excitement of Chinese dining. All dishes can be placed on the table at the beginning of the meal, making a very colorful array.

Dinner for Six

Chicken with Watercress Soup
Moo Shu Pork
Pressed Duck
Aromatic Spiced Beef
Stir-Fry Zucchini and Black Mushrooms with Cherry Tomatoes
Rice
Oriental Oranges

Dinner for Eight

Add Steamed Fish and Black Beans

ADVANCE PREPARATION

1 to 2 Months Ahead:
1. Prepare Pressed Duck. Freeze before frying.
2. Make Chinese Pancakes. Freeze.

2 to 3 Days Ahead:
1. Prepare Aromatic Spiced Beef. Refrigerate.
2. Prepare sauce for Oriental Oranges.

Morning of Party:
1. Cook Moo Shu Pork (For optimum results, cook egg 1 hour in advance of serving.)
2. Prepare ingredients for Zucchini and Black Mushrooms with Cherry Tomatoes. Mix sauce. Wrap in self-locking plastic bag. Stir-fry if serving chilled.
3. Prepare oranges. Chill.
4. Cut up chicken. Wash watercress and cut up. Prepare soup base.
5. Fry almonds for duck. Wash lettuce.
6. (If serving fish) Prepare fish. Cut up scallions. Make sauce mixture.

1 to 2 Hours Before Serving:
1. Cook egg for Moo Shu Pork.
2. Place Aromatic Spiced Beef on serving platter. Bring to room temperature.
3. Put Hoisin sauce in a serving dish.
4. Fry Pressed Duck. Place lettuce on serving platter. Cover with plastic wrap. Refrigerate. Prepare Pressed Duck sauce.
5. Prepare rice.

20 to 25 Minutes Before Serving
Steam fish.

15 Minutes Before Serving:
1. Fry Pressed Duck again until heated through. Let stand for 10 minutes. Cut into serving pieces. Reheat sauce.
2. Reheat Moo Shu Pork. Add egg. Keep warm on low heat.
3. Steam Chinese Pancakes until heated through.
4. Stir-fry zucchini and black mushrooms with cherry tomatoes. Prepare soup.

ELEGANT BUFFET FOR TEN

Chinese food lends itself to American sideboard-style buffet entertaining because everything is bite-sized, suitable for eating with chopsticks or forks without needing knives. The colors of this menu are glorious; the foods are rich and festive. When you want a different buffet for New Year's Eve, an anniversary, or any celebration, this spread will tempt all guests.

Shrimp Stuffed Black Mushrooms
Phoenix Dragon Chicken (double recipe)
Red-Cooked Fresh Ham
Five Treasure Vegetable Platter
Yangchow Fried Rice
Peking Dust

ADVANCE PREPARTION
1 to 2 Months Ahead:
Stuff chicken breasts with ham. Wrap and freeze.

2 to 3 Days Ahead:
1. Cook rice for Yangchow Fried Rice.
2. Prepare Red-Cooked Fresh Ham.
3. Cook nuts for Peking Dust.
4. Make Szechuan peppercorn salt.

1 Day Ahead:
Cut up ham, clean shrimp, shred lettuce and chop scallions for fried rice. Put in self-sealing plastic bags. Refrigerate.

Morning of Party:
1. Fry chicken breasts.
2. Blanch vegetables for Five Treasure Vegetable Platter. Prepare sauce.
3. Stuff mushrooms. Blanch broccoli until slightly undercooked. Prepare sauce for black mushroom recipe.
4. Prepare Peking Dust. Refrigerate.

1 to 2 Hours in Advance:
1. Stir-fry fried rice.
2. Unmold Peking Dust. Garnish with whipped cream.

30 Minutes Before Party:
1. Steam black mushrooms and keep warm in steamer.
2. Reheat ham.

15 Minutes Before Party
1. Reheat fried rice.
2. Fry chicken second time until heated throughout.
3. Reheat broccoli for stuffed mushrooms by steaming. Reheat sauce.
4. Reheat vegetables for Five Treasure Vegetable Platter by steaming or by reheating each vegetable separately in sauce mixture. Arrange vegetables on serving platter. (Vegetables may also be served at room temperature.) At serving time, reheat sauce. Pour hot sauce over vegetables.)

TWO ONE-DISH MEALS

These two cold noodle combinations make wonderful one-dish meals all year-round. Once you have made them, they are certain to enter your permanent repertoire of dishes. They make a fine summer dinner or an elegant picnic, as well as being perfect for a Chinese buffet any time of the year.

Peking Noodles with Meat Sauce is spicy and may be served hot or at room temperature. The noodles are placed in the center of the table along with the meat sauce and the cold vegetables. Each guest fills his bowl half full of noodles and adds the meat sauce and vegetables of his choice. Cold Noodles with Chicken and Shrimp makes a very pleasant light meal. Both recipes can easily be doubled or tripled. Crisp Scallion Cake prepared ahead and frozen, and fresh fruit for dessert complete your meal.

Peking Noodles with Meat Sauce

ADVANCE PREPARATION
2 to 3 Days Ahead:
Cook the sauce and refrigerate.

One Day Ahead:
Cook the noodles. Drain and rinse. Toss with 1 tablespoon Chinese sesame oil. Place in a self-sealing plastic bag. Seal tightly.

Morning of Dinner:
1. Prepare vegetables and ham and place in serving dishes. Cover with plastic wrap.
2. Prepare fruit. Defrost scallion cake.

30 Minutes Before Serving:
Bring noodles and sauce to room temperature if serving at room temperature.

15 Minutes Before Serving:
If serving hot, plunge noodles into a large pot of boiling water. Heat through. Reheat sauce. Place prepared vegetables and ham on serving table. The sauce and noodles may be kept warm on a hot tray. Heat scallion cake in oven.

Cold Noodles with Chicken and Shrimp

ADVANCE PREPARATION

1 Day Ahead:
1. Wash vegetables; drain.
2. Marinate chicken breast.
3. Cook chicken breast. Cover and refrigerate.

Morning of Dinner:
1. Cut up vegetables. Cover with plastic wrap or wrap in a self-sealing plastic bag.
2. Marinate shrimp. Cook shrimp. Cool. Refrigerate.
3. Cook noodles. Drain. Rinse with cold water. Toss with Chinese sesame oil. Arrange on serving platter. Cover with plastic wrap. Chill.
4. Chop peanuts.
5. Make sauce mixture.

1 Hour Before Serving:
Assemble salad. Cover with plastic wrap.

10 Minutes Before Serving:
Pour sauce over salad. Sprinkle with chopped peanuts. Serve. Toss at the table.

SUMMER MENUS

Summer is an ideal time for Chinese entertaining. There are many wonderful room temperature do-ahead dishes which can be prepared well in advance. These dishes may also be served as a refreshing part of a winter buffet table.

Summer Buffet for Six

Hot and Sour Shrimp
Lemon Chicken
Minced Pork with Lettuce Packages
Chinese Fruit Bowl

Summer Buffet for Eight

Add Tangy Noodles with Vegetables

ADVANCE PREPARATION:
1 Day Ahead:
1. Cook shrimp. Prepare sauce. Refrigerate.
2. Steam chicken. Refrigerate.
3. (If serving Tangy Noodles) Prepare noodles completely. Cover with plastic wrap. Refrigerate.

Morning of the Party:
1. Prepare cucumbers and red pepper. Assemble the dish. Cover with plastic wrap and refrigerate.
2. Prepare lemon sauce for chicken in wok. Add chicken. Cook until heated through.
3. Cut up vegetables for Tangy Noodles. Cover with plastic wrap.
4. Stir-fry pork mixture. Refrigerate. Deep-fry walnuts and bean threads. Wash lettuce. Put in a plastic bag. Refrigerate lettuce.
5. Prepare Chinese Fruit Bowl.

1 Hour Before Serving:
1. Pour sauce on Hot and Sour Shrimp.
2. Place lettuce on a platter. Place chicken and sauce on lettuce.
3. Place lettuce and bean threads on platter. Put plum sauce in serving bowl.
4. Put noodles, vegetables, and sauce in serving containers for Tangy Noodles.

15 Minutes Before Serving:
Reheat pork. Place on bean threads. Garnish with scallions and walnuts.

Summer Picnic for Six

Tea Eggs
Cold Rice Noodle Rolls with Hot Spicy Sauce
Hacked Chicken
Chilled Red Radishes
Fresh Fruit

1 Day Ahead:
1. Prepare tea eggs. Refrigerate.
2. Prepare and assemble Rice Noodle Rolls. Cover with plastic wrap. Refrigerate. Slice scallions. Chop peanuts. Prepare sauce mixture. Cover and refrigerate.
3. Cook chicken. Cool. Cover with plastic wrap. Refrigerate. Prepare sauce mixture. Refrigerate.
4. Prepare radishes. Cover with plastic wrap. Refrigerate.

Morning of Picnic
1. Prepare cucumbers and scallions for chicken. Cover with plastic wrap. Refrigerate. Fry peanuts. Chop.
2. Wash fruit.

Ingredients for Picnic Basket
1. Tea eggs.
2. Assembled Rice Noodle Rolls, scallions, chopped peanuts, prepared sauce mixture.
3. Chicken, cucumbers, scallions, peanuts, sesame sauce mixture.
4. Radishes.
5. Fruit.

Serving Time
1. Pour sauce over Rice Noodle Rolls.
2. Pour sauce over Hacked Chicken. Toss.

Summer Barbecue for Six

Smoked Tea Chicken
Barbecued Ribs
Tangy Noodles
Hot and Sour Cucumbers
Fresh Fruit

ADVANCE PREPARATION
1 Day Ahead:
1. Steam chicken. Smoke chicken on barbecue if serving cold. Cover with plastic wrap. Refrigerate.
2. Marinate ribs.
3. Prepare Tangy Noodles completely. Cover with plastic wrap. Refrigerate.
4. Prepare Hot and Sour Cucumbers. Cover with plastic wrap. Refrigerate.

Morning of Dinner:
Wash fruit.

1 Hour Before Dinner:
1. Barbecue ribs on outdoor grill.
2. Smoke chicken on covered barbecue grill if serving hot.
3. Place chicken on serving platter.
4. Put Tangy Noodles on serving dish.
5. Place cucumbers in a serving bowl.
6. Arrange fresh fruit bowl.

17

Chinese Ingredients

人 ANISE, STAR.   Small dry brown seed cluster or clove shaped like
角   an 8-point star. It has a licorice flavor and is used sparingly
in red-cooked simmered and braised dishes. When a
recipe calls for 1 whole star anise, it means 8 individual
pods. Anise extract may be substituted.

筍 BAMBOO SHOOTS.   An ivory-colored vegetable available in
cans either whole or sliced. They add sweetness to a dish.
There are 2 varieties—winter and summer. The winter
bamboo shoot is smaller and more tender. Whole bamboo
shoots packed in water and not brine are best. Occasionally, fresh bamboo shoots can be found. Prepare fresh
bamboo shoots by removing the tough outer skin and
cooking them in boiling water for 15 minutes. Canned
bamboo shoots will keep a few days refrigerated. The
water must be changed every day. Substitute a coarse-
textured vegetable such as celery, green pepper, carrots,
or young cabbage for the bamboo shoots.

豆 BEAN CURD (TOFU).   Commonly known as tofu, bean curd is
腐   made from soybeans which are soaked, boiled, then
drained until the curd forms. Bean curd is high in protein,
low in calories, and very inexpensive. It comes in squares
2½ or 3 inches to a side and is white with the consistency
of firm custard. It will keep a week refrigerated if sub-
merged in water. The water must be changed daily. Bean
curd is conducive to all types of cooking. It can be boiled,
steamed, stir-fried, baked, marinated, pressed, shallow-
fried and deep-fried. It combines well with almost every
food.

BEAN CURD, DRIED.   Made of dried skin of soybean milk. Used in soups and vegetarian dishes.

白
豆
腐
干

BEAN CURD, PRESSED.   Water is extracted from fresh bean curd, making it firm and compact. It is simmered in water with soy sauce, star anise, and sugar. The resilient texture is quite unusual.

豆
鼓

BEANS, FERMENTED BLACK (SALTED BLACK BEANS).   Dried, oval black beans preserved by fermentation with salt and spices. They are used as a flavoring ingredient and are salty with a distinct flavor. They will keep indefinitely in a tightly closed jar. Rinse before using.

原
牲
鼓

BEAN SAUCE (BROWN BEAN SAUCE, BROWN BEAN PASTE). Bean sauce comes in 2 forms—whole bean and ground bean. Whole bean sauce is best. Made from fermented soybeans, salt, flour and water, it is a salty, thick brownish sauce. Bean sauce is available in cans. Once opened, it should be transferred to a glass jar and will keep indefinitely in the refrigerator.

芽
菜

BEAN SPROUTS.   Grown from mung beans. Always purchase fresh, crisp white bean sprouts. Never use canned. They add texture and a delicate taste to meat, rice, noodle dishes, salads, soups, etc. Cook briefly to retain the texture and taste. Avoid brownish bean sprouts.

粉
絲

BEAN THREAD OR CELLOPHANE NOODLES.   Dry, thin white noodles made from ground mung peas. They puff up immediately when dropped in hot oil. They must be soaked first for all other types of cooking. Soak in warm water for 20 minutes or until soft. They become transparent, thus are called cellophane noodles.

苦
瓜

BITTER MELON.   Cucumber-like vegetable with shiny, pebbly skin. It tastes acid at first because of its quinine content, but it is cool and refreshing. Scoop out the pulp and seeds before cooking. Parboil 3 minutes, otherwise the taste will be bitter.

白菜 BOK CHOY.   A Chinese vegetable with white stems and green leaves. Smaller bunches are more tender. The taste is similar to Swiss chard.

酸菜 CABBAGE, PICKLED (PICKLED MUSTARD GREENS).   Whole mustard cabbage packed in brine and fermented. Adds tang to dishes. Rinse well with cold water. Wring dry. Slice diagonally.

紹菜 CELERY CABBAGE (NAPA).   There are two varieties—a short, thick, roundish white type with light green tops, and a long light green type with broad leaves. It has a light, clear taste. Celery cabbage is used in soups, is stir-fried, or pickled.

CELLOPHANE NOODLES.   *See* BEAN THREAD.

栗子 CHESTNUTS, DRIED.   Shelled, dried chestnuts are used as a flavoring in stuffings and braised dishes. They can take the place of fresh chestnuts in desserts. Soak in hot water for a few hours or overnight to remove the skin covering, simmer for 1 hour in 5 cups water per pound.

CHILI PEPPER OIL. *See* Hot Chili Oil.

辣椒干 CHILI PEPPERS, DRIED.   Thin, dried, bright red peppers about 2 inches long. Sold in Chinese, Italian, or Greek grocery stores. They are extremely hot and are used to season oil before the ingredients are added in a stir-fry dish. Chili pepper oil is made from red chili peppers. When seasoning, 4 chili peppers are medium hot, 6 are hot and 8 are devastating in most recipes. Substitute Tabasco sauce.

辣椒醬 CHILI SAUCE or PASTE.   This sauce is made from crushed fresh chili peppers and salt, often with garlic and sometimes with black beans or soybeans. It is very hot and should be used sparingly. It will keep indefinitely in a glass jar, refrigerated. Tabasco sauce may be substituted, if necessary.

芥末粉 **CHINESE MUSTARD POWDER.**   Use yellow mustard powder available in Chinese grocery stores or English mustard powder or Coleman's mustard. For mustard sauce, mix the powder to a medium-thick paste with water. To enhance the flavor, add vinegar.

四川榨菜 **CHINESE PICKLES (SZECHUAN PRESERVED MUSTARD GREENS).** Many types of Chinese vegetables are pickled. One of the most popular is Szechuan preserved mustard greens. They are very spicy and are packed in cans or plastic bags with salt, chili, and spices. They need to be rinsed before being used. They are sour tasting, hot and salty in flavor, and crunchy in texture. They are used in small amounts and can be refrigerated in a tightly closed jar for months.

CHINESE RADISH (ICICLE RADISH, CHINESE TURNIP). *See* TURNIP.

香腸 **CHINESE SAUSAGE.**   Slender pork sausages in links about 6 inches long tied together in pairs. Sweet and savory. To store, wrap in plastic and freeze.

木耳 **CLOUD EARS.**   This Chinese fungus grows on trees. They have a unique, unusual texture. Cloud ears provide a slight earthy flavor and a contrast in color to a dish. Soak in hot water for 20 minutes until soft. Trim stems.

芫荽 **CORIANDER.**   Also known as cilantro or Chinese parsley, this is a bright green herb with slender, delicate stems and a small serrated flat leaf.

五香粉 **FIVE-SPICE POWDER (FIVE-FRAGRANCE POWDER).**   A powdered blend of star anise, cinnamon, cloves, fennel, and anise pepper. Fragrant, slightly sweet, and pungent. Substitute allspice.

薑 **GINGER.**   A gnarled, spicy root of the ginger plant. It is an essential ingredient in Chinese cooking. Purchase a root that is smooth and firm, which indicates freshness and juiciness. Has a pungent, fresh spicy taste. Used as a seasoning in soups, meats, vegetables, and sweet dishes. It neutralizes fishy odors and is frequently used with sea-food. If the ginger is very fresh, it does not need to be peeled. Younger roots have very thin skins. To use, lightly scrape or peel. Then crush, mince, or shred according to the recipe. Two quarter-sized pieces of ginger equal 1 teaspoon chopped ginger. (A quarter-sized piece is the size of an American twenty-five-cent coin.) Powdered ginger or dried ginger may not be substituted.

白
果

GINGKO NUTS.   Small fruit of the gingko tree. The nuts come dried or in cans. The dried nuts must be shelled and blanched for 5 to 10 minutes so the membrane can be pulled off.

糯
米

GLUTINOUS RICE (SWEET RICE).   Short-grained rice which becomes sticky when cooked. Use in pearl balls, sweets, and stuffings. Must be washed and soaked before use until soft, about 4 hours or overnight.

GOLDEN NEEDLES. *See* **TIGER LILY BUDS.**

火
腿

HAM.   Ham is an important seasoning in Chinese cooking. It is used in small amounts to improve the flavor of soups and many dishes. Smithfield ham closely resembles the ham in China. It is very salty with a strong taste. This ham may be purchased by the slice in Chinatown. Since it is cured, it will keep a long time in the refrigerator or freezer. Another substitute is Westphalian ham. Remove the rind before using.

海
鮮
醬

HOISIN SAUCE (DUCK SAUCE, RED SEASONING SAUCE).   This is one of the most popular Chinese prepared sauces. It is made from soybeans, flour, sugar, salt, garlic, chili peppers, and spices. It has a dark, brownish-red color and a slightly sweet hot flavor. Hoisin sauce is used in cooking, served as a dip with Peking Duck and Moo Shu Pork. It is sold in cans. Transfer it to a jar and refrigerate. It will last for a long time.

辣
油
HOT CHILI OIL (CHILI PEPPER OIL, HOT OIL).   Used in salads, dips, or added during cooking. Indispensable to a kitchen liking spicy food. To make hot chili oil, see Chapter 15. Substitute Tabasco Sauce.

HOT OIL.   See HOT CHILI PEPPER OIL.

LILY STEMS (GOLDEN NEEDLES, TIGER LILY BUDS). See TIGER LILY BUDS.

荔
枝
LICHEE FRUIT.   Small, delicate oval-shaped fruit available fresh or in cans. Delicious when chilled.

蓮
葉
LOTUS LEAF.   Dried lotus leaves are used to enclose stuffings as a wrapping for foods to be steamed. They should be soaked for an hour in warm water until they are soft, then drained and dried of excess moisture. The leaf imparts a delicate flavor to the food wrapped. It is not to be eaten. Bamboo leaves can be substituted for lotus leaves. They must be soaked overnight.

蓮
根
LOTUS ROOT.   Reddish brown stem of the water lily. It has 2 or 3 sections about 8 inches per section and 2 inches in diameter. About 5 to 7 tunnels run through the length of each section, forming a lacy pattern. Lotus root is used as a vegetable and is crispy in texture. It can be stir-fried, used in soups or salads. Fresh lotus root is available from July through February. It is also available canned.

味
精
MONOSODIUM GLUTAMATE (ACCENT).   A chemical not necessary for Chinese cooking. I do not approve of its use.

冬
菇
MUSHROOMS, DRIED BLACK CHINESE.   Meaty, succulent, and chewy in texture. The best mushrooms are thick with light skins and highly cracked surfaces. They must be soaked in hot water until soft and the hard stems cut off. Dried mushrooms are sold by weight and keep indefinitely in a dry container. Substitute dried mushrooms from central Europe and Italy. Use less as their flavor is stronger.

草
菇
MUSHROOMS, STRAW.　　Straw mushrooms are available canned and dried. They are small yellow mushrooms crisp in texture, fragrant, and very tasty. The dried mushrooms must be soaked until soft.

MUSTARD.　　*See* CHINESE MUSTARD POWDER.

NAPA.　　*See* CELERY CABBAGE.

麵
NOODLES.　　Freshly made egg noodles can be purchased in Chinatown. You can make your own or substitute American or Italian packaged noodles or spaghettini or linguine.

排
米
粉
NOODLES, RICE OR RICE STICKS.　　Known as rice sticks and made from rice flour. Soak in warm water until soft for 20 minutes. Used for soups or stir-fried dishes. Also deep-fried and used as a garnish for dishes. Heat oil to 375°. Deep-fry 1 or 2 seconds until they puff up. Substitute bean threads.

NOODLES, TRANSPARENT OR CELLOPHANE.　　See BEAN THREAD.

NORI.　　*See* PURPLE LAVER.

OIL, SESAME.　　*See* SESAME OIL.

蠔
油
OYSTER-FLAVORED SAUCE.　　Thick brown sauce made of oysters and spices. It has a light brown caramel color and a "meaty" flavor. A good brand does not taste fishy. Sauce comes in bottles and large cans and keeps indefinitely refrigerated.

PICKLED MUSTARD GREENS.　　*See* CABBAGE, PICKLED.

酸
梅
醬
PLUM SAUCE.　　Made from plums, chili, ginger, spices, vinegar, and sugar. Used as a table condiment. It is often used as a dip for Spring Rolls, Roast Duck, or Roast Pork. Sold in jars or cans.

紫
菜
PURPLE LAVER (NORI, SEAWEED, DRIED).   Tissue thin, dried pressed purple seaweed sold in packages. Tightly sealed, it keeps indefinitely.

米
粉
RICE FLOUR (RICE POWDER).   Made of glutinous rice, used in dough wrappers for desserts or snacks. It is also used to coat deep-fried foods.

RICE WINE.   *See* SHAOHSING WINE.

豆
椒
SALTED BLACK BEANS.   *See* BEANS, FERMENTED, BLACK.

麻
油
SESAME OIL.   Amber-colored oil made from toasted sesame seeds. Used as a flavoring. Use Chinese sesame oil only. Sold in most grocery stores.

芝
蘇
擂
蘭
SESAME PASTE (SESAME SEED PASTE).   Aromatic, rich, tasty paste made from ground sesame seeds. Similar in taste and texture to peanut butter. Used in sauces and cold chicken dishes. Substitute creamy-style peanut butter mixed with a little sesame oil.

酒
SHAOSHING WINE (RICE WINE). Brewed from glutinous rice and has a bouquet like a rich sherry. It is incomparable for flavor in cooking. Dry sherry can be substituted.

蝦
片
SHRIMP CHIPS.   Thin slices of dried dough made from shrimp and starch. When they are deep fried in hot oil, they puff up and become crisp and brittle like potato chips. They are served as hors d'oeuvres and snacks and are quick and easy to prepare.

蝦
米
SHRIMP, DRIED.   Salted and dried shrimp highly valued as a seasoning. Dried shrimp must be soaked in hot water for 30 minutes before being simmered with other ingredients and longer if it is being stir-fried. The shrimp have a strong flavor concentrated by the drying process. They will keep well stored in a tightly covered jar.

生老
抽抽 SOY SAUCE. Soy sauces are made from fermented soybeans, wheat, yeast, salt, and sugar. There are two main types of soy sauce, light also called thin soy sauce and dark also called black or thick soy sauce. Light soy sauce is light colored and should not be muddy in color. It is used for delicate dishes. It is also used in soups and dips and is combined with other sauces. Dark, black, or thick soy sauce is rich and thick with a sweet aroma. It is used in red-cooked dishes. Good quality soy sauce is necessary for good sauces and marinades. Best soy sauce is from China. Domestic soys made by a chemical process are highly concentrated, salty, and bitter. Store in a cool place.

STAR ANISE. *See* ANISE, STAR.

冰
糖 SUGAR, ROCK. Amber-colored crystallized sugar made from raw sugar. Used in red cooking of meats and poultry. Crystals are sweet, but subtle and produce a beautiful glaze. Crush with a hammer or mallet.

四
川
花 SZECHUAN PEPPERCORNS. Reddish-brown peppercorns with a distinctive aroma. They are spicier than black peppercorns and numb the tongue rather than burn.

花四
椒川
粉 SZECHUAN PEPPERCORN POWDER. Prepared from Szechuan peppercorns. Heat Szechuan peppercorns in a skillet over low heat, shaking occasionally until they are aromatic. Cool and crush gently in the blender, food processor, or with a rolling pin between waxed paper. Store in a tightly covered jar.

SZECHUAN PRESERVED VEGETABLES. *See* CHINESE PICKLES.

SZECHUAN PEPPERCORN SALT. *See* Chapter 15: Dipping Salts and Sauces.

果
皮 **TANGERINE PEEL.**   Used as a sesasoning, contains a deep citrus flavor. Peel is used for roasting ducks, simmering meats. It is usually discarded except in Szechuan dishes in which it is shredded or minced and stir-fried in the sauce. The older the skin, the more prized it is. You can make your own—sun dry tangerine or orange peels until they have completely hardened or heat in a 200° oven until hard. Use more homemade peel as it is not as strong.

金
針 **TIGER LILY BUDS. (GOLDEN NEEDLES, LILY STEMS).**   Dried, elongated lily buds about 2 to 3 inches long. They have a mild, flowery fragrance, a soft texture, and add an interesting texture and shape to stir-fry dishes. Pale gold in color, fragile, and highly nutritious. Soak in hot water 15 minutes or until soft, and trim away the tough stems.

蘿
白 **TURNIP.**   (CHINESE RADISH, ICICLE RADISH). Long, white cylindrical vegetables. They are spicy and absorb the flavor of the sauce of the dish in which they are cooked. They are used in soups or cold salads and are also known as Japanese radish or Daikon.

黑
醋 **VINEGAR, CHENKONG RICE (CHINESE BLACK VINEGAR).** Chenkong vinegar is black in color with a mellow flavor. Used for cooking as well as a dipping sauce. Red wine vinegar may be substituted; however the taste is not comparable.

馬
蹄 **WATER CHESTNUTS.** Fresh water chestnuts are sweet and crisp. They grow in water and are covered with mud. They must be washed and peeled before eating. Eaten raw, they are delicious. Substitute canned water chestnuts.

馬
蹄
粉 **WATER CHESTNUT FLOUR.**   Made of ground water chestnuts. Used for coating and gives an extremely light crust. Store tightly closed. Substitute cornstarch.

Index

A

Anise-Boiled Peanuts, 39
Ants Climbing a Tree, 201
Aromatic Spiced Beef, 57
Asparagus Sesame Salad, 68

B

Bamboo Shoots in Hoisin Sauce, 188
Bananas, Fried Rolls, 243
Bananas, Shrimp Stuffed, 116
Barbecued Pork, 44
Barbecued Pork-Filled Buns, 154–55
Barbecued Pork Lo Mein, 206
Barbecued Ribs, 98
Barbecuing, 23
Basic Chinese Chicken Broth, 224
Basic Hot Water Dough, 86
Bean Curd
  Steamed Chicken, 172
  Stuffed, 124–25
  Three Flavor, 170–71
Bean Sprout Salad, 69
Beef
  Aromatic Spiced, 57
  Cinnamon-Flavored, 56

Flank Steak with Rice Sticks, 207
Fried Noodles and Bok Choy, 209
In Broth with Transparent
  Noodles, 213
Jerky, 55
Meat and Vegetable-Filled Buns, 156
  Minced, Northern Style, 200
  Mongolian, 181
  Red-Cooked Stew, 211
  Sesame Strips, 111
  Steak Kow in Oyster Sauce, 180
  Szechuan Dry-Fried Shreds,
    134–35
Bird's Nest, 221
Black Mushrooms Stuffed with
  Shrimp on Broccoli, 164–65
Blanching, 22
Breads, 31
Broth
  Basic Chinese Chicken, 224
  Shanghai Fish Balls, 230
Brown Sauce for Pressed Duck, 110
Buffet for Ten, 276–77
Buns
  Barbecued Pork-Filled, 154–55
  Meat and Vegetable Filled, 156
  Plain, 152

C

Cabbage
  Creamed Chinese, 184
  Hot and Sour, 183
  Stir-Fried, 74
  Stuffed Rolls, 157
Cakes, scallion, 90
Caramelized Raisin Sesame
    Noodles, 236
Cashews, Sweet-Fried Nuts, 40
Char Shiu Bao, 154–55
Chicken
  and Watercress Soup, 225
  Basic Chinese Broth, 224
  Cold Noodles, 74–75
  Cold Szechuan Sesame Shred
    Noodles, 76–77
  Curried with Tomatoes and
    Green Peppers, 175
  Drunken, 51
  Fried Noodles with Shrimp, 210
  Hacked, Szechuan Style, 52–53
  In a Bird's Nest, 222
  Kung Pao, 178
  Lemon, 50
  Lollipops, 105
  Lotus-Leaf Rice, 158–59
  Mustard Sauce, 54
  Paper-Wrapped, 102–3
  Phoenix Dragon, 104–5
  Phoenix Dragon with Vegetables,
    129
  Plum on Snow, 177
  Red-Cooked Pine Nut, 130–31
  Red-Cooked with Chestnuts, 219
  Salt-Roasted, 106–107
  Skewered with Bacon, 101
  Smoked Tea, 46
  Spicy Dumplings, 100
  Spicy in Lettuce Packages, 198–99
  Spicy Tangerine, 179
  Steamed with Bean Curd, 172
  Steamed wih Chinese Sausages,
    220
  Stuffed Wings, 132–33
  White Cooked, 47
  With Snow Peas, Black
    Mushrooms and Bamboo
    Shoots, 176
Chilled Red Radishes, 73
Chinese Buffet, 3
Chinese Dinner, 274–75
Chinese Fruit Bowl, 236
Chinese Pancakes, 192
Chopsticks, 8
Cinnamon Dipping Salt, 267
Cinnamon-Flavored Beef, 56
Cleaver, 9, 12–17
Cooking methods, 17–23
Cooking tips, 35–37
Cold Lamb in Aspic, 58
Cold Noodles with Chicken and
    Shrimp, 74, 278
Crab
  In Lettuce Packages, 202
  Steamed Eggs, 162
  With Bean Threads, 189
Crabmeat Corn Soup, 232
Creamed Chinese Cabbage, 184
Crispy Pepper Skin Duck, 258–59
Crushing, 17
Cubing, 15
Cucumbers, Hot and Sour, 67
Curried Chicken with Tomatoes
    and Green Peppers, 175
Custard Tarts, 245

D

Date and Pine Nut Rolls, 239
Deep-Fried Sweet Sesame Balls, 241
Deep Frying, 19–20
Desserts
  Caramelized Raisin Sesame
    Noodles, 236
  Chinese Fruit Bowl, 237
  Custard Tarts, 245
  Date and Pine Nut Rolls, 238

Deep-Fried Sweet Sesame Balls, 241
Fried Banana Rolls, 243
Fried Sugar Knots, 244
Oriental Oranges, 235
Peking Dust, 265
Sesame Bean Paste Puffs, 240
Steamed Buns with Date Filling, 239
Steamed Pears, 234
Sweet Potato Dumplings, 242
Dicing, 15, 16–17
Dips
  Chili Soy, 268
  Hoisin, 269
  Soy Oil, 267
  Soy Vinegar, 267
  Soy Vinegar Sesame, 267
  Spicy Soy Vinegar, 268
Dough, 86
Duck
  Brown Sauce, 110
  Crispy Pepper Skin, 258–59
  Peking, 254–57
  Pressed, 108
Dumplings
  Four-Happiness Shao-Mai, 150
  Har Gow, 166–67
  Peking Pan Fried, 84
  Shao-Mai, 148–49
  Spicy Chicken, 100
  Sweet Potato, 242
  Taro, 92–93
  Turnip, 91
Drunken Chicken, 51
Dry-Frying, 22
Dry Ingredients, 24

E

Egg Balls, 161–62
Egg Noodles, 80–81
Egg Pancakes, 193
Eggplant
  Spiced, 66

Stuffed Slices, 96
Stuffed Slices with Fish-Flavored Sauce, 125
Szechuan Style, 141
Egg rolls, 80–81
Eggs
  Gold Coin, 123
  Steamed with Crab, 162
  Tea, 41
Egg Wrappers, 193
Equipment, 5

F

Fine Dicing, 16–17
Fish, 27
  Basic Balls, 118
  Cakes, 119
  Deep-Fried Balls, 118
  Hot and Sour Balls, 139
  Rolls with Scallion Sauce, 169
  Scallion Smoked, 64
  Steamed wtih Black Beans, 168
  Sweet and Sour, 260–61
Five-Spice Dipping Salt, 267
Five-Treasure Vegetable Platter, 142
Flank Steak with Rice Sticks, 207
Flat slicing, 14
Flower Peppercorn Powder, 266
Flower Rolls, 152–53
Flower Soup, 248–49
Four Happiness Shao-Mai, 150
Fried Banana Rolls, 243
Fried Noodle Cake, 208
Fried Noodles with Beef and Bok Choy, 209
Fried Noodles with Chicken and Shrimp, 210
Fried Sugar Knots, 244
Fruit, Chinese Fruit Bowl, 236
Frying, 79–80

G

Ginger Sauce for Shrimp, 269
Gold Coin Eggs, 123

Green Beans
  Szechuan Dry-Cooked, 140
  With Peanuts, 73
Green Peppers, Stuffed, 136–37

H

Hacked Chicken, Szechuan Style,
  52–53
Ham Steamed Rice Noodle Rolls, 42
Happy Shrimp Rolls, 60
Har Gow, 166–67
Hoisin Dip, 269
Hot and Sour Cabbage, 183
Hot and Sour Cucumbers, 67
Hot and Sour Fish Balls, 139
Hot and Sour Ribs, 99
Hot and Sour Shrimp, 62
Hot and Sour Soup, 226
Hot and Sour Zucchini, 186
Hot Chili Oil, 268

I

Ingredients, 283–92

J

Jade Salad, 72
Jade Pearl Balls, 97
Jerky, Beef, 55

K

Kung Pao Chicken, 178

L

Ladle, 7
Lamb
  Cold in Aspic, 58
  Skewered, 112
Lemon Chicken, 50
Lettuce, Stir-Fry with Straw
  Mushrooms, 187
Lion's Head, 216–17

Lotus Leaf Rice, 158–59
Lotus Root Salad, 71

M

Marinade
  Beef, 134–35
  Chicken Wing, 132–33
  Mushroom, 164–65
  Pork, 44
Marinating, 23
Mealtime, 2
Meat and Vegetable Filled Buns,
  156
Meat-Filled Omelets, 126–27
Menus, 270–81
Minced beef, Northern Style, 200
Minced Pork with Bean Threads in
  Lettuce Packages, 194
Mincing, 16
Mongolian Beef, 181
Mongolian Hot Pot, 262–64
Moo Shu Pork, 196–97
Mustard Sauce, 269

N

Noodle Rolls, Steamed, 42
Noodles, 28–30
  Barbecued Pork Lo Mein, 206
  Beef in Broth, 213
  Caramelized Raisin Sesame
    Noodles, 237
  Chicken Shred, 76–77
  Cold Szechuan Sesame, 76
  Cold with Chicken and Shrimp,
    278
  Fried Cake, 208
  Fried with Beef and Bok Choy,
    209
  Fried with Chicken and Shrimp,
    210
  Egg, 80–81
  Peking with Meat Sauce, 277–78
  Pork with Bean Thread, 143
  Singapore Stir-Fried, 144–45

Steamed Rolls, 42
Szechuan Red-Cooked Beef, 215
Tangy, 77
Tangy with Vegetables, 78
With Beef, 214
With Chicken and Shrimp, 74–75
With Meat Sauce, 205

O

Oil, 36, 37
Omelets, Meat Filled, 126–27
One-Dish Meals, 277–78
One Hundred Corner Deep-Fried
    Shrimp Balls, 114
Oriental Oranges, 235

P

Pancakes
  Chinese, 192
  Egg, 193
Paper-Wrapped Chicken, 102–3
Pasta machine, 12
Peanuts, Anise-Boiled, 39
Pearl Balls, 147
Pearl Balls, Jade, 97
Peking Duck, 254–57
Peking Dust, 265
Peking Noodles with Meat Sauce,
    205, 277–78
Peking Pan-Fried Dumplings, 84–85
Phoenix Dragon Chicken, 104
Phoenix Dragon Chicken with
    Vegetables, 129
Pine Nut Meat Patties, 218
Plain Buns, 152
Plum Chicken on Snow, 177
Pork, 25–26
  Ants Climbing a Tree, 201
  Barbecued, 44
  Barbecued Ribs, 98
  Deep-Fried Jade Meatballs, 97
  Eggplant, Szechuan Style, 141
  Filled Buns, 154–55

Fried Won Tons, 82–83
  Hot and Sour Ribs, 99
  Lion's Head, 216–17
  Meat and Vegetable-Filled Buns,
    156
  Meat-Filled Omelets, 126–27
  Minced with Bean Threads in
    Lettuce Packages, 194
  Moo Shu, 196–97
  Pearl Balls, 147
  Pine Nut Meat Patties, 218
  Red-Cooked, 212
  Red-Cooked Fresh Ham, 252–53
  Shao-Mai, 148–49
  Shredded Egg Balls, 161–62
  Shreds in Hoisin Sauce, 195
  Spiced Ribs in Pumpkin, 250–51
  Spicy with Peanuts, 174
  Steamed Rice Noodle Rolls, 42
  Stuffed Cabbage Rolls, 157
  Stuffed Eggplant Slices, 96
  Stuffed Green Peppers, 136–37
  Twice Cooked, 128
  With Bean Thread Noodles, 143
Pork and Cucumber Soup, 227
Pork and Shrimp Fried Won Tons, 82
Pot Stickers, 84–85
Poultry, 26
Pressed Duck, 108–9

Q

Quail Egg Pastries, 247

R

Radishes, Chilled Red, 73
Red-Cooked Beef Stew, 211
Red-Cooked Chicken with
    Chestnuts, 219
Red-Cooked Fresh Ham, 252–53
Red-Cooked Pine Nut Chicken,
    130–31
Red-Cooked Pork, 212
Red Cooking, 21–22

Ribs
  Barbecued, 98
  Hot and Sour, 99
  Spiced Rice Coated, 160
  Spiced Ribs in Pumpkin, 250
Rice, 27–28
  Lotus Leaf, 158–59
  Steamed Noodle Rolls, 42
  Yangchow-Fried, 120–21
Roasting, 22
Roll Cutting, 14
Rolls
  Flower, 152–53
  Fried Flower, 153
  Spring, 87–89
  Vegetable, 87–89
  Water Chestnut, 95

S

Salads
  Asparagus Sesame, 68
  Bean Sprout, 69
  Jade, 72
  Lotus Root, 71
  Spicy Vegetable, 70
  Szechuan Mixed Vegetable, 203
  Tomato and Cucumber, 71
Salt Roasted Chicken, 106–7
Salts
  Cinnamon Dipping, 267
  Five-Spice Dipping, 267
  Szechuan Peppercorn, 266
  Szechuan Peppercorn Powder, 266
Sauces
  Brown for Pressed Duck, 110
  Cinnamon-Flavored, 56
  Fish-Flavored, 125
  Ginger, 137
  Ginger for Shrimp, 269
  Ginger Scallion Dipping, 49
  Hoisin, 188, 195
  Hot and Sour, 62, 139
  Hot Spicy, 42

  Mustard, 54, 163, 269
  Scallion, 169
  Spicy, 42, 48
Scallion brushes, 257
Scallion Cakes, 90
Scallion Smoked Fish, 64
Scoring, 17
Seafood
  Fried Won Tons, 83
Seasonings, 24–25
Sesame Bean Paste Puffs, 240
Sesame Beef Strips, 111
Sesame Seed Buns, 94
Shanghai Fish Balls in Broth, 230
Shao-Mai, 148–49, 150
Shredded Egg Balls, 161–62
Shredded Pork with Szechuan
    Cabbage Soup, 231
Shredding, 15
Shrimp
  Balls in Ginger Sauce, 137
  Ball Soup, 229
  Balls Steamed or Fried, 115
  Balls with Snow Peas, 138
  Cold Noodles, 74–75
  Fried Noodles with Chicken, 210
  Fried Won Tons, 82–83
  Happy Rolls, 60
  Hot and Sour, 58
  Lotus Leaf Rice, 158–59
  One Hundred Corner Deep-Fried
    Balls, 114
  Shao-Mai, 148–49
  Shao-Mai, Four Happiness, 150
  Singapore Stir-Fried Noodles,
    144–45
  Steamed Dumplings, 166–67
  Steamed in Mustard Sauce, 163
  Steamèd Stuffed Black
    Mushrooms on Broccoli,
    164–65
  Stuffed Bananas, 116
  Szechuan, 182
  Toast, 113

With Scallions, 59
Singapore Stir-Fried Noodles, 144
Skewered Chicken with Bacon, 101
Skewered Lamb, 112
Skimmer, 8
Slant Cutting, 14
Slicing, 13, 14
Smoked Tea Chicken, 46
Smoking, 23
Snow Peas
  Shrimp Balls, 138
  Spicy Vegetable Salad, 70
Soup
  Chicken and Watercress, 225
  Crabmeat Corn, 232
  Flower, 248–49
  Hot and Sour, 226
  Pork and Cucumber, 227
  Shredded Pork with Szechuan
    Cabbage, 231
  Shrimp Ball, 229
  Won Ton, 228
Soups, 31
Soy Mayonnaise, 65, 269
Soy Oil Dip, 267
Soy Vinegar Dipping Sauce, 267
Soy Vinegar Sesame Dipping Sauce,
  267
Spatula, 7
Spareribs, Spiced Rice Cooked, 16
Spiced Eggplant, 66
Spiced Ribs in Pumpkin, 250–51
Spiced Rice-Coated Spareribs, 160
Spicy Chicken in Lettuce Packages,
  198–99
Spicy Pork with Peanuts, 174
Spicy Soy Vinegar Dipping Sauce,
  268
Spicy Tangerine Chicken, 179
Spicy Vegetable Salad, 70
Spinach, Deep-Fried Jade
  Meatballs, 70
Spinach Jade Salad, 72
Spinach, Stir-Fried, 184

Spring Rolls, 87–89
Staples, 24–34
Steak Kow in Oyster Sauce, 180
Steamed Buns with Date Filling, 239
Steamed Eggs with Crab, 162
Steamed Pears, 234
Steamed Rice Noodle Rolls, 42
Steamed Shrimp Balls, 115
Steamed Shrimp in Mustard Sauce,
  163
Steamer, 9–11
Steaming, 20–21
Steeping, 22
Stir Frying, 1, 18–19
Strainer, 8
Stuffed Bean Curd, 124–25
Stuffed Cabbage Rolls, 157
Stuffed Chicken Wings, 132–33
Stuffed Eggplant Slices, 96
Stuffed Eggplant Slices with Fish-
  Flavored Sauce, 125
Stuffed Green Peppers, 136–37
Summer Menus, 278–81
Sweet and Sour Fish, 260–61
Sweet Fried Nuts, 40
Sweet Potato Dumplings, 242
Sweets, 31–32
Szechuan Dry-Cooked Green
  Beans, 140
Szechuan Dry-Fried Beef Shreds,
  134–35
Szechuan Mixed Vegetable Salad,
  203
Szechuan Peppercorn Powder, 266
Szechuan Peppercorn Salt, 266
Szechuan Red-Cooked Beef
  Noodles, 215
Szechuan Shrimp, 182

T

Taro Dumplings, 92–93
Tea, 32–34
Tea Eggs, 41
Three-Flavor Bean Curd, 170–71

Tomato and Cucumber Salad, 71
Tortilla Press, 12
Turnip Dumplings, 91
Twice-Cooked Pork, 128

V

Vegetable, Five-Treasure Platter, 142
Vegetable Rolls, 63
Vegetables, 25

W

Water Chestnut Rolls, 95
White-Cooked Chicken, 47–49
Wines, 34

Wok, 5–7, 11
Won Tons, 80–81
    Pork and Shrimp Fried, 82–83
    Fried Seafood, 83
Won Ton Soup, 228
Wrap-Up Party, 272-74

Y

Yangchow Fried Rice, 120–21
Yeast Dough, 150–51

Z

Zucchini
    Stir-Fried, 185
    Hot and Sour, 186